philips
minigroove
second extended version of the european discography

compiled by john hunt 2008

Contents

Introduction / page 5

00100 / page 9

00200 / page 24

00300 / page 36

00400 / page 50

00500 / page 62

00600 / page 71

00700 / page 85

00900 / page 95

02000 / page 95

03000 / page 135

04000 / page 143

05000 / page 145

06000 / page 151

09000 / page 162

10000 / page 166

200 000 / page 167

400 000 / page 170

610 000 / page 171

663 000 / page 173

675 000 / page 175

695 000 / page 176

697 000 / page 178

698 000 / page 181

700 000 / page 190

835 000 / page 193

836 000 / page 209

838 000 / page 212

802 000 / page 212

839 000 / page 231

894 000 / page 241

European recordings made or issued by Philips for American Columbia / page 245

Re-issue categories / page 267

Index of conductors and orchestras / page 268

Index of instrumentalists and chamber groups / page 280

Index of singers / page 290

Philips Minigroove Second Edition
Published by John Hunt.
© 2008 John Hunt
reprinted 2009
ISBN 978-1-901395-23-5

Sole distributors:
Travis & Emery,
17 Cecil Court,
London, WC2N 4EZ,
United Kingdom.
(+44) 20 7 459 2129.
sales@travis-and-emery.com

Philips minigroove: introduction to the second extended version

The first edition of this particular discography in 2003 (ISBN 1 901395 13 8) traced the early history of Europe's youngest classical music label in the 1950s. Those first ten years of Philips produced such a vast cornucopia of recorded material that further research seemed inevitable: this will now take us up to the end of the 1960s, in fact to just before the point when the company abandoned its tried and tested 5- and 6-digit numbering systems in favour of the 7-digit international one, starting with the 6500 000 series.

Although Philips originally intended a strict numerical and chronological sequence in the LP numbering system, starting at 00100 and with suffixes "L" and "R" denoting 12-inch (30cm) and 10-inch (25cm) formats respectively, separate sequences were soon introduced for the 10-inch format (00600 and 00700), with the result that precise chronology was abandoned. This was even more the case in the early stereophonic era, for example when the full-price 835 000 series was followed by 802 000.

Whilst the period from 1955 saw the expansion of the label to embrace issues from the American Columbia catalogue (and later Mercury and Vanguard), I have decided to exclude these from the new survey. Major figures from those catalogues like Antal Dorati, Leonard Bernstein and Eugene Ormandy are currently receiving attention from me in their own discographies. Instead, I have pursued my original intent to account for as many as possible of the numbers which contained the recorded material of Dutch (and very soon also European) origin. However, a smallish numbers of LPs recorded by Philips in Europe and for some reason then allocated numbers from the American Columbia sequence, are included.

The change from 5-digit (00100-09900) to 6-digit catalogue numbers (the already mentioned 835 000) hinged mainly upon the introduction in the late 1950s of stereophonic recording, when it was obviously felt, for prestige reasons, that a new and instantly recognisable system was needed. Indeed, Philips was alone among the major labels in publishing its very earliest stereo efforts in that form only, with no equivalent mono one. This may have been intended to coerce the public into changing over to stereo, but it was soon decided to let collectors make their own choice over a longer period of time (mono versions actually continued to appear until 1966-1967). Therefore where mono and stereo versions of a recording coexist, the LP is listed numerically under its mono number.

Already remarked upon in my first edition was the reluctance of the British and American branches of Philips to embrace the European numbering system, preferring in the UK 4-digit numbers with prefixes ABL (later AL), NBL, SBL, SABL (later SAL) and so on. These are therefore included in the discography, as are the various American catalogue numbers LC and BC (Epic) and later PHM, PHS and WS.

By the 1960s the prestige of a classical recording company demanded the inclusion of a Beethoven symphony cycle, among other things, in its catalogue. Decca boasted one by the *Wiener Philharmoniker* under conductor Hans Schmidt-Isserstedt, Deutsche Grammophon had Herbert von Karajan and EMI Otto Klemperer (I refer here only to integral cycles which were recorded and issued as such). It was not until towards the end of the decade that Philips presented its own modern cycle by the *Concertgebouworkest* under Eugen Jochum. Previously individual Beethoven symphony records on the Philips label had been shared between the likes of Paul van Kempen, John Pritchard, Willem van Otterloo, Eduard van Beinum, Igor

Markevitch and Wolfgang Sawallisch. An early development in the historical category, however, was the transfer to Philips LPs of Dutch Radio broadcasts of most of the symphonies by the legendary Willem Mengelberg.

By placing the known recording data in italics immediately under the catalogue number and title, it has become possible to reduce my previous 3-column discography layout to 2 columns: the first of these gives conductor, orchestra and major soloists, whilst the second is devoted to catalogue numbers (the term *excerpts* indicates not only parts of a major work but also complete short works which may have been extracted from the original recital or compilation). As many different issues as possible are included for each recording, with reissues both on domestic Philips and in other territories, and a not unimportant part of the research has been the cross-referencing among those various reissues. A guide to editions and categories is provided, as is a listing of the main Philips contract artists (this was, after all, the heyday of conductors and soloists being exclusive to one label).

Philips material reissued for CD has appeared continuously since 1985 from what is now known as the Universal group (Philips, Decca and Deutsche Grammophon). In addition, as copyright starts to expire, a multitude of other CD labels has begun issuing original Philips recordings.

I am always pleased to hear from collectors who can add to my information, and already have to thank Michael Gray for providing so many recording details, as well as Maurits Clement, Syd Gray, John Hancock, Bill Holland, Otto Ketting, Klaus Heinze, Roderick Krüsemann, Philip Stuart, Malcolm Walker and Jaco van Witteloostuyn.

John Hunt 2008

A 00100 R/haydn symphony no 92 "oxford"
recorded in the concertgebouw amsterdam on 28-29 december 1950
otterloo further lp issue: SBL 5201/S04008L
residentie cd: challenge records CC 72142
orkest

N 00101 L/grieg peer gynt suites nos 1 and 2
recorded in the concertgebouw amsterdam on 30 december 1950
otterloo 78 rpm issue: N11137-11140G
residentie further lp issues: ABR 4027/A00734R/S06101R/
orkest 695 004KL/G03000L/G05312R/832 004WGY/
  MGW 14043/SRW 18043
  cd: 462 0992
  excerpts
  78 rpm issue: N12056G
  45 rpm issue: ABE 10051/400 038AE
  lp: SBL 5636/S04042L/S06010R

A 00102 L/beethoven symphony no 5
recorded in the jesus-christus-kirche berlin-dahlem on 28-30 may 1951
jochum further lp issues: NBR 6030/N00766R/GBL 5556/
berliner G05332R/LC 3002
philharmon- cd: tahra TAH 238
isches orchester

A 00103 R/mahler kindertotenlieder
recorded in the concertgebouw amsterdam on 24-25 january 1951
otterloo further lp issues: S06028R/695 093KL
residentie cd: PHCP 5113/challenge records CC 72142
orkest
schey

A 00104 L/works for flute and piano by schubert, gaubert and caplet *recorded in amsterdam on 19 january 1951*
barwahser 78 rpm issue A11148-11149G (schubert only)
de nobel

A 00105 R/palestrina missa papae marcelli
recorded in amsterdam on 3 july 1952
de nobel further lp issues: NBL 5033/LC 3045
netherlands
chamber choir

A 00106 R/piano works by chopin
recorded in amsterdam on 12 february 1951
de groot

N 00107 R/works by schubert and bruch
recorded in the concertgebouw amsterdam between 25 january-1 february 1951
otterloo   **rosamunde entr'acte in b flat and ballet in g**
residentie   45 rpm issue: 494 026CE
orkest   further lp issues: 675 012KR/832 095PGY/
    SFL 14028/700 135WGY
    cd: challenge records CC 72142
otterloo   **kol nidrei for cello and orchestra**
residentie   78 rpm issue: N12015-12016G
orkest   45 rpm issue: 494 029CE
de machula   cd: 462 0912

A 00108 L/piano works by schubert and schumann
recorded in amsterdam on 8 june 1951
haskil   **piano sonata no 21 d960**
    further lp issues: ABL 3029/ABL 3356/A00484L/
    A02087L/695 089KL/6588 008/6590 089/
    6733 002/6747 055/LC 3031/PHC 9076
    cd: 442 6352/442 6852/456 8292/documents LV 959/
    andromeda ANDRCD 5102
    bunte blätter
    45 rpm issue: ABE 10037/400 010AE
    further lp issues: ABL 3029/A00372L/835 936AY/
    6598 274/6747 055/LC 3031/GCL 54
    cd: 420 8512/426 9642/442 6352/442 6852/
    475 7739

A 00109 L/chopin the 24 préludes
recorded in amsterdam on 13-14 february 1951
de groot   further lp issues: ABR 4042/LC 3017/700 070WGL
    cd: 462 5272
    excerpts
    78rpm issue: A11240G

A 00110 L/tchaikovsky symphony no 4
recorded in the concertgebouw amsterdam on 7-8 june 1950
otterloo   further lp issues: GBL 5538/G03036L
residentie   cd: challenge records CC 72142
orkest

A 00111 R / orchestral works by mozart
recorded in the jesus-christus-kirche berlin-dahlem on 20-21 february 1951

lehmann	**symphony no 35 "haffner"**
berliner	further lp issues: SBL 5201/S04008L/G03008L/
philharmon-	695 014KL/200 044WGY/LC 3006
isches orchester	**march in d k249**
	further lp issues: SBL 5201/S04008L

A 00112 R / mozart violin sonatas k301 and k304
recorded in amsterdam between 6-15 june 1951

de klijn	further lp issue: S04012L
heksch	cd: globe GLO 6039

A 00113 L / piano works by chopin
recorded in amsterdam on 18-20 january 1952

uninsky	*excerpts from the recital*
	45 rpm issues: ABE 10114/400 063AE
	further lp issues: G05310R/S06004R

A 00114 L / works by liszt
recorded in the concertgebouw amsterdam on 24 march 1951

otterloo	**piano concerto no 1**
residentie	78 rpm issue: A11182-11183G
orkest	further lp issues: ABL 3026/A00200L/S04001L/
de groot	GBL 5545/G03002L/695 003KL/200 037WGY/
	LC 3020
	cd: 462 8962/462 8952
otterloo	**les préludes**
residentie	78 rpm issue: N11152-11153G
orkest	45 rpm issue: 400 031AE
	further lp issues: NBR 6014/N00702R/S06126R/
	S06190R/GBL 5527/G03007L/675 005KR/
	200 013WGY/LC 3032

A 00115 R/works by cherubini, poot, sibelius and weber
recorded in the jesus-christus-kirche berlin-dahlem on 21-23 february 1951

lehmann	**anacreon overture**
berliner	78 rpm issue: A11159G
philharmon-	**ouverture joyeuse**
isches orchester	78 rpm issue: A11161G
	valse triste
	78 rpm issue: A11161G
	45 rpm issue: SBF 135
	euryanthe overture
	78 rpm issue: A11160G
	further lp issues: GBL 5556/G03052L

A 00116 R/overtures and choruses by wagner and verdi
recorded in the concertgebouw amsterdam on 16-17 january 1951

kempen	**lohengrin preludes acts 1 and 3**
netherlands	**and treulich geführt**
radio orchestra	78 rpm issue: N11143-11144G
netherlands	45 rpm issue: NBE 11028/402 035NE
opera chorus	**gloria all' egitto/aida**
	78 rpm issue: N12012G
	45 rpm issue: NBE 11009/402 014NE
	further lp issues: G05376R/N00649R/S06018R
	la forza del destino overture
	78 rpm issue: N11151G

N 00117 R/piano music by kunc, tajcevic and papandopulo
recorded in amsterdam on 3 april 1951

lorkovic	78 rpm issue: A11184-11186G

N 00118 L/organ music by bach, mendelssohn, rheinberger and grison *recorded in amsterdam on 22 march 1951*

asma	78 rpm issue: N11167-11168G
	excerpts
	further lp issue: S06017R
	cd: 441 9632

N 00119 L/operatic music by weber, mascagni and leoncavallo
recorded in the concertgebouw amsterdam on 15-17 january 1951 (orchestral pieces) and 14-15 april 1951 (arias)

kempen	**oberon overture**
netherlands	78 rpm issue: N11142G
radio orchestra	further lp issues: S06003R/200 028WGL
	cavalleria rusticana intermezzo
	78 rpm issue: N12011G
	45 rpm issue: SBF 103/NBE 11018/402 010NE
	i pagliacci intermezzo
	78 rpm issue: N12011G
	45 rpm issue: NBE 11018/402 010NE
kempen	**ozean du ungeheuer/oberon**
netherlands	78 rpm issue: N12057G
radio orchestra	further lp issues: SBR 6206/S06136R
brouwenstijn	cd: 462 0712/preiser 89692
	voi lo sapete/cavalleria rusticana
	78 rpm issue: N11169G
	45 rpm issues: NBE 11018/402 010NE
	further lp issues: G03147L/695 052KL
	cd: 462 0712
kempen	**vesti la giubba/i pagliacci**
netherlands	45 rpm issues: NBE 11018/402 010NE
radio orchestra	
vroons	

A 00120 L/tchaikovsky symphony no 6 "pathétique"
recorded in the concertgebouw amsterdam on 23 may 1951

kempen	further lp issues: ABL 3000/ABL 3127/GBL 5507/
concertgebouw	A00253L/G03009L/695 006KL/LC 3003
orkest	cd: 438 3102

A 00121 L/mozart masonic music
recorded in the musikverein vienna between 7-15 november 1953

paumgartner	**maurerische trauermusik**
wiener	45 rpm issues: NBE 11005/400 004NE
symphoniker	further lp issues: ABL 3022/LC 3062/836 930DY
wiener	**eine kleine freimaurerkantate; dir seele**
kammerchor	**des weltalls; die maurerfreude**
christ, majkut,	further lp issues: ABL 3022/LC 3062/836 930DY
berry	

A 00123 L/berlioz symphonie fantastique
recorded in the jesus-christus-kirche berlin-dahlem between 18-25 june 1951
otterloo further lp issues: ABL 3019/A00254L/GBL 5547/
berliner G03026L/LC 3005
philharmon- cd: retrospective RET 037
isches orchester

A 00124 L/piano works by chopin
recorded in amsterdam on 18-20 january 1951
uninsky *excerpts from the recital*
further lp issue: G05310R

N 00125 R/music for violin and piano by pugnani, bloch and ravel *recorded in amsterdam on 28 june 1951*
magyar
hielkema

N 00126 R/piano music by fauré, pijper, voormolen and orthel
recorded in amsterdam on 4 july 1951
van der pas

N 00127 R/choral works by delden, voormolen, dresden and sweelinck *recorded in amsterdam on 3-7 july 1950*
de nobel
netherlands
chamber choir

A 00128 R/tchaikovsky romeo and juliet, fantasy overture
recorded in the concertgebouw amsterdam on 17-18 july 1951
kempen further lp issues: SBL 5217/S04027L/S06029R/
concertgebouw G03084L/WL 1131/LC 3008
orkest cd: 438 3102

A 00129 L/chopin the 4 ballades
recorded in amsterdam on 24-25 september 1951
de groot 78 rpm issue: A11232-11233G (ballades 1 & 2)
further lp issue: LC 3037

A 00130 L/works by morton gould
recorded in the concertgebouw amsterdam on 13 september 1951
otterloo	**interplay for piano and orchestra**
residentie	78 rpm issue: N11197-11198G
orkest	further lp issue: N00677R
de groot	cd: challenge records CC 72142
otterloo	**spirituals for orchestra**
residentie	further lp issue: N00677R
orkest	cd: challenge records CC 72142

A 00131 R/piano music by albeniz and de falla
recorded in amsterdam on 25-26 september 1951
de groot   further lp issues: 695 095KL/LC 3175
           excerpts
           78 rpm issue: A11202-11204G

A 00132 L/beethoven violin concerto
recorded in the concertgebouw amsterdam on 25-26 february 1952
otterloo   further lp issues: S04000L/675 000KR/
residentie   695 027KL/832 009PGY/LC 3023
orkest
krebbers

A 00133 L/beethoven piano concerto no 5 "emperor"
recorded in the concertgebouw amsterdam on 23 november 1951
otterloo   further lp issues: ABL 3032/S04005L/675 001KR/
residentie   695 025KL/200 002WGY/LC 3014
orkest   cd: 462 0762
de groot

A 00134 R/schumann piano concerto
recorded in the concertgebouw amsterdam on 12 september 1951
otterloo   further lp issues: ABR 4080/S06120R/S04033L/
residentie   GBR 6504/G05308R/G03001L/6598 274/
orkest   6747 055/695 088KL/200 066WGY/LC 3020
haskil   cd: 420 8512/426 9642/442 6312/442 6852

A 00135 R/tchaikovsky piano concerto no 1
recorded in the concertgebouw amsterdam on 12-13 october 1951
otterloo   further lp issues: ABR 4020/A00672R/S06114R/
residentie   675 002KR/695 003KL/200 017WGY/LC 3010/
orkest   G05313R
uninsky

A 00136-00137 R/piano works by liszt
recorded in amsterdam on 1-2 october 1951
uninsky further lp issues: S04034L/LC 3027/LC 3066
excerpts
78 rpm issue: A11212G

A 00138 R/bloch schelomo, rhapsody for cello and orchestra
recorded in the concertgebouw amsterdam on 11 october 1951
otterloo further lp issue: LC 3072
residentie cd: 462 0912
orkest
de machula

A 00139 L/johann strauss waltzes: wiener blut, an der schönen blauen donau, g'schichten aus dem wienerwald and frühlingsstimmen *recorded in the musikverein vienna on 2-3 february 1952*
moralt further lp issues: ABL 3002/GBL 5549/
wiener G03045L/695 008KL/LC 3004
symphoniker *excerpts*
78 rpm issues: A11237-11239G
45 rpm issues: NBE 11034/402 002NE
further lp issues: S06006-06007R
cd: retrospect RET 045

A 00140 L/works for violin and orchestra by bach and beethoven
recorded in the concertgebouw amsterdam on 11 november 1951 (beethoven) and 24 november 1951 (bach)
otterloo **bach concerto for 2 violins**
residentie further lp issues: S06105R/695 057KL/
orkest 832 005PGY/G05462R/MGW 14044/
krebbers, SRW 18044/LC 3036
olof cd: 462 5532
otterloo **beethoven violin romances nos 1 and 2**
residentie 78 rpm issue: A11218-11219G
orkest 45 rpm issues: SBF 102/SBF 151
krebbers further lp issues: S06000R/695 027KL/
200 031WGL/200 031WGY/832 005PGY/
G05462R/MGW 14044/SRW 18044/
LC 3036/675 011ER

A 00141 L/tchaikovsky symphony no 5
recorded in the concertgebouw amsterdam on 3-5 december 1951
kempen further lp issues: ABL 3007/A00252L/G03024L/
concertgebouw LC 3013/200 052WGL
orkest cd: 420 8582/438 3102

A 00142 L/debussy préludes, 1er livre
recorded in amsterdam on 13-15 november 1951
henkemans further lp issue: A00489L
cd: 462 0832
excerpts
78 rpm issue: A11177G/A11216G
further lp issues: ABR 4023/SBL 5200/S04007L

A 00143 R/piano works by scarlatti and ravel
recorded in amsterdam on 8-9 september 1951
haskil **sonatas K193 (L142), K87 (L33) and K386 (L171)**
45 rpm issue: 400 170AE
further lp issues: L02087L/6747 055/695 090KL/
melodiya M10 42589-42590
cd: 442 6352/442 6852/475 7739
melodiya lp contains only K87 (L33) and K386 (L171)
sonatine
further lp issues: 6747 055/695 090KL/melodiya
M10 42589-42590
cd: 442 6352/442 6852/475 7739/
andromeda ANDRCD 5102

N 00144 L/franck symphony in d minor
recorded in the concertgebouw amsterdam on 2-3 january 1952
otterloo further lp issues: GBL 5544/G03042L/
residentie 695 037KL/LC 3019
orkest cd: 462 8992/462 8952

A 00145-00146 L/beethoven symphony no 9 "choral" and overtures
recorded in the concertgebouw amsterdam on 3-4 may 1952
otterloo **symphony no 9**
residentie further lp issues: ABL 3030-3031/A00220-00221L/
orkest L00439L/SBL 5227/S04040L/GBL 5548/
toonkunst G03030L/695 000KL/WL 1061
choir cd: challenge records CC 72142
spoorenberg
von ilosvay,
vroons, schey
otterloo **egmont and coriolan**
residentie 78 rpm issues: N11154G/N12058G
orkest 45 rpm issues: 411 908SE/SBF 158
further lp issues: S06001R/S06119R/GBL 5514/
GBR 6259/G03012L/G05306R/695 020KL/
200 028WGY (egmont)

N 00147 L/organ music by bach, handel, mendelssohn and driffili
recorded in amsterdam on 29-30 may 1952
asma *excerpts*
        45 rpm issue: SBF 219
        cd: 441 9632

A 00148 L/debussy préludes, 2eme livre
recorded in amsterdam on 6-7 june 1952
henkemans   further lp issue: A00489L
        cd: 462 0832
        excerpts
        78 rpm issue: A11177G
        further lp issues: SBL 5200/S04007L

N 00149 L/works by weber and schubert
recorded in the concertgebouw amsterdam on 11 october 1951
otterloo   **der freischütz overture**
residentie   further lp issue: S06003R
orkest   **rosamunde overture**
        78 rpm issue: N11120G
        further lp issues: S06002R/SBL 5236/S04042L
otterloo   **leise leise/der freischütz**
residentie   78 rpm issue: N12054G
orkest   further lp issues: S06019R/SBR 6200/S06100R
brouwenstijn   cd: 462 0712/preiser 89692
otterloo   **der hirt auf dem felsen, arrangement**
residentie   78 rpm issue: N12053G
orkest   45 rpm issues: 312 097NF/313 080SF
spoorenberg
huckriede

A 00150-00153 L/bach matthäus-passion
recorded live in the concertgebouw amsterdam on 2 april 1939
mengelberg   further lp issues: ABL 3035-3038/A00320-00322L/
concertgebouw   6747 168/SL 179
orkest   cd: 416 2062/462 0922/462 8712/468 6362
toonkunst choir   *excerpts*
zanglust choir   45 rpm issues: 400 176AE/400 177AE/113 518YE
vincent, durigo,   further lp issues: L09913L/G05301R/G05388R/
erb, tulder,   turnabout TV 4445-4446
ravelli, schey   cd: 464 5222
        also published in various pirated editions

A 00154 L / dvorak symphony no 9 "from the new world"
recorded in the concertgebouw amsterdam on 17 october 1952
dorati further lp issues: ABL 3021/G03153L/LC 3001
residentie
orkest

A 00155-00156 L / bach french suites and 20 little preludes
recorded in the musikverein vienna between 9-21 december 1951
ahlgrimm *excerpts*
  further lp issues: SBR 6209/S06040R/ML 4746

A 00157-00159 L / bach wohltemperiertes klavier, book one
recorded in the musikverein vienna between 9-21 december 1951
ahlgrimm further lp issue: SL 191
  excerpts
  further lp issues: SBR 6209/S06040R

A 00160 L / orchestral works by debussy and ravel
recorded in the salle apollo paris on 19-20 november 1952
fournet **trois nocturnes**
conservatoire further lp issue: LC 3048
orchestra
ensemble vocal
fournet **rapsodie espagnole**
conservatoire further lp issue: LC 3048
orchestra **menuet antique**
  45 rpm issue: 400 001AE
  further lp issue: LC 3048

A 00161 L / orchestral works by chabrier
recorded in the salle apollo paris on 17-18 november 1952
fournet **fete polonaise/le roi malgré lui**
orchestre further lp issues: NBL 5000/SBR 6234/SBR 6235/
lamoureux S06159R/S06184R/LC 3028
brasseur choir
germain
fournet **marche joyeuse; suite pastorale**
orchestre further lp issues: NBL 5000/LC 3028
lamoureux **gwendoline overture**
  further lp issues: NBL 5000/S06034R/LC 3028
  espana
  45 rpm issue: 400 001AE
  further lp issues: NBL 5000/GBL 5500/
  G03004L/LC 3028

A 00162 L/works by rachmaninov
recorded in the concertgebouw amsterdam on 12-13 december 1952

otterloo	**piano concerto no 2**
residentie	further lp issues: ABL 3014/695 026KL/G05300R/
orkest	MGW 14040/SRW 18040/LC 3009
de groot	
de groot	**mélodie op 3 no 3; prélude op 32 no 10**
	78 rpm issue: A11248G
	further lp issues: ABL 3014/LC 3009

A 00163-00164 L/strauss salome
recorded in the musikverein vienna between 4-11 december 1953
moralt   further lp issues: ABL 3003-3004/6747 406/SL 126
wiener   cd: 438 6642
symphoniker
wegner, milinkovic,
d.hermann, szemere,
kmennt, metternich

N 00165 L/gamelan music
recorded in amsterdam on 23-24 january 1953
netherlands
study group

A 00166 L/mozart flute concertos nos 1 and 2
recorded in the musikverein vienna on 28-29 january 1953
pritchard   further lp issues: ABL 3059/6530 046/G03046L/
wiener   G05352R (no 1 only)/832 007PGY/LC 3033/
symphoniker   698 094CL
barwahser

A 00167 L/mozart bastien und bastienne
recorded in the musikverein vienna between 25-31 january 1953
pritchard   further lp issues: ABL 3010/839 308VGY/
wiener   6540 015
symphoniker
i.hollweg, kmennt,
berry

A 00168 L/chopin piano sonatas nos 2 and 3
recorded in amsterdam on 18-20 january 1952
uninsky   further lp issue: 200 011WGY (no 2 only)

A 00169-00171 L/bach the english suites
recorded in amsterdam between 23 may-10 june 1952
ahlgrimm *excerpts*
further lp issues: SBR 6209/S06040R

A 00172-00174 L/bach the partitas
recorded in amsterdam between 23 may-10 june 1952
ahlgrimm *excerpts*
further lp issues: SBR 6209/S06040R

A 00175 L/orchestral music by french composers
recorded in the salle apollo paris on 9-11 february 1953
martinon **roussel le festin de l'araignée; honegger**
orchestre **pastorale d'été; fauré pavane**
lamoureux further lp issue: LC 3058
 dukas l'apprenti sorcier; debussy prélude
 a l'apres-midi d'un faune
 further lp issues: S06011R/LC 3058

A 00176 L/beethoven symphony no 6 "pastoral"
recorded in the musikverein vienna on 22-23 february 1953
otterloo further lp issues: ABL 3043/GBL 5514/G03012L/
wiener 675 003KR/695 020KL/200 005WGY/LC 3011
symphoniker *some reissues incorrectly named orchestra as residentie orkest*

A 00177 L/beethoven symphony no 3 "eroica"
recorded in the jesus-christus-kirche berlin-dahlem on 26-28 may 1951
kempen further lp issues: ABL 3013/GBL 5514/G03013L/
berliner G03058L/695 001KL/832 008PGY/LC 3016
philharmon- cd: 438 5332/PHCP 1268-1269
isches orchester

A 00178 L/johann strauss der zigeunerbaron, abridged version
with narration *recorded in the musikverein vienna on 7-8 april 1953*
moralt further lp issue: LC 3041
wiener *overture only*
symphoniker further lp issues: SBR 6212/S06088R/S06012R/
wiener N00631R
kammerchor
barabas, milinkovic,
christ, kmennt,
braun, edelmann,
liewehr

A 00179 L/symphonies by beethoven
recorded in the musikverein vienna on 1-2 june 1953 (symphony no 1) and in the jesus-christus-kirche berlin-dahlem on 28-29 april 1953 (symphony no 8)

pritchard	**symphony no 1**
wiener	further lp issues: S06037R/GBL 5539/G03003L/
symphoniker	G03037L/LC 3095
kempen	**symphony no 8**
berliner	further lp issues: A00220-00221L/ABL 3030-3031/
philharmon-	GBL 5539/GBR 5601/G03003L/G05303R/
isches orchester	LC 3095
	cd: 438 5332/PHPC 1268-1269/

A 00180 L/beethoven symphony no 7
recorded in the jesus-christus-kirche baerlin-dahlem on 30 may-1 june 1953

kempen	further lp issues: ABL 3017/GBL 5510/G 03050L/
berliner	6747 234/695 034KL/700 045WGY/LC 3026
philharmon-	cd: 438 5332/PHCP 1268-1269
isches orchester	

A 00181 L/haydn symphonies nos 53 "l'impériale" and 67
recorded in the musikverein vienna between 14-23 april 1953

sacher	further lp issues: ABL 3075/LC 3038
wiener	
symphoniker	

N 00182 L/organ works by césar franck
recorded in amsterdam on 16-17 july 1953

asma	further lp issues: NBL 5004/LC 3051

N 00183 L/overtures and preludes from wagner operas
recorded in the musikverein vienna on 13 may 1953

moralt	**tannhäuser and die meistersinger von nürnberg**
wiener	further lp issues: S06063R/GBL 5540/G03038L/
symphoniker	200 020WGY
	der fliegende holländer and tristan und isolde
	further lp issues: S06009R/GBL 5540/G03038L/
	200 020WGY

A 00184 L/mozart piano concerti no 18 k456 and 19 k459
recorded in the musikverein vienna between 17-24 march 1953

pritchard	further lp issues: LC 3047/695 070KL (no 18 only)
wiener	
symphoniker	
henkemans	

A 00185-00187 L/bach wohltemperiertes klavier, book two
recorded in amsterdam in june and july 1953
ahlgrimm further lp issue: SL 191

A 00188-00189 L/bizet les pecheurs de perles
recorded in paris between 5-12 october 1953
fournet further lp issues: 6747 404/SC 6002
orchestre cd: 434 7822/462 2872
lamoureux *excerpts*
brasseur choir 45 rpm issues: ABE 10119/NBE 11065/402 100AE/
alarie, bianco, 402 074NE
simoneau, further lp issues: ABL 3255/A02000L/H72 AX205/
depraz GBL 5574/GL 5674/G03067L/G03426L/
700 472WGY

A 00190 L/massenet scenes pittoresques and scenes alsaciennes
recorded in the salle apollo paris on 15 september 1953
fournet further lp issues: SBL 5202/S04010L/LC 3053
orchestre
lamoureux

A 00191 L/orchestral music by berlioz
recorded in the salle apollo paris on 30 september-2 october 1953
otterloo further lp issues: S06043R/GBL 5542/G03040/
orchestre LC 3054
lamoureux cd: retrospective recordings RET 037

A 00192-00194 L/debussy pelléas et mélisande
recorded in the salle apollo paris between 14-24 september 1953
fournet further lp issues: ABL 3076-3078/SC 6003
orchestre
lamoureux
brasseur choir
micheau, gorr,
maurane, roux,
depraz

A 00195 L/brahms paganini variations and handel variations
recorded in amsterdam on 20-21 october 1953
simon

A 00196 L/orchestral works by lalo
recorded in the salle apollo paris on 16-17 june and on 25 september 1953
fournet **namouna suite no 1; rapsodie norvégienne**
orchestre further lp issue: LC 3049
lamoureux **le roi d'ys overture**
further lp issues: S06034R/SBR 6235/S06184R/
LC 3049
SBR 6235 and S06184R incorrectly named conductor as otterloo

A 00197 L/concert arias by mozart
recorded in the musikverein vienna on 21-22 november 1953
paumgartner
wiener
symphoniker
kmennt

A 00198 L/brahms symphony no 1
recorded in the concertgebouw amsterdam between 4-12 december 1953
otterloo further lp issues: S04006L/GBL 5536/G03034L/
residentie 200 053WGL
orkest cd: challenge records CC 72142

A 00199 L/violin concerti by mozart
recorded in the musikverein vienna on 23-24 november 1953
moralt **concerto no 3 k216**
wiener further lp issues: ABL 3040/G05343R/695 048KL/
symphoniker LC 3060/eterna 820 132
grumiaux cd: 473 1042
concerto no 4 k218
further lp issues: ABL 3040/G05344R/
695 035KL/894 105ZKY/LC 3060/eterna 820 132
cd: 473 1042
cd edition incorrectly names conductor as paumgartner

A 00200 L/piano concerti by liszt
recorded in the concertgebouw amsterdam on 22 december 1953 (concerto no 2)
concerto no 1 *see 00114*
otterloo **concerto no 2**
residentie further lp issues: ABL 3026/S04001L/GBL 5545/
orkest G03002L/695 017KL/200 037WGY/LC 3145
de groot cd: 462 8962/462 8952

N 00201 L/puccini scenes from tosca
recorded in milan in april 1954
guarnieri　　　　further lp issues: NBL 5001/GBL 5537/S04004L
rai milano
orchestra
malagrida,
franzini, salsedo

N 00203 L/schubert rosamunde, complete incidental music
recorded in the musikverein vienna on 29-31 january 1954
loibner　　　　further lp issues: NBL 5007/G03149L/LC 3063
wiener
symphoniker
wiener kammerchor

A 00204 L/beethoven piano sonatas nos 17 and 18
recorded in hilversum on 11-12 march 1954
de groot　　　　cd: 462 0762 (no 17 only)

A 00205-00206 L/bach organ works
heiller　　　　further lp issues: LC 3132/LC 3261

A 00207 L/operatic and concert arias by mozart
recorded in the musikverein vienna on 24-26 january 1954
paumgartner　　　　further lp issue: LC 3135
wiener　　　　cd: preiser 90335
symphoniker
zadek

N 00208 L/telemann suite for flute and strings; haydn flute concerto in d
recorded in the musikverein vienna on 22-23 january 1954
paumgartner　　　　further lp issue: LC 3075
wiener
symphoniker
barwahser

N 00209 L/bartok 44 violin duos
recorded in amsterdam on 3-4 may 1954
krebbers, olof

N 00210 L/ballet suites by tchaikovsky
recorded in the musikverein vienna on 24-26 march 1953 (sleeping beauty) and 26-28 may 1953 (casse noisette)

moralt	**casse noisette**
wiener	further lp issues: NBL 5005/S06050R/GBL 5526/
symphoniker	G03000L/G03022L/675 013KR/200 051WGY/
	LC 3078
	excerpts
	45 rpm issues: ABE 10103/NBE 11029/
	400 086AE/402 016NE
otterloo	**sleeping beauty**
wiener	further lp issues: NBL 5005/S06051R/GBL 5526/
symphoniker	G03022L/675 013KR/LC 3078
	excerpts
	45 rpm issues: ABE 10103/NBE 11029/
	400 086AE/402 016NE

A 00211 L/mozart wind divertimenti k252, k253, k270 and k289
recorded in the musikverein vienna on 10-13 december 1953
paumgartner further lp issue: G05379R (k270 and k289 only)
members of
wiener
symphoniker

A 00212 L/haydn symphonies nos 44 "trauer" and 85 "la reine"
recorded in the musikverein vienna on 6-8 january 1954
sacher further lp issue: LC 3059
wiener
symphoniker

N 00213 L/works for flute and orchestra by quantz, gluck and mozart
recorded in the musikverein vienna on 21-22 january 1954
paumgartner 45 rpm issue: 400 074AE (gluck)
wiener further lp issues: NBL 5031/G05353R (quantz and
symphoniker gluck)/LC 3134/695 078KL/698 094CL (mozart)
barwahser

A 00214-00215 L/bach brandenburg concerti nos 1-5*
recorded in the musikverein vienna between 12-22 april 1954
sacher 45 rpm issues: 400 040AE (no 3)/400 047AE (no 4)
basler kammer- further lp issues: S06106R (no 1)/S06107R (nos 2 and 5)/
orchester S06108R (nos 3 and 4)/695 010KL (nos 1, 2 and 3)/
 695 011KL (nos 4 and 5)/200 033WGL (nos 1, 2 and 3)/
 200 034WGL (nos 4 and 5)/LC 3166 (nos 1, 2 and 3)/
 LC 3167 (nos 4 and 5)/SC 6008
 *concerto no 6 appeared on A00719R

A 00218 L/brahms symphony no 2
recorded in the concertgebouw amsterdam on 17-19 may 1954
beinum further lp issues: ABL 3020/GBL 5596/G03087L/
concertgebouw LC 3098/200 071WGL
orkest cd: 462 5342

A 00219 L/works by contemporary dutch composers
recorded in the concertgebouw amsterdam between 20-29 may 1954
beinum **henkemans violin concerto**
concertgebouw further lp issue: LC 3093
orkest cd: donemus CVCD 7/BFO-A3
olof
beinum **pijper piano concerto**
concertgebouw further lp issues: A02242L/LC 3093
orkest
henkemans
beinum **pijper six epigrams**
concertgebouw further lp issues: A02242L/LC 3093
orkest

A 00220-00221 L/ *see 00145-00146 and 00179*

A 00223-00224 L/organ works by bach
heiller further lp issues: LC 3261/LC 3367

A 00225 L/mélodies by duparc
recorded in paris on 21-22 april 1953
maurane
bienvenu

A 00226-00227 L/mahler symphony no 8 "symphony of a thousand"
recorded at a concert in the ahoy hal rotterdam on 3 july 1954
flipse
rotterdam
philharmonic
and brabant
orchestras
and choirs
kupper, zadek,
bijster, hermes,
l.fischer, woud,
fehenberger,
vroons, hollestelle,
schey, frick
further lp issues: ABL 3024-3025/SC 6004/
GL 5773-5774
cd: eduard-flipse-stichting EFS 100/
scribendum SC 010

A 00228 L/lalo symphonie espagnole; chausson poeme; ravel tzigane
recorded in the salle apollo paris on 21-22 june 1954
fournet
orchestre
lamoureux
grumiaux
further lp issues: ABL 3126/695 091KL/LC 3082/
G05348R (lalo)
cd: 473 1042

A 00229-00230 L/janacek aus einem totenhaus
recorded at a performance in the stadsschouwburg amsterdam on 25 june 1954
krannhals
netherlands
opera orchestra
and chorus
jongsma, scheffer,
mantgem, bröcheler,
wozniak, genemens,
holthaus
further lp issues: ABL 3119-3120/SC 6005

A 00231 L/brahms cello sonatas nos 1 and 2
recorded in hilversum on 9-10 march and 20 june 1954
de machula
mikkilä

A 00232 L/mozart string quartets k499 and k589
recorded in amsterdam on 4-5 july 1954
netherlands further lp issues: ABL 3080/LC 3100
string quartet cd: globe GLO 6037

A 00233 L/saint-saens piano concerto no 2; d'indy symphonie cévénole
recorded in the salle apollo paris on 16-18 december 1953
fournet further lp issues: A00509L (d'indy)/LC 3096
orchestre
lamoureux
doyen

A 00234 L/beethoven violin sonatas nos 5 and 6
recorded in amsterdam on 20-21 july 1954
de klijn
heksch

A 00235 L/handel concerti grossi op 6: nos 1, 2, 6 and 7
recorded in the musikverein vienna on 9-13 april 1954
pritchard further lp issues: ABL 3075/LC 3097/
wiener 200 075WGL/695 079KL
symphoniker

A 00237 L/debussy études
recorded in amsterdam on 28-29 march and in july 1954
henkemans

A 00238 L/bach solo violin partitas nos 2 and 3
recorded in the bachzaal amsterdam between 7-15 july 1955
magyar

A 00239 L/mozart piano concerti nos 17 k453 and no 27 k595
recorded in the musikverein vienna on 7-8 april 1954
pritchard further lp issues: 695 036KL/LC 3117
wiener
symphoniker
henkemans

N 00241 L/widor organ symphony no 5
recorded in amsterdam on 1-3 september 1954
asma further lp issue: LC 3156

A 00242-00243 L/bach die kunst der fuge
recorded in vienna between april and november 1953
ahlgrimm
bretschneider

A 00244 L/mozart piano concerto no 22 k482; variations k460
recorded in the musikverein vienna on 14-16 april 1955 (concerto) and on 15 may 1955 (variations)
paumgartner
wiener
symphoniker
heksch

A 00245 L/clementi piano trios nos 1, 3, 6 and 32
recorded in october 1954
trio di bolzano further lp issue: LC 3351

A 00246 L/ravel the 2 piano concerti
recorded in the salle apollo paris on 15-18 november 1954
fournet further lp issue: LC 3123/836 926DSY
orchestre
lamoureux
doyen

N 00247 L/greek chamber music by skalkottas, varvoglis and kalomiris

N 00248 L/tchaikovsky the seasons, piano suite
recorded in amsterdam on 3-4 november 1954
osieck *excerpts*
45 rpm issue: 402 025NE

A 00249-00250 L/ orchestral works by bruckner
recorded in the musikverein vienna on 23-26 march 1954 (symphony) and in the concertgebouw amsterdam on 23 october 1954 (overture)

otterloo	**symphony no 7**
wiener symphoniker	further lp issue: SC 6006
otterloo	**overture in g minor**
residentie orkest	further lp issue: SC 6006 cd: challenge records CC 72142

A 00251 L/ works by roussel
recorded in the salle apollo paris on 20-22 september 1954

sacher	**petite suite; concert pour petit orchestre; sinfonietta for strings**
orchestre lamoureux	further lp issue: LC 3129
sacher	**piano concerto**
orchestre lamoureux gousseau	further lp issue: LC 3129

A 00252 L/ *see 00141*   **A 00253 L/** *see 00120*

A 00254 L/ *see 00123*

N 00255 L/ schubert fantasy in f minor and danses hongroises
recorded in paris on 19-22 november 1954

schnabel piano duo	45 rpm issue: NBE 11004/402 024NE (danses)

A 00256-00257 L/ chopin the nocturnes
recorded in paris on 1-3 october 1954

smeterlin	further lp issues: LC 3151-3152/SC 6007 *excerpts* 45 rpm issue: SBF 155 further lp issues: G05318R/695 049KL

A 00258 L/ violin concerti by mozart
recorded in the musikverein vienna on 12-13 october 1954

paumgartner	**concerto no 2 k211**
wiener symphoniker	further lp issues: ABL 3099/695 071KL/LC 3157 cd: 473 1042
grumiaux	**concerto no 5 k219** further lp issues: ABL 3099/G05345R/ 695 048KL/LC 3157 cd: 473 1042

A 00259 L/works for piano and orchestra by mozart
recorded in the musikverein vienna on 8-10 october 1954

sacher	piano concerto no 9 k271
wiener	further lp issues: ABL 3143/695 068KL/6599 068/
symphoniker	6747 055/6768 366/LC 3162/M10 52589-52590
haskil	cd: 420 7822/426 9642/442 6312/442 6852/
	475 7739/476 8322

paumgartner	concert rondo k386
wiener	45 rpm issue: 400 083AE
symphoniker	further lp issues: ABL 3143/SBR 6200/S06100R/
haskil	695 068KL/6747 055/6768 366/LC 3162/
	MG 50413/SR 90413
	cd: 420 7822/426 9642/442 6312/442 6852/
	454 6862/475 7739/476 8322/ermitage ERM 175

A 00260 L/mozart thamos in ägypten, incidental music
recorded in the musikverein vienna on 25-26 june 1954
paumgartner   further lp issue: ABL 3089
wiener
symphoniker
wiener kammerchor
i.hollweg,
kmennt, berry

A 00261 L/schmidt symphony no 4
recorded in the musikverein vienna on 7-9 september 1954
moralt
wiener
symphoniker

A 00262 L/franck psyché, symphonic poem in 3 parts
recorded in the concertgebouw amsterdam on 21-22 october 1954

otterloo	further lp issues: ABL 3114/LC 3146
residentie	cd: 462 8992/462 8952
orkest	
netherlands	
chamber choir	

A 00263 L/concerti for violin and orchestra
recorded in the musikverein vienna on 26-28 march 1954 (paganini) and in the concertgebouw amsterdam on 20-21 december 1954 (vieuxtemps)

otterloo	**paganini violin concerto no 1**
wiener	further lp issues: A02426L/G05443R/LC 3143
symphoniker	cd: 462 5212
krebbers	*LC 3143 incorrectly named orchestra as wiener philharmoniker*
otterloo	**vieuxtemps violin concerto no 4**
residentie	further lp issue: 641 400AXL
orkest	cd: 462 5212
krebbers	

A 00265 L/bach sonatas for flute and harpsichord
recorded in the musikverein vienna between 27 maqy-2 june 1954
pfersmann
ahlgrimm

N 00266 L/smetana scenes from the bartered bride
recorded in the musikverein vienna on 23-24 may 1954

loibner	further lp issues: NBL 5024/GL 5695/
wiener	G03183L/LC 3181
symphoniker	*excerpts*
zadek, hopf,	45 rpm issues: NBE 11019/NBE 11042/
edelmann	400 027NE/402 062NE/402 048NE
	cd: preiser 90498/89695

A 00267-00268 L/bach goldberg variations
recorded in the musikverein vienna between january and may 1954
ahlgrimm

A 00269 L/violin concerti by sibelius and glazunov
recorded in the concertgebouw amsterdam on 11-14 february 1955
otterloo   further lp issue: LC 3184
residentie
orkest
magyar

A 00271 L/orchestral works by tchaikovsky
recorded in the salle apollo paris on 31 january-2 february 1955

kempen	**serenade for strings**
orchestre	further lp issues: GBL 5564/G03503L/LC 3213/
lamoureux	200 023WGL
	cd: 438 3102
	excerpts
	45 rpm issue: SBF 135
	further lp issue: GL 5687
	suite no 4 "mozartiana"
	further lp issue: LC 3213
	cd: 438 3102

N 00272 L/palestrina missa brevis; missa ad fugam
recorded in amsterdam on 17 february 1955

de nobel	further lp issue: NBL 5033/LC 3359
netherlands	
chamber choir	

A 00273 L/bruckner symphony no 3
recorded in the musikverein vienna on 11-13 january 1955

andreae	further lp issues: GL 5697/G03171L/LC 3218
wiener	
symphoniker	

A 00274 L/mozart piano trios k502 and k564
recorded in the mozarteum salzburg between 6-11 december 1954
mozarteum trio

A 00275-00276 L/bach orgelbüchlein
heiller

A 00277-00278 L/bach organ chorales
heiller

A 00280-00282 L/mozart don giovanni
recorded in the musikverein vienna between 2-13 may 1955

moralt	further lp issues: ABL 3069-3071/GL 5753-5755/
wiener	6768 033/SC 6010
symphoniker	cd: 438 6742
wiener	*excerpts*
kammerchor	45 rpm issues: ABE 10121/400 003AE/402 101NE
jurinac, zadek,	further lp issues: ABL 3254/A02001L/SBR 5200/
sciutti, simoneau,	SBR 6235/SBR 6236/S06100R/S06149R/
london, weber,	S06184R/G03068L/695 058KL/H72-AX 205
ernster, wächter	

A 00283 L/mozart symphonies nos 25 and 33
recorded in the mozarteum salzburg on 6-9 september 1954
paumgartner
camerata
academica

A 00284-00285 L/verdi messa da requiem
recorded in the teatro argentina rome between 30 april-7 may 1953
kempen   cd: 442 2532/preiser 20047
santa cecilia   *excerpts*
orchestra   cd: preiser 89670
and chorus
brouwenstijn,
ilosvay, munteanu,
czerwenka

A 00286 L/mozart symphonies nos 29 and 34
recorded in the concertgebouw amsterdam on 25-26 april 1955
otterloo
residentie
orkest

A 00288 L/recital of arias by handel, haydn and purcell
sacher
wiener
symphoniker
zadek

A 00290 L/mozart piano concerti nos 12 k414 and 13 k415
recorded in the musikverein vienna on 24-26 march 1955
otterloo   further lp issues: 695 075KL/LC 3214
wiener
symphoniker
de groot

A 00291 L/mozart wind serenades k375 and k388
paumgartner
wiener
symphoniker

A 00292 L/harpsichord music by marchand and clérambault
recorded in paris on 1-2 march 1955
charbonnier

A 00293 L/couperin l'apothéose de lully; corrette concerto in g
recorded in paris on 13-16 september 1954
hewitt further lp issue: LC 3383
hewitt chamber
orchestra

A 00294-00295 L/symphonies by bruckner and schubert
recorded in the concertgebouw amsterdam on 6-9 june 1955
beinum **bruckner symphony no 8**
concertgebouw further lp issues: ABL 3086-3087/SC 6011
orkest cd: 442 7302/464 9502
 schubert symphony no 3
 further lp issues: ABL 3086-3087/A00436L/
 SC 6011
 cd: 442 7302/462 7242/475 6353

A 00297-00298 L/mahler symphony no 6
recorded at a concert in the concertgebouw amsterdam on 25 june 1955
flipse further lp issue: SC 6012
rotterdam cd: eduard-flipse-stichting EFS 100
philharmonic
and brabant
orchestras

A 00299 L/mozart sinfonia concertante k364; adagio k261; rondos k269 and k373
recorded in the musikverein vienna on 16 april 1954
paumgartner further lp issues: 695 057KL/LC 3197
wiener
symphoniker
de klijn, godwin

A 00300 L/bach das musikalische opfer
recorded in the musikverein vienna between 27 may-4 june 1955
ahlgrimm

A 00301 L/835 030AY/vivaldi le 4 stagioni
recorded in the concertgebouw amsterdam on 18-21 july 1955
i musici further lp issues: ABL 3128/LC 3216
excerpts
45 rpm issues: 400 110AE/400 111AE/
400 112AE/400 113AE
this appears to be the first philips mono lp for which a stereo version was also prepared

A 00302 L/torelli concerti grossi from op 8
recorded in the concertgebouw amsterdam on 22-26 july 1955
i musici further lp issue: LC 3217
excerpts
45 rpm issue: 400 024AE
further lp issue: S06081R

A 00303 L/corelli concerti grossi from op 6
recorded in the concertgebouw amsterdam on 12-16 july 1955
i musici further lp issue: LC 3264

A 00304 L/franck string quartet in d
recorded in paris on 25-27 may 1955
loewenguth further lp issue: LC 3227
quartet

A 00305 L/mozart piano concerti nos 6 k238 and 14 k449
recorded in the musikverein vienna on 14-17 may 1955
paumgartner further lp issues: ABL 3135/695 070KL (no 14)/
wiener 695 094KL (no 6)/LC 3226
symphoniker
henkemans

A 00306 L/mozart the 4 flute quartets
recorded in amsterdam on 5-6 july 1955
members of further lp issue: LC 3368
netherlands
string quartet
barwahser

A 00307 L/symphonies by mozart
recorded in the musikverein vienna on 7-8 april 1955

otterloo	**symphony no 36 "linz"**
wiener	further lp issues: GBL 5529/G03020L/695 014KL/
symphoniker	200 044WGL/LC 3233
	symphony no 38 "prague"
	further lp issues: G03008L/GBL 5529/G03020L/
	LC 3233

A 00308-00311 L/bach organ works
heiller

A 00312 L/choral works by stravinsky
recorded in the concertgebouw amsterdam in july 1954 (les noces) and on 25-26 january and 2 july 1955 (other works)

de nobel	**les noces**
netherlands	further lp issues: ABL 3124/LC 3231
chamber choir	
bijster, canne-meyer,	
haefliger, schey	
de nobel	**mass; pater noster; ave maria**
netherlands	further lp issues: ABL 3124/LC 3231
chamber choir	

A 00313 L/mozart violin concerti nos 1 k207 and 7 k271a
recorded in the musikverein vienna on 18-21 may 1955

paumgartner	further lp issues: ABL 3147/695 035KL (no 1)/
wiener	695 067KL (no 7)/894 105ZKY (no 1)/LC 3230
symphoniker	cd: 473 1042
grumiaux	

A 00315 L/piano concerti by mozart
recorded in the musikverein vienna between 8-11 october 1954

paumgartner	**concerto no 20 k466**
wiener	further lp issues: ABL 3129/A00752R/GBR 6517/
symphoniker	G05334R/6527 093/LC 3163/MG 50413/SR 90413
haskil	cd: 442 6312/442 6852/475 7739/476 8322
sacher	**concerto no 23 k488**
wiener	further lp issues: ABL 3129/A00753R/A02084L/
symphoniker	GBR 6518/G05335R/695 068KL/6527 093/
haskil	LC 3163/MG 50413/SR 90413
	cd: 442 6312/442 6852/475 7739

A 00316 L/marcello sonatas for viola da gamba and harpsichord
recorded in april 1955
scholz, giordani

A 00317 L/tansman the prophet isaiah, symphonic oratorio
recorded in the concertgebouw amsterdam in 1955
kempen   further lp issue: LC 3298
netherlands
radio orchestra
and chorus
kalkman

A 00318 L/symphonies by mozart
recorded in the concertgebouw amsterdam between 19-27 september 1955
böhm   **symphony no 41 "jupiter"**
concertgebouw   further lp issues: ABL 3102/G03014L/G05440R/
orkest   695 086KL/6540 077/6527 035/LC 3229/
                   200 068WGL
                   cd: 438 9562/477 5296
                   symphony no 26
                   further lp issues: ABL 3102/GBR 6505/
                   G05314R/LC 3229
                   cd: 438 9562/477 5296
                   symphony no 32
                   further lp issues: ABL 3102/LC 3229
                   cd: 438 9562/477 5296

A 00319 L/symphonies by mozart
recorded in the concertgebouw amsterdam between 19-27 september 1955
böhm   **symphony no 39**
concertgebouw   further lp issues: 6833 214/LC 3357
orkest   cd: 438 9562/477 5296
                   symphony no 40
                   further lp issues: GBL 5578/GBR 6505/G03064L/
                   G05314R/695 086KL/6540 077/6527 035/
                   LC 3357/200 068WGL
                   cd: 438 9562/477 5296

A 00320-00322 L/ *see 00150-00153*

A 00323-00324 L/donizetti don pasquale
recorded in the teatro san carlo naples between 8-17 september 1955
molinari- further lp issues: ABL 3140-3141/SC 6016
pradelli *excerpts*
san carlo further lp issues: GBL 5519/G03023L/
orchestra S06157R/H72-AX 205
and chorus
rizzoli, munteanu,
valdengo, capecchi

A 00325 L/beethoven piano sonatas nos 8, 14 and 23
recorded in the concertgebouw amsterdam on 7-10 november 1955
richter-haaser further lp issues: A02017L/ABL 3192/GL 5683
 (no 23)/GBR 6503 (nos 8 and 14)/G05307R
 (nos 8 and 14)/200 001 (no 23)
 cd: 442 7472

A 00326 L/mozart works for piano duet k381, k448 and k501
recorded in the bachzaal amsterdam on 28-29 october 1955
schnabel
piano duo

A 00327 L/bach sonatas for viola da gamba and harpsichord
recorded in the musikverein vienna between january and june 1955
harnoncourt
ahlgrimm

A 00329-00330 L/mussorgsky sorochintsky fair
recorded in ljubljana on 27-30 november 1955
hubad further lp issues: ABL 3148-3149/SC 6017
slovenian opera
orchestra
and chorus
bukovetz, korosec,
stritar

A 00331-00332 L/prokofiev the love of three oranges
recorded in ljubljana on 2-10 december 1955
leskovic   further lp issues: ABL 3150-3151/SC 6013
slovenian opera
orchestra
and chorus
khochevar, korosec,
lipuscek, chuden

A 00333 L/harpsichord sonatas by galuppi
sartori

A 00334 L/seventeenth-century harpsichord music
sartori

A 00335 L/bach two- and three-part inventions
recorded in the musikverein vienna in january and march 1954
ahlgrimm

A 00338 L/mozart violin sonatas k454 and k526
recorded in amsterdam on 2-5 january 1956
grumiaux   further lp issues: ABL 3144/6500 323/
haskil   6768 366/6780 017/LC 3299
        cd: 416 4782/442 6252/442 6852

A 00339 L/mozart piano concerti nos 24 k491 and 25 k503
recorded in the musikverein vienna on 4-8 october 1955
moralt   further lp issues: G05444R (no 24)
wiener   G05445R (no 25)/695 094KL (no 25)
symphoniker   *695 094KL incorrectly named conductor as paumgartnrt*
henkemans

A 00340 L/mozart concerti for 2 and 3 pianos k365 and k242
recorded in the musikverein vienna on 25-26 november 1955
paumgartner   further lp issues: 695 054KL/LC 3259
wiener
symphoniker
schnabel piano duo
alpenheim

A 00341 L/mozart piano quartet k452; oboe quartet k370; bassoon and cello sonata k292
recorded in the musikverein vienna between 28 january-1 fbruary 1955 and on 12 december 1955
members of
wiener
symphoniker
wollmann

A 00342 L/symphonies by haydn and schubert
recorded in the concertgebouw amsterdam on 10 may 1954 (haydn) and in the musikverein vienna on 13-14 january 1956 (schubert)

zecchi	**symphony no 100 "military"**
concertgebouw orkest	further lp issues: G03156L/LC 3258
zecchi	**symphony no 5**
wiener symphoniker	further lp issues: G03156L/LC 3258

A 00343-00344 L/mozart la finta semplice
recorded in the mozarteum salzburg on 30 january-3 february 1956
paumgartner   further lp issues: ABL 3106-3107/SC 6021
camerata
academica
siebert, maran,
pernerstorfer

A 00346-00347 L/chamber music from versailles
recorded in paris on 7-9 february 1955
hewitt
hewitt chamber
orchestra
micheau, sénéchal,
depraz

A 00348 L/violin sonatas by debussy and lekeu
recorded in amsterdam on 12-15 december 1955
grumiaux   further lp issue: LC 3667
castagnone

A 00349 L/chamber music from versailles
recorded in paris on 5-7 october 1955
hewitt
hewitt chamber
orchestra
collard, munteanu,
maurane, roux,
depraz

A 00350-00351 L/bach the four orchestral suites
recorded in the concertgebouw amsterdam on 31 may-2 june 1955 (nos 1 and 2), on 3 april 1956 (no 3) and on 10 april 1956 (no 4)
beinum further lp issues: ABL 3136-3137/SC 6024/
concertgebouw LC 3194 (nos 1 and 2)/LC 3332 (nos 3 and 4)/
orkest G05320R (no 2)/G05322R (no 3)/695 081KL
(nos 1 and 2)/695 082KL (nos 3 and 4)
cd: 420 8572 (no 2)/466 5432 (no 2)/475 6353/
retrospective recordings RET 034-035

A 00353 L/orchestral works by bartok and kodaly
recorded in the concertgebouw amsterdam on 13-14 october 1955 (bartok) and on 11-12 april 1956 (kodaly)
beinum **music for strings, percussion and celesta**
concertgebouw further lp issues: ABL 3163/A00433L/
orkest 6768 023/LC 3274
cd: retrospective recordings RET 036
hary janos suite
further lp issues: ABL 3163/6768 023
cd: retrospective recordings RET 036

A 00354-00356/smetana the bartered bride
recorded in the national theatre ljubljana between 14-21 april 1956
gebré further lp issues: ABL 3179-3181/SC 6020
slovenian opera *exscerpts*
orchestra further lp issue: S06177R
and chorus
bukovetz, brajnik,
lipuseck, koroshetz,
janko

A 00357-00359 L/mozart le nozze di figaro
recorded in the musikverein vienna between 16-22 april 1956
böhm further lp issues: GL 5777-5779/6706 006/
wiener SFL 14012-14014/SC 6022
symphoniker cd: 438 6702
chor der wiener *excerpts*
staatsoper 45 rpm issues: ABE 10129/NBE 11065/402 074NE
jurinac, streich, further lp issues: SBR 6235/GL 5666/G03069L/
ludwig, berry, H72-AX 205
schöffler

A 00360-00362 L/charpentier louise
recorded in the salle apollo paris between 21-31 may 1956
fournet further lp issue: SC 6018
opéra-comique cd: 442 0822
orchestra *excerpts*
and chorus further lp issues: GL 5649/G03118L
monmart, michel,
laroze, musy

A 00363-00364 L/gluck orfée et euridice
recorded in the salle apollo paris on 20-24 april 1956
rosbaud further lp issues: ABL 3359-3360/SC 6019
orchestre cd: 438 7842/468 5372
lamoureux
blanchard choir
alarie, danco,
simoneau

A 00365 L/hindemith 4 temperaments; 5 pieces from schulwerk; funeral music for viola and strings
recorded in the concertgebouw amsterdam between 7-21 october 1955 and on 12 june 1956
goldberg
netherlands
chamber orchestra
fleisher, godwin

A 00366 L/bach fantasias for harpsichord
recorded in the musikverein vienna between march 1954 and january 1955
ahlgrimm

A 00367 L/masses by mozart
recorded in the mozarteum salzburg on 8-9 march 1956 (credo-messe) and in the musikverein vienna on 30-31 may 1956 (missa brevis)

paumgartner	**credo-messe k257**
camerata	further lp issues: GL 5787/LC 3323/
academica	698 078CL/200 056WGL
and chorus	
cahnbley, schretter,	
maran, raninger	
moralt	**missa brevis k275**
wiener	further lp issues: GL 5787/LC 3415/
symphoniker	698 078CL
sängerknaben	
majkut, berry	

A 00368 L/beethoven piano sonatas nos 21 and 28
recorded in the concertgebouw amsterdam on 3-5 march 1956
richter-haaser   cd: 442 7472

A 00369 L/wind concerti by mozart
recorded in the musikverein vienna on 14 september 1953 (clarinet concerto) and on 7-8 march 1955 (horn and bassoon concerti)

paumgartner	**clarinet concerto**
wiener	further lp issues: ABR 4033/A00698R/
symphoniker	L09010L/695 022KL
schönhofer	
paumgartner	**horn concerto no 3**
wiener	further lp issues: L09010L/G05337R/
symphoniker	A00779R
koch	
paumgartner	**bassoon concerto**
wiener	further lp issues: L09010L/G05337R/
symphoniker	A00779R
czernak	

A 00370 L/works by prokofiev
recorded in the salle apollo paris on 28-29 june 1953 (symphony and suite) and in the concertgebouw amsterdam on 8 april 1953 (piano concerto)

martinon	**symphony no 1; suite from love of 3 oranges**
orchestre	45 rpm issue: NBE 11046/400 015NE (symphony)
lamoureux	further lp issue: G03011L
otterloo	**piano concerto no 3**
residentie	further lp issues: ABR 4022/A00650R/G03011L
orkest	cd: challenge records CC 72142
uninsky	

A 00371 L/works by de falla
recorded in the salle apollo paris on 7-9 november 1955

martinon	**el amor brujo**
orchestre	further lp issues: SBL 5213/S04028L/LC 3305
lamoureux	
vozza	
martinon	**noches en los jardines de espana**
orchestre	further lp issues: SBL 5213/S04028L/LC 3305
lamoureux	
del pueyo	

A 00372 L/piano works by schumann
recorded in amsterdam on 4 june 1951 (abegg variations) and 26 may 1955 (kinderszenen) and in hilversum on 5-6 may 1954 (waldszenen)

haskil
- **abegg variations**
  78 rpm issue: A11213G
  45 rpm issue: ABE 10037/400 010AE
  further lp issues: 835 936/6590 088/6747 055/ longanesi GCL 54
  cd: 420 8512/426 9642/442 6352/442 8292/475 7739
- **kinderszenen**
  45 rpm issue: ABE 10080/400 076AE
  further lp issues: A00775R/835 936/6598 274/ 6747 055/695 008KL/LC 3358/longanesi GCL 54
  cd: 420 8512/426 9642/442 6352/442 8292/ 475 7739/476 2668/andromeda ANDRCD 5102
- **waldszenen**
  further lp issues: A00775R/835 936/6747 055/ 695 089KL/LC 3358
  cd: 420 8512/426 9642/442 6352/442 8292/ 475 7739/476 2668/andromeda ANDRCD 5102
  longanesi edition was incorrectly dated 1954

A 00373 L/rimsky-korsakov scheherazade, symphonic suite
recorded in the concertgebouw amsterdam on 17 july 1956

beinum
concertgebouw
orkest

further lp issues: ABL 3194/S06013R/6768 023/ G03006L/G05407R/LC 3300

A 00374 L/mozart selection of dances and marches
recorded in the mozarteum salzburg on 16-17 june 1955

paumgartner
camerata
academica

A 00375 L/masses by mozart
recorded in vienna between 2-10 september 1955 (coronation mass) and in the mozarteum salzburg between 20-27 october 1955 (missa brevis)

moralt	**coronation mass k317**
wiener	further lp issues: G03189L/G05403R/
symphoniker	695 072KL/LC 3415/200 056WGL
sängerknaben	*excerpts*
majkut, berry	further lp issues: SBR 6200/S06100R
paumgartner	**missa brevis k194**
camerata	further lp issue: LC 3323
academica	
and chorus	

A 00376 L/mahler symphony no 4
recorded in the concertgebouw amsterdam on 7-9 may 1956

otterloo	further lp issues: GL 5811/G03226L/
residentie	695 051KL/698 027CL/LC 3304
orkest	cd: retrospective recordings RET 041/
stich-randall	challenge records CC 72142

A 00377 L/beethoven incidental music for die geschöpfe des prometheus
recorded in the concertgebouw amsterdam on 14-15 may 1956

otterloo	further lp issue: ABL 3183
residentie	cd: challenge records CC 72142
orkest	*excerpts*
	45 rpm issue: CFE 15062/495 036CE
	further lp issue: L00453L

A 00378 L/mozart ballet music for les petits riens; german dances
recorded in the musikverein vienna on 20-23 june 1955

paumgartner	further lp issues: 200 032WGL/
wiener	695 028KL (german dances)
symphoniker	

A 00379 L/organ music by frescobaldi
recorded in the istituto pontifica rome on 16-18 april 1954
vignanelli

A 00380 L/violin sonatas by tartini, corelli, vitali and veracini
recorded in amsterdam on 16-19 july 1956

grumiaux	45 rpm issue: ABE 10090/400 069AE
castagnone	further lp issue: LC 3414
	cd: 438 5162

A 00381 L/franck piano quintet; prélude, chorale et fugue
recorded in paris on 8-10 september 1953 (prélude chorale et fugue) and on 23-25 may 1955 (piano quintet)
loewenguth
string quartet
eymar

A 00382 L/mozart divertimenti k131, k136, k137 and k138
recorded in the mozarteum salzburg on 24-26 october 1955
paumgartner
camerata
academica

A 00383 L/violin concerti by vivaldi
i musici

A 00384 L/five concerti by marcello
recorded in rome between 26 april-5 may 1956
i musici further lp issue: LC 3380

A 00385 L/works for voice and harpsichord by caccini, peri, luzzaschi and gagliano
recorded in rome between 20-24 april 1956
nicolai, carteri,
nobile, sartori

A 00386 L/operatic arias from tannhäuser, lohengrin, der fliegende holländer, don carlo, il trovatore and la forza del destino
recorded in the musikverein vienna between 8-12 april1956
moralt cd: 462 0712/preiser 89692
wiener
symphoniker
brouwenstijn

A 00388-00389 L/piano music by granados
recorded on 29-30 august 1956
del pueyo

A 00390 L/bruckner symphony no 9
recorded in the concertgebouw amsterdam on 17-19 september 1956
beinum further lp issues: L09011L/6540 008/
concertgebouw 894 050ZKY/LC 3401
orkest cd: 442 7312/464 9502

A 00392 L/mozart complete ballet music for idomeneo
recorded in the mozarteum salzburg on 2-5 june 1955
paumgartner further lp issue: 698 084CL
camerata
academica

A 00393-00395 L/rossini mosé
recorded in the teatro san carlo naples between 3-20 june 1956
serafin further lp issues: ABL 3201-3203/6700 013
san carlo *excerpts*
orchestra further lp issues: S06193R/GBL 5519/GL 5696/
and chorus G03023L/G03184L
mancini, rizzoli,
filippeschi, taddei,
rossi-lemeni

A 00396-00397 L/mozart zaide; lo sposo deluso; l'oca del cairo
recorded in the mozarteum salzburg on 4-5 june 1956
paumgartner
camerata
academica
and chorus
boesch, majkut,
raninger

A 00398 L/works by mozart
recorded in the concertgebouw amsterdam on 22-25 may 1956
beinum **posthorn serenade**
concertgebouw further lp issues: ABL 3174/G05415R/
orkest 642 107DXL/LC 3354
cd: 475 6353/retrospective recordings RET 046
symphony no 29
further lp issues: ABL 3174/6768 023/LC 3354
cd: 462 5252/retrospective recordings RET 046

A 00399 L/works by tchaikovsky and smetana
recorded in the concertgebouw amsterdam between 10-15 september 1956
dorati	**symphony no 4**
concertgebouw	further lp issues: ABL 3195/200 050WGY/LC 3421
orkest	**the moldau/ma vlast**
	see 09003-09004

A 00400 L/beethoven violin sonatas nos 2, 3 and 8
recorded in amsterdam on 16-18 september 1956
grumiaux	further lp issues: ABL 3199/GL 5857/836 961/
haskil	6733 001/6580 090 (nos 2 and 3)/6580 032 (no 8)/
	LC 3488/SC 6030
	cd: 422 1402/442 6252/442 6852/475 8460

A 00402 L/liturgical chants from russian cathedrals
recorded in paris on 13-14 february 1953
spassky
russian orthodox
cathedral choir

A 00403 L/works by albeniz, bizet and rimsky-korsakov
recorded in the salle apollo paris between 9-17 december 1953 (albeniz and bizet)
and on 16 june 1954 (rimsky-korsakov)
toldra	**iberia suite**
orchestre	further lp issue: A00699R
lamoureux	
fournet	**carmen suite no 1**
orchestre	further lp issues: S06012R/GBL 5500/G03004L/
lamoureux	LC 3068
	capriccio espagnol
	45 rpm issue: ABE 10050/400 020AE
	further lp issue: LC 3432

A 00405 L/chopin études op 10
recorded in amsterdam between 22 february-3 march 1954
uninsky	further lp issues: A00710-00711R/LC 3065

A 00409 L/beethoven violin sonatas nos 1, 4 and 5
recorded in amsterdam on 2-5 january 1957
grumiaux further lp issues: ABL 3204/A00790R (nos 1 and 2)/
haskil GL 5858/836 962/6733 001/LC 3400/SC 6030
cd: 422 1402/442 6252/442 6852/475 8460

A 00410-00411 L/works by mahler
recorded in the concertgebouw amsterdam between 3-12 december 1956
beinum **das lied von der erde**
concertgebouw further lp issues: GL 5798/G03161L/894 120ZKY/
orkest 6780 013/SC 6023
merriman cd: 462 0682
haefliger
beinum **lieder eines fahrenden gesellen**
concertgebouw 45 rpm issue: ABE 10169/400 117AE
orkest further lp issues: 6780 013/SC 6023
merriman cd: 462 0682

A 00412 L/beethoven violin sonatas nos 7 and 10
recorded in amsterdam on 28-30 december 1956
grumiaux further lp issues: ABL 3207/GL 5859 (no 10)/
haskil 836 963/6733 001/LC 3381/SC 6030
cd: 422 1402/442 6252/442 6852/475 8460

A 00413-00414 L/d'albert tiefland
recorded in the musikverein vienna on 7-14 january 1957
moralt further lp issues: 6768 026/SC 6025
wiener cd: 434 7812
symphoniker *excerpts*
chor der wiener further lp issues: GL 5672/G03100L
staatsoper
brouwenstijn,
hopf, kmennt,
schöffler, wächter,
czerwenka

A 00415-00416 L/bach toccatas and fugues
ahlgrimm

A 00417-00419 L/mozart cosi fan tutte
recorded in the musikverein vienna between 23-29 november 1956

moralt	further lp issues: GL 5703-5705/G03177-03179L/
wiener	PHC 3005
symphoniker	*excerpts*
chor der wiener	lp: SBR 6235/S06184R
staatsoper	
stich-randall,	
malaniuk, sciutti,	
kmennt, berry,	
ernster	

A 00420 L/works for violin and orchestra by saint-saens
recorded in the salle apollo paris on 21-23 june 1954 (concerto) and on 26-29 november 1956 (other works)

fournet	**violin concerto no 3**
orchestre	further lp issues: A00465L/G05354R/
lamoureux	695 091KL/LC 3399
grumiaux	**introduction and rondo capriccioso**
	45 rpm issue: SBF 161
	further lp issue: LC 3399
	cd: 473 1042
	havanaise
	further lp issues: G05406R/695 092KL/LC 3399
	cd: 473 1042

A 00421 L/debussy works for piano
recorded in amsterdam between 10-18 january 1957

henkemans	*excerpts*
	78 rpm issues: A11217G/A11247G
	cd: 462 8972/462 8952

A 00422 L/violin concerti by tchaikovsky and bruch
recorded in the musikverein vienna on 29 october-1 november 1956

leskovic	further lp issue: LC 3365
wiener	
symphoniker	
grumiaux	

A 00423-00425 L/ donizetti linda di chamonix
recorded in the teatro san carlo naples between 7-19 september 1956
serafin further lp issues: 6706 005/M3L-403
san carlo *excerpts*
orchestra 45 rpm issue: ABE 10130/400 124AE
and chorus further lp issues: GL 5519/G03023L/
stella, valletti, H72-AX 205/preiser PR 9832
capecchi, taddei,
modesti

A 00427 L/ album de musique: songs collected by rossini
recorded in florence on 7-10 october 1956
danco
molinari-pradelli

A 00428 L/ cherubini requiem in c minor
toffolo
trieste
philharmonic
giuseppe verdi
chorus

A 00429 L/ chopin 14 valses
recorded in amsterdam on 11-14 february 1957
uninsky *excerpts*
 45 rpm issue: 400 026AE
 further lp issue: G03005L

A 00430 L/ beethoven violin sonatas nos 6 and 9
recorded in amsterdam on 26-28 september 1957
grumiaux further lp issues: ABL 3326/GL 5860 (no 6)/
haskil GL 5859 (no 9)/GBR 5636 (no 9)/G05351R (no 9)/
 695 073KL (no 9)/836 944/6733 001/LC 3458/
 SC 6030
 cd: 422 1402/442 6252/442 6852/475 8460

A 00432 L/mozart violin sonatas k301, k304, k376 and k378
recorded in basel on 19-20 november 1958
grumiaux further lp issues: 6747 055/6768 366/6780 017/
haskil LC 3602/SC 6034/melodiya C10 13439-13440
cd: 412 2532/442 6252/442 6852

A 00433 L/works by stravinsky and bartok
recorded in the concertgebouw amsterdam on 22 may 1956 (stravinsky)
beinum **le chant du rossignol**
concertgebouw further lp issues: S06130R/6768 023/LC 3274
orkest cd: retrospective recordings RET 044
music for percussion strings and celesta
see 00353

A 00434 L/beethoven violin concerto
recorded in the concertgebouw amsterdam on 4 june 1957
beinum further lp issues: 894 048ZKY/6530 018/
concertgebouw LC 3420/eterna 820 126
orkest
grumiaux

A 00435 L/mozart requiem
recorded in the musikverein vienna in november 1956
böhm further lp issues: GL 5709/G03088L/LC 3507/
wiener 200 072WGL
symphoniker cd: 420 7722/477 5296
chor der wiener *also issued in a pirated cd edition by classical collection*
staatsoper
stich-randall, malaniuk,
kmennt, böhme

A 00436 L/symphonies by mendelssohn and schubert
recorded in the concertgebouw amsterdam on 2-4 june 1955 (mendelssohn)
beinum **mendelssohn symphony no 4 "italian"**
concertgebouw further lp issues: SBR 6202/S06073R/GBL 5578/
orkest G03064L/G05329R/6768 023/LC 3411
schubert symphony no 3
see 00294-00295

A 00437 L/works by mussorgsky-ravel and stravinsky
recorded in the concertgebouw amsterdam on 21-22 february 1952 (mussorgsky-ravel) and 6 april 1956 (stravinsky)

dorati	**pictures from an exhibition**
concertgebouw orkest	further lp issues: ABR 4013/A00607R/S06165R/ GBR 6521/G05309R/LC 3015
beinum	**oiseau de feu, suite**
concertgebouw orkest	further lp issues: S06130R/6768 023/LC 3290 cd: retrospective RET 044

A 00439 L/ *see 00145-00146*

A 00440 L/concerti by mozart
recorded in the concertgebouw amsterdam on 29 may 1957 (clarinet concerto) and 6 june 1957 (flute and harp concerto)

beinum	**concerto for flute and harp**
concertgebouw orkest barwahser berghout	further lp issues: ABL 3217/894 018ZKY/LC 3456 cd: 462 5252/475 6353/etcetera KTC 2024
beinum	**clarinet concerto**
concertgebouw orkest de wilde	further lp issues: ABL 3217/G05333R/ 894 018ZKY/LC 3456

A 00441 L/835 001AY/works by debussy
recorded in the concertgebouw amsterdam on 27-28 may 1957

beinum	**trois nocturnes**
concertgebouw orkest collegium choir	further lp issues: 836 916DSY/894 005ZKY/ 6530 016/6768 023/LC 3464/BC 1020 cd: 462 0692/475 6353/retrospective RET 040
beinum	**la mer**
concertgebouw orkest	further lp issues: 836 916DSY/G05466R/ 894 005ZKY/6530 016/6812 102/ LC 3464/BC 1020 cd: 462 0692/475 6353/retrospective RET 040
	berceuse héroique
	further lp issues: ABL 3324/SABL 103/835 003AY/ 835 009AY/G05466R/6768 023 cd: 438 7422
	marche écossaise
	further lp issues: ABL 3324/SABL 103/835 003AY/ 835 009AY/6768 023/LC 3477

berceuse héroique and marche écossaise appeared on mono lp 00441 but not on the stereo equivalent 835 001

A 00443 L/vivaldi three violin concerti
recorded in rome on 2-4 may 1956
i musici further lp issue: LC 3343
  excerpts
  further lp issue: GBL 5621

A 00444-00445 L/puccini la boheme
recorded in the teatro san carlo naples between 31 may-14 june 1957
molinari- further lp issues: 6720 008/M2L-401
pradelli cd: 442 1062
san carlo *excerpts*
orchestra 45 rpm issues: ABE 10124/ABE 10130/
and chorus 402 104AE/400 125AE
stella, rizzoli, further lp issues: GBL 5653/G03070L/
poggi, capecchi, S06187R/H72-AX 205
mazzini, modesti,
luise

A 00446 L/pergolesi stabat mater; salve regina
recorded in the teatro communale florence on 11-15 october 1956
molinari- further lp issue: LC 3460
pradelli
teatro communale
orchestra
and chorus
rizzoli, carbe

A 00447 L/geminiani five concerti from op 7
recorded in rome on 5-7 march 1957
i musici further lp issue: LC 3467

A 00448 L/manfredini six concerti from op 3
recorded in rome between 1-6 may 1957
i musici further lp issue: LC 3514

A 00449 L/bonporti four concerti from op 11
recorded in rome on 13-17 january 1957
i musici further lp issue: LC 3542
  excerpts
  45 rpm issue: 400 141AE

L 00450-00454 L/ *sampler lps for the philips classical catalogue*

A 00456 L/835 090AY/schumann carnaval; liszt paganini études
recorded in amsterdam on 4-6 april 1961
magaloff

A 00457-00458 L/symphonies by beethoven
recorded in the maison de la chimie paris in october 1960 (no 1) and between 20 january-2 february 1961 (no 9)

markevitch	**symphony no 9 "choral"**
orchestre	further lp issues: A02090-02091L/A02328-02329L/
lamoureux	835 087-835 088AY/835 091-835 092AY/
karlsruhe	835 206-835 207AY/836 918DSY/693 500ZVL/
oratorio choir	AM 004/AS 004/6539 006/6580 006/MDW 14050/
güden, heynis,	SRW 18050/melodiya D 011255-011258
uhl, rehfuss	cd: 464 0912
	symphony no 1
	cd: 464 0942

A 00459 L/symphonies by haydn and mozart
recorded in the concertgebouw amsterdam on 6-10 december 1960 (haydn) and 6-9 june 1961 (mozart)

goldberg	**haydn symphony no 83 "la poule"**
netherlands	further lp issues: 835 093AY/SFL 14039/
chamber	700 101WGL/LC 3810/BC 1148
orchestra	cd: retrospective 93407
	mozart symphony no 21
	further lp issues: 835 093AY/SFL 14073
	cd: retrospective 93407
	mozart symphony no 5
	further lp issue: SFL 14073
	cd: retrospective 93407

A 00460 L/835 094AY/sacred arias by bach and handel

gillesberger	further lp issue: 894 061ZKY/6530 038
wiener	cd: 426 1092/438 7722/462 0842/462 1022
symphoniker	*excerpts from the recital*
heynis	further lp issue: 610 123VL

A 00461 L/835 097AY/schubert lieder recital
recorded in the bachzaal amsterdam between 18-24 june 1961
souzay further lp issues: ABL 3408/SABL 214/
baldwin 894 064ZKY/6527 103/500 007/900 007
cd: 422 4182
excerpts from the recital
45 rpm issues: 400 247AE/400 248AE
further lp issues: 610 143VL/836 260VZ/
894 079ZKY/6580 011

A 00462 L/miscellaneous concerti by vivaldi
i musici

A 00463-00464 L/puccini tosca
recorded in the teatro san carlo naples between 5-13 september 1957
serafin further lp issues: 6720 007/WL 1197-1198/M2L-402
san carlo *excerpts*
orchestra 45 rpm issues: ABE 10125/ABE 10130/
and chorus 400 124AE/402 105NE
stella, poggi, further lp issues: G03073L/695 032KL/
taddei preiser PR 9832

A 00465 L/violin concerti by paganini and saint-saens
recorded in the salle apollo paris on 8-10 november 1954 (paganini)
gallini **paganini concerto no 4**
orchestre further lp issues: ABR 4024/A00714R/A02426L/
lamoureux 894 017ZKY/836 931VZ/GBL 5576/G03062L/
grumiaux G05327R/LC 3143
cd: 473 1042
saint-saens concerto no 3
see 00420

A 00469 L/song cycles by britten, ravel and debussy
sacher **les illuminations**
orchestre further lp issue: 641 112AXL
lamoureux
micheau
fournet **shéhérazade**
orchestre further lp issue: 641 112AXL
lamoureux
micheau
fournet **don quichotte a dulcinée; ballades de**
orchestre **francois villon**
lamoureux further lp issue: 641 112AXL
maurane

A 00470 L/benvenoli   messe solennelle pour 53 voix
recorded in vienna on 6 june 1952
messner   further lp issue: A00622-00623R
wiener
symphoniker
salzburger domchor

A 00472 L/scarlatti   keyboard sonatas
sartori

A 00474 L/835 063AY/piano concerti by schumann and grieg
recorded in the musikverein vienna on 18-21 january 1958
moralt   **schumann**
wiener   further lp issues: ABL 3224/SABL 180/GL 5814/
symphoniker   SGL 5814/G03215L/G05476R/837 041GY/
richter-haaser   610 806VL/836 251VZ/SDAL 500/SFL 14093/
                     700 182WGY/MGW 14049/SRW 18049
                     grieg
                     further lp issues: ABL 3224/SABL 180/GL 5814/
                     SGL 5814/G03215L/837 041GY/6539 018/
                     GBR 6516/G05323R/SFL 14093/
                     700 182WGY/MGW 14049/SRW 18049

A 00475 L/incidental music by mendelssohn and schubert
recorded in the concertgebouw amsterdam on 2-4 december 1957
szell   **a midsummer night's dream overture, scherzo,**
concertgebouw   **nocturne and wedding march**
orkest   further lp issues: ABL 3238/835 006AY/GBL 5677/
                     G05324R/SFM 23006/839 511/894 044ZKY/
                     6580 027/LC 3433/BC 1023
                     cd: 432 2282/442 7272/475 6780
                     excerpts
                     45 rpm issue: ABE 10078/400 858AE/SBF 152
                     rosamunde overture, entr'acte in b minor
                     (ballet music no 1), entr'acte in b flat and
                     ballet in g (ballet music no 2)
                     further lp issues: ABL 3238/835 064AY/
                     G 05331R/G05449R/894 069ZKY/SFM 23006/
                     839 511/839 516VGY/6530 054/LC 3433/BC 1023
                     cd: 432 2282/442 7272/475 6780
                     excerpts
                     45 rpm issue: 400 059AE

A 00476 L/835 002AY/violin concerti by vivaldi
recorded in rome between 1-10 january 1958
i musici further lp issues: LC 3480/BC 1021
excerpts
45 rpm issue: 400 108AE
further lp issues: GL 5621/BAL 31/SBAL 31

A 00478 L/beethoven piano sonatas 24, 25 and 32; rondo op 51/1
recorded in amsterdam on 15-16 april 1956 and on 26-27 april 1957
henkemans

A 00479 L/835 005AY/vivaldi flute concerti from op 10
recorded in rome between 1-10 january 1958
i musici further lp issues: LC 3541/BC 1014
tassinari *excerpts*
further lp issue: G05321R

A 00484 L/piano sonatas by mozart and schubert
recorded in amsterdam on 5-6 may 1954 (mozaqrt)
haskil **mozart sonata no 10 k330**
further lp issues: ABL 3356/A02084L/A00724R/
695 090KL/6733 002/6768 366
cd: 442 6352/442 6852/456 8292/475 7739
schubert sonata no 21 d960
see 00108

A 00486 L/reger mozart variations; eine romantische suite
recorded in the concertgebouw amsterdam on 9-10 march 1956 (suite)
and on 26-27 march 1957 (variations)
otterloo further lp issue: G03148L
residentie cd: challenge records CC 72142
orkest

A 00487 L/works by henk badings
recorded in the concertgebouw amsterdam on 28-30 november 1955
otterloo	**symphony no 3**
residentie	cd: challenge records CC 72142
orkest	
otterloo	**concerto for two violins**
residentie	further lp issue: A02242L
orkest	
krebbers, olof	

A 00488 L/835 129AY/christmas concerti by torelli, corelli, manfredini and locatelli
recorded in rome between 1-10 january 1958
i musici   further lp issues: L09006L/500 025/900 025

A 00489 L/ *see 00142 and 00148*

A 00490 L/choral music for christmas
de nobel
netherlands
chamber choir

A 00491 L/835 004AY/handel the water music
recorded in the concertgebouw amsterdam on 1-5 july 1958
beinum   further lp issues: ABL 3249/SABL 125/
concertgebouw   894 007ZKY/6540 068/6598 893/
orkest   LC 3551/LC 3749/BC 1016/
                 BC 1112/eterna 825 133
                 cd: 420 8572/466 5432/475 6353
                 excerpts
                 45 rpm issue: 400 119AE
                 further lp issues: A02299L/835 175AY

A 00492 L/string quartets by flothuis and landré
recorded in amsterdam on 14-18 june 1958
netherlands
string quartet

A 00493 L/mozart scenes from la finta giardiniera
paumgartner
camerata
academica
protero, nixa,
seywald, perl

A 00494 L/operas by mozart and pergolesi
paumgartner   der schauspieldirektor
camerata
academica
harvey, brinck,
seywald, perl
paumgartner   la serva padrona
camerata
academica
protero, raninger

A 00495 L/haydn lo speziale
paumgartner
camerata
academica
schönauer, zur eck,
smid-kowar

A 00499 L/works for violin and piano by schubert
recorded in amsterdam between 14-23 july 1958
grumiaux   **sonatinas d384 and d408**
castagnone   further lp issue: LC 3609
                  cd: 438 5162
                  excerpts
                  further lp issues: SBR 6230/S06082R
                  sonatina d385 and duo d574
                  further lp issues: SBR 6230/S06082R/LC 3609
                  cd: 438 5162

A 00501 L/concerti for one and two harpsichords by bach
fiala   **concerti bwv1056 and bwv1058**
amati orchestra   further lp issue: G05353R
ahlgrimm
fiala   **concerti bwv1060 and bwv1061**
amati orchestra
ahlgrimm, bretschneider

A 00502 L/835 000AY/works by brahms
recorded in the concertgebouw amsterdam on 1-3 may 1958 (symphony) and on 26-27 september 1958 (overture)

beinum	**symphony no 4**
concertgebouw	further lp issues: ABL 3310/SABL 100/894 003ZKY/
orkest	LC 3563/BC 1019/SC 6033/BSC 103
	cd: 462 5342
	academic festival overture
	further lp issues: ABL 3310/835 013AY/894 003ZKY/
	LC 3563/BC 1019/SC 6033/BSC 103
	cd: retrospective RET 039

academic festival overture appeared on mono lp 00502 but not on the stereo equivalent 835 000

A 00504 L/835 015AY/brahms symphony no 1
recorded in the concertgebouw amsterdam on 6-7 october 1958

beinum	further lp issues: ABL 3283/SABL 124/894 036ZKY/
concertgebouw	SC 6033/BSC 103
orkest	cd: 420 8542/462 5342/475 6353

A 00505 L/835 019AY/works by beethoven
recorded in the beethovenhaus bonn on 17-20 september 1958

horszowski	**horn sonata arranged for cello and piano**
casals	further lp issues: 6747 103/6833 054
	cd: 420 8552
horszowski	**piano trio op 1 no 3**
vegh	further lp issue: G05364R
casals	cd: 426 1052

A 00506 L/835 020AY/beethoven piano trio no 7 "archduke"
recorded in the beethovenhaus bonn on 17-20 september 1958

horszowski	further lp issues: GBL 5639/G03601L/6701 038/
vegh	6747 103/500 016/900 016
casals	cd: 420 8552

A 00507 L/beethoven cello sonatas nos 2 and 5
recorded in the beethovenhaus bonn on 17-20 september 1958
horszowski
casals

A 00509 L/works for piano and orchestra
fournet fauré ballade
orchestre further lp issues: N00704R/802 776LY
lamoureux **franck variations symphoniques**
doyen further lp issues: 695 037KL/802 776LY
d'indy symphonie cévénole
see 00233

A 00514 L/835 016AY/mozart eine kleine nachtmusik; serenata notturna; divertimento in d k136
i musici further lp issues: ABL 3323/SABL 127/G05412R/
836 203VZ/610 109VR (eine kleine nachtmusik)/
836 223VZ (eine kleine nachtmusik)/LC 3613/BC 1040

A 00516 L/835 017AY/handel concerti grossi op 6: nos 9, 10 and 12
i musici further lp issues: ABL 3325/SABL 129/
LC 3591 (nos 9 and 10)/LC 3644 (no 12)/
BC 1030 (nos 9 and 10)/BC 1061 (no 12)

A 00517 L/khachaturian piano concerto; solo works by scriabin, khachaturian, rachmaninov, prokofiev and balakirev
otterloo further lp issue: ABR 4039 (concerto)
residentie
orkest
boukoff

A 00518 L/beethoven piano sonatas nos 8, 14 and 23
recorded in amsterdam between 6-12 january 1960
boukoff further lp issues: GBL 5598/G03059L/SFL 14082/
700 139WGY/894 038ZKY

A 00519 L/835 007AY/bach concerti bwv 1041, bwv 1042 and bwv 1043
i musici further lp issues: ABL 3259/SABL 142/A02037L
(bwv 1043)/835 042AY (bwv 1043)/G05347R
(bwv 1043)/L09008L/610 112VR (bwv 1041)/
610 106VR (bwv 1042 and bwv 1043)/
836 217VZ (bwv 1042 and bwv 1043)/
6589 021/LC 3553/BC 1018

A 00520 L/835 018AY/chopin selection of polonaises
uninsky

A 00526 L/symphonies by cherubini and weber
zecchi   **cherubini symphony in d**
wiener   further lp issue: LC 3402
symphoniker
otterloo   **weber symphony no 2**
residentie   further lp issue: LC 3402
orkest

A 00527 L/concerti by mozart and haydn
recorded in vienna in may 1956 (mozart) and in amsterdam on 2 october 1956 (haydn)
loibner   **mozart oboe concerto**
wiener   further lp issue: 695 022KL/894 053ZKY
symphoniker   cd: 462 5522
j.stotijn
goldberg   **haydn oboe concerto in d**
netherlands   further lp issues: 6530 062/MG 50396/SR 90396/
chamber   894 053ZKY
orchestra   cd: 462 5522/retrospective 93407
h.stotijn

A 00528 L/835 022AY/dittersdorf doktor und apotheker
recorded in the mozarteum salzburg in february 1959
paumgartner
camerata academica
lowrencewic,
harvey, vrooman,
smid-kovar, welz,
perl

A 00529 L/835 023AY/gluck der betrogene kadi
recorded in the mozarteum salzburg in february 1959
paumgartner
camerata academica
nixa, djeri,
schönauer, vrooman,
smid-kovar

A 00533 L/835 026AY/cantatas by bach and ritter
recorded at a concert in the janskerk gouda on 1 july 1959

horst	**bach cantata no 169 "gott alleine soll mein**
netherlands	**herze haben"**
chamber	further lp issues: LC 3683/BC 1077
orchestra	cd: 438 7722
and chorus	**ritter o amantissime sposo jesu**
heynis	45 rpm issue: 400 175AE
	further lp issues: LC 3683/BC 1077
	cd: 462 0842/retrospective 93407

retrospective incorrectly describes conductor as szymon goldberg

A 00536 L/835 027AY/russian and french orchestral works
recorded in the concertgebouw amsterdam on 16-18 june 1959

fournet	**mussorgsky night on bare mountain;**
concertgebouw	**borodin in the steppes of central asia**
orkest	further lp issues: ABL 3231/SABL 144/
	G05359R/836 211VZ/LC 3636/BC 1054/
	836 902DSY (bare mountain)
	chabrier espana
	further lp issues: ABL 3231/SABL 144/
	LC 3636/BC 1054
	debussy prélude a l'apres-midi d'un faune;
	dukas l'apprenti sorcier
	further lp issues: ABL 3231/SABL 144/S06011R/
	G05401R/836 209VZ/894 011ZKY/
	LC 3636/BC 1054

A 00539 L/835 029AY/albinoni concerti from op 2 and op 9
recorded in rome between 29 april-6 may 1959
i musici further lp issues: ABL 3321/SABL 158/
LC 3682/BC 1076
excerpts
further lp issues: BAL 31/SBAL 31/GBL 5621

A 00544 L/835 031AY/piano concerti by liszt
somogyi **concerto no 1**
wiener further lp issues: 610 114VR/G05408R/SFL 14034/
symphoniker 700 156WGY/MGW 14066/SRW 18066/
boukoff 894 009ZKY
concerto no 2
further lp issues: 610 114VR/G05408R/SFL 14050/
700 172WGY/MG 14066/SRW 18066/WL 1134/
894 009ZKY

A 00545 L/835 032AY/dvorak symphony no 9 "from the new world"
recorded in the concertgebouw amsterdam on 21-22 september 1959
dorati further lp issues: ABL 3309/SABL 161/GL 5848/
concertgebouw SGL 5848/G03247L/837 075GY/839 502VGY/
orkest 610 113VR/836 214VZ/836 237VZ/894 006ZKY/
SFL 14030/827 075GY/6500 218/6580 072/
6582 014/6582 502/6701 006
cd: 442 4012/454 5382

A 00546 L/835 033AY/dvorak symphony no 7; 4 slavonic dances
recorded in the concertgebouw amsterdam on 16-17 september 1959
haitink 45 rpm issue: 400 180AE (3 dances only)
concertgebouw further lp issues: ABL 3367/SABL 196/
orkest LC 3668/BC 1070
cd: 462 0772

A 00547 L/835 034AY/symphonies by beethoven
recorded in the maison de la chimie paris in october 1959
markevitch **symphony no 5**
orchestre further lp issues: GL 5807/G03223L/610 133VR/
lamoureux 836 205VZ/DY 88253/6527 026/6806 086/
836 928DSY/G05414R/894 016ZKY
cd: 464 0902
symphony no 8
further lp issues: GL 5807/G03223L/894 016ZKY
cd: 464 0902

A 00548 L/recital of piano music for the left hand
recorded in amsterdam in november 1959
de groot   *excerpts*
                    cd: 462 0762

A 00555 L/835 478AY/concerti by vivaldi
duhamel
orchestra

A 00556 L/835 479AY/organ toccatas by bach
cochereau

A 00557-00558 L/835 481-482AY/bach the 4 orchestral suites
redel   further lp issue: 894 030-894 031ZKY
munich pro arte
orchestra

A 00559 L/works by stravinsky and mussorgsky
recorded in moscow in 1962
markevitch   **symphonie de psaumes**
ussr state   further lp issues: AL 3430/SAL 3430/A02232L/
orchestra   835 120AY/835 482AY/6511 022
state academy
choir
markevitch   **songs for soprano and orchestra**
ussr state   further lp issues: AL 3430/SAL 3430/A02232L/
orchestra   A02250L/835 120AY/835 482AY/6511 022
vishnevskaya   cd: 446 2122

A 00560 L/recital of songs by kilpinen
borg
koskimies

A 00561 L/quartets by dittersdorf, richter, rosetti and asplmayr
oistersek
string quartet

A 00563 L/835 483AY/offenbach scenes from la belle hélene
rosenthal further lp issues: GL 5664/SGL 5664/
orchestra G03493L/837 498GY
rhodes, plantey,
giraudeau

A 00564 L/835 484AY/pierre henry orphée, drame chorégraphique
henry

A 00565-00566 L/835 485-486AY/panorama of experimental music
henry

A 00567 L/835 487AY/musique concrete
henry

A 00568 L/835 488AY/organ works at notre dame
cochereau
andré

A 00569 L/835 489AY/concerti by stölzel, leopold mozart and telemann
faerber
württemberg
chamber
orchestra

A 00570 L/835 490AY/recital of music for two guitars
presti,
lagoya

A 00571 L/835 491AY/works by couperin
recorded in the liederhalle stuttgart in july 1958
couraud
stuttgart soloists

A 00572 L/835 492AY/concerti by rameau
recorded in the liederhalle stuttgart in july 1958
couraud
stuttgart soloists

A 00574 L/music for christmas
delzant
various choirs

A 00575 L/835 499AY/milhaud les 4 saisons
milhaud
orchestre further lp issues: american decca DL 1959/DL 1962
lamoureux

A 00576 L/835 474AY/liszt the two piano concerti
recorded in the town hall walthamstow on 19-21 july 1961
kondrashin further lp issues: ABL 3401/SABL 207/6504 015/
london 6580 071/500 000/900 000/eterna 826 276/
symphony melodiya D 013747-013748/C 0867-0868
richter cd: 412 0062/434 1632/454 2002

A 00579 L/works by messiaen and daniel lesur
kreder

A 00581 L/mussorgsky pictures from an exhibition
recorded at a concert in sofia on 24 february 1958
richter further lp issues: ABL 3314/GBL 5752/G03497L/
  6768 219/6780 502/american columbia ML 5600/
  Y-32223
  cd: 420 7742/454 1662/454 1672
  also published on lp by melodiya

A 00582 L/preludes and fugues from wohltemperiertes klavier
engel

A 00584 L/schubert impromptu d899 no 4; moment musical no 1;
liszt 2 valses oubliées; études transcendantes nos 5 and 11
recorded at a concert in sofia on 24 february 1958
richter 45 rpm issues: ABE 10199 (études transcendantes)/
  ABE 10211 (valses oubliées)/ABE 10212 (schubert)/
  further lp issues: ABL 3301/6768 219 (schubert and
  études transcendantes)/6780 502/american
  columbia ML 5396
  cd: 420 7742/454 1662/454 1672/456 9462
  also published on lp by melodiya

A 00592L/schumann faschingsschwank aus wien; fantasiestücke
engel

A 00594-00596 L/anthology of zarzuelas torroba
zarzuelas
orchestra

A 00600 R/piano music by debussy
recorded in amsterdam on 12-14 november 1951
henkemans further lp issue: ABR 4023
excerpts
78 rpm issue: A11216G
45 rpm issue: 400 002AE
cd: 462 8972/462 8952

N 00601 R/piano music by satie, auric, honegger and poulenc
thyrion

N 00602 R/lalo cello concerto
recorded in the concertgebouw amsterdam on 3-4 january 1952
otterloo further lp issue: 698 093CL
residentie cd: 462 0912
orkest
de machula

A 00603 R/orchestral works by tchaikovsky
recorded in the concertgebouw amsterdam on 18 july 1951 (1812) and on 3-5 december 1951 (capriccio italien)

kempen
concertgebouw
orkest

ouverture solennelle 1812
78 rpm issue: A11195-11196G
45 rpm issue: ABE 10054/400 046AE
further lp issues: ABR 4003/SBL 5217/S04027L/ S06078R/G03084L/WL 1131/LC 3008
cd: 438 3102
capriccio italien
45 rpm issue: 400 029AE
further lp issues: ABR 4023/S00788R/S06078R/ S06190R/SBL 5217/S04027L/200 017WGY/ LC 3008
cd: 420 8582/438 3102

A 00604 R/schubert symphony no 8 "unfinished"
recorded in the concertgebouw amsterdam on 21-22 april 1952

jochum
concertgebouw
orkest

further lp issues: ABR 4021/GBL 5501/ G03014L/G05366R/LC 3006
cd: tahra TAH 238

N 00605 R/virtuoso violin pieces
recorded in amsterdam on 31 january 1952

magyar
hielkema

excerpts
78 rpm issues: N11226G/N11227G/N11228G/ N11230G
45 rpm issue: 402 001NE

N 00606 R/choral arrangements of mozart, schubert and johann strauss

wiener
sängerknaben

further lp issue: NBR 6007

A 00607 R/ *see 00437*

A 00608 R/strauss don juan; till eulenspiegels lustige streiche
recorded in the concertgebouw amsterdam on 24-25 april 1952

jochum
concertgebouw
orkest

further lp issues: ABR 4009/LC 3032

A 00609 R/beethoven piano sonatas nos 8 and 14
recorded in amsterdam on 17 april 1952
van der pas further lp issue: S06067R

A 00610 R/recital of lieder and songs
recorded in amsterdam on 15-16 may 1952
vincent further lp issues: S06204R/695 074KL
de nobel cd: 464 5222
excerpts
78 rpm issue: A11242G
45 rpm issue: 313 016SF

A 00611 R/recital of songs by mozart
recorded in amsterdam on 19-20 june 1952
margono further lp issue: S06035R
wering *excerpts*
78 rpm issue: N12043G

N 00612 R/jugoslav folksongs
recorded on 7 july 1952
jugoslav
theatre chorus

A 00613 R/viola sonatas by honegger and milhaud
recorded in amsterdam on 11-12 july 1952
boon
de groot

A 00614 R/mozart violin sonatas k378 and k379
de klijn further lp issue: S04012L
heksch cd: globe GLO 6039

N 00615 R/smetana string quartet no 1 "aus meinem leben"
recorded in amsterdam on 26-27 june 1952
netherlands
string quartet

N 00616 R/saxophone arrangements of french music
recorded in amsterdam on 9 july 1952
adolphe sax
quartet

N 00617 R/choral arrangements by french, belgian, dutch and american composers
recorded in amsterdam in september 1952
maastricht royal
male chorus

N 00618-00619 R/european christmas carols
recorded in amsterdam in september 1952
maastricht royal
male chorus

N 00620 R/orchestral works by smetana and dvorak
recorded in the concertgebouw amsterdam on 22 september 1952 (moldau)
and in september 1953 (slavonic rhapsosy)
dorati   the moldau/ma vlast
concertgebouw   further lp issues: NBR 6010/S00708R/S06053R/
orkest   G05328R/200 035WGY/LC 3015
dorati   **slavonic rhapsody no 3**
residentie   further lp issues: NBR 6010/S06053R/G05328R/
orkest   200 039WGL/LC 3015

N 00621 R/piano music by mendelssohn
recorded in amsterdam on 10-11 september 1952
de groot   *excerpts*
                78 rpm issue: N12063G
                further lp issue: GBL 5594/G03082L

A 00622-00623 R/choral works for salzburg cathedral
messner   **hymn to saint rupert "plaudite timpana"**
wiener
symphoniker   **benvenoli messe solennelle for 53 voices**
salzburger   *see 00470*
domchor

N 00624 R/choral music by italian composers
recorded in vienna in december 1952
wiener
sängerknaben

N 00625 R/recital of lieder by brahms and ballads by loewe
recorded in amsterdam on 10-11 november 1952

schey	**4 ernste gesänge**
de nobel	78 rpm issues: N12068-12069G
	further lp issue: 695 093KL
	cd: PHCP 5113
	4 ballads
	45 rpm issue: 402 053NE
	further lp issue: 695 093KL
	cd: PHCP 5113
	excerpts
	78 rpm issue: N12070G

N 00626 R/santorsolo guitar concerto and solo pieces by sor, sarrega and savio

sacher	further lp issue: LC 3055
wiener	*excerpts*
symphoniker	78 rpm issue: N11223G
walker	

A 00627 R/piano music by debussy
recorded in amsterdam on 15-16 december 1952

henkemans	**estampes**
	further lp issues: SBL 5200/S04007L
	cd: 462 8972/462 8952
	childrens' corner
	45 rpm issues: NBE 11020/402 054NE
	excerpts
	45 rpm issue: 400 002AE

N 00628 R/waltzes by josef and johann strauss

salmhofer	**aquarellen**
wiener	45 rpm issues: NBE 11040/402 045NE
symphoniker	further lp issues: NBR 6008/200 029WGY
	accelerationen
	further lp issues: NBR 6008/S06007R
	wo die zitronen blüh'n; kusswalzer
	45 rpm issues: NBE 11040/402 045NE (zitronen)/
	NBE 11034/402 002NE (kusswalzer)
	further lp issues: NBR 6008/200 029WGY

N 00629 R/arias and choruses by beethoven and weber

loibner	**gott welch dunkel hier!/fidelio**
wiener	further lp issues: NBR 6027/S06020R
symphoniker	**wehen mir lüfte ruh'/euryanthe; durch die**
vroons	**wälder/der freischütz**
	further lp issue: NBR 6027
loibner	**o welche lust!/fidelio; was gleicht wohl**
wiener	**auf erden/der freischütz**
symphoniker	further lp issues: NBR 6027/695 016KL
wiener	
kammerchor	

N 00630 R/wagner scenes from tannhäuser, holländer and parsifal

moralt	further lp issues: NBR 6030/A01252L
wiener	cd: preiser 90498
symphoniker	
edelmann	

N 00631 R/operetta overtures by johann strauss and suppé

moralt	**die fledermaus**
wiener	further lp issues: SBR 6212/S06012R/S06088R
symphoniker	**boccaccio; dichter und bauer**
	further lp issues: SBR 6212/S06088R/S06162R
	der zigeunerbaron *see 00178*

N 00632 R/piano recital
recorded in amsterdam on 5-6 january 1953

de groot	*excerpts*
	45 rpm issues: NBE 11016/402 019NE

N 00633 R/music by french and belgian composers for 1 and 2 harps
recorded in amsterdam on 12-14 january 1953

spier	further lp issue: 695 107KL
berghout	*excerpts*
	78 rpm issues: N12072-12073G

N 00634 R/operatic choruses by donizetti, verdi and mascagni
moralt further lp issue: NBR 6003
residentie *excerpts*
orkest further lp issue: S06018R
netherlands
opera chorus

N 00635 R/bizet l'arlésienne, suites nos 1 and 2
fournet further lp issues: S06089R/GBL 5500/G03004L/
orchestre G05377R/200 008WGY/LC 3018
lamoureux *excerpts*
45 rpm issues: NBE 11027/402 003NE

N 00636 R/ballet music by gounod and rabouf
fournet **faust ballet music**
orchestre further lp issues: NBR 6000/SBL 5203/S04013L/
lamoureux GBL 5567/G03054L/695 019KL
fournet **marouf ballet/savetier du caire**
paris opéra further lp issue: NBR 6000
orchestra

N 00637 R/piano music for 4 hands by ravel and fauré
marika
smadja

N 00638 R/délibes scenes from lakmé
recorded in the salle apollo paris on 25-26 february 1953
dervaux further lp issue: S06091R
orchestre cd: 477 0222
lamoureux
alarie,
simoneau

N 00639 R/verdi scenes from la traviata
recorded in the salle apollo paris on 24-25 february 1953
dervaux further lp issue: S06092R
orchestre cd: 477 0222
lamoureux *excerpts*
morales, 45 rpm issues: ABE 10178/402 066AE
simoneau

N 00640 R/recital of guitar music
walker further lp issue: LC 3055
excerpts
78 rpm issue: A11225G

N 00641 R/piano music by israeli composers
granetman

A 00642 R/j. c. bach sinfonias op 18 nos 1 and 4
sacher further lp issues: ABR 4005/S04003L/SFL 14130/
wiener 700 440WGY
symphoniker cd: retrospective recordings RET 034-035

N 00643 R/recital of songs by mexican composers
puig
frid

N 00644 R/sacred pontifical liturgy from the russian orthodox church
russian orthodox
cathedral choir

N 00645 R/recital of keyboard music by bach
hengeveld

A 00646 R/beethoven piano concerto no 3
otterloo further lp issues: ABR 4047/A06115R/GBL 5594/
wiener G03082L/G05330R/200 036WGL
symphoniker
de groot

N 00647 R/schumann carnaval
tagliaferro

N 00648 R/recital of piano music by ravel
bruins

N 00649 R/operatic arias by saint-saens, thomas, bizet and verdi
recorded in the musikverein vienna in 1952
loibner   cd: preiser 89670
wiener   *excerpts*
symphoniker   78 rpm issue: N12079G
ilosvay   **gloria all' egitto/aida** *see 00116*

A 00650 R/ *see 00370*

A 00651 R/chopin piano concerto no 1
otterloo   further lp issues: GBR 6500/G05302R/835 700AY/
residentie   675 004ER/200 010WGL
orkest
uninsky

N 00652 R/mussorgsky pictures from an exhibition
uninsky

A 00653 R/chopin selection of nocturnes and polonaises
uninsky   *excerpts from the recital*
                  45 rpm issue: 400 000AE

A 00654 R/mozart piano sonata k457 and fantasia k475
recorded in amsterdam on 31 march-1 april 1953
henkemans

A 00655 R/scenes from wagner and strauss operas
moralt   further lp issue: ABR 4004
wiener   cd: preiser 90335
symphoniker
zadek

N 00656 R/mozart piano sonatas k332 and k333
recorded in amsterdam on 27-28 january 1954
haebler

A 00657 R/mozart 4 concert arias
recorded in the musikverein vienna on 11-13 april 1953
pritchard   further lp issue: ABR 4054
wiener
symphoniker
hollweg

A 00658-00659 R/bruckner symphony no 4 "romantic"
recorded in the concertgebouw amsterdam on 6-7 may 1953
otterloo further lp issue: 695 083KL
residentie cd: challenge records CC 72142
orkest

A 00660 R/chopin the 24 préludes
de groot further lp issue: ABR 4042

N 00661 R/franck le chasseur maudit; rédemption
fournet
orchestre
lamoureux

N 00662 R/contemporary dutch music
recorded in the concertgebouw amsterdam on 8 may 1953
otterloo **sam dresden dance flashes for orchestra**
residentie further lp issue: donemus 8303
orkest cd: challenge records CC 72142
diepenbrock elektra, symphonic suite
cd: challenge records CC 72142

N 00663 R/operatic arias by french composers
recorded in the salle apollo paris on 21-22 april 1953
dervaux further lp issue: S06094R
orchestre *excerpts*
lamoureux 45 rpm issues: NBE 11024/402 005NE
alarie

N 00664 R/saint-saens piano concerto no 5
fournet further lp issue: LC 3057
orchestre
lamoureux
tagliaferro

A 00665 R/ravel daphnis et chloé, first and second suites
recorded in the concertgebouw amsterdam on 4-5 may 1953
otterloo further lp issue: ABR 4019
residentie cd: challenge records CC 72142
orkest

N 00666 R/piano music by french composers
recorded on 8-9 june 1953
thyrion

N 00667 R/kodaly dances from galanta; dances of marossek
moralt further lp issue: NBR 6009
wiener
symphoniker

A 00668 R/baroque concerti
recorded in the musikverein vienna on 23 march 1953 and 30 april 1953
pritchard **concerti by manfredini and corelli**
wiener further lp issue: ABR 4014/200 043WGL
symphoniker **handel concerto grosso op 6 no 12**
further lp issues: ABR 4014/S06105R

A 00669 R/fauré requiem
recorded in paris on 25-27 june 1953
fournet further lp issues: ABR 4012/G03101L
orchestre *excerpts*
lamoureux cd: 477 0222
brasseur choir
alarie, maurane

A 00670 R/ *see 00370*

N 00671 R/schumann fantasy in c minor
boukoff

A 00672 R/ *see 00135*

N 00673 R/schumann études symphoniques
boukoff

N 00674 R/ballet suites by délibes
fournet **sylvia**
orchestre 45 rpm issue: NBE 11076/402 089NE
lamoureux further lp issues: NBR 6005/SBL 5203/S04013L/
S06095R/GBL 5567/G03054L/G05325R/
695 015KL
excerpts
45 rpm issue: NBE 11027/402 003NE
coppélia
further lp issues: NBR 6005/SBL 5203/S04013L/
S06095R/GBL 5567/G03054L/G05325R/
695 019KL/200 008WGL
excerpts
45 rpm issues: NBE 11027/402 003NE

A 00675 R/j. c. bach sinfonia concertante in a; harpsichord concerto in e flat
sacher further lp issues: ABR 4029/S04003L/
wiener 695 050KL/SFL 14130/700 440WGY
symphoniker
leonhardt

A 00676 R/mozart cassations k63 and k99
sacher further lp issues: ABR 4010/LC 3043
wiener
symphoniker

N 00677 R/ *see 00130*

N 00678 R/songs from the renaissance
de nobel
netherlands
chamber choir

N 00679 R/choral music by poulenc, martin and hopkins
de nobel
netherlands
chamber choir

N 00680 R/wagner scenes from die meistersinger von nürnberg
loibner further lp issue: A01252L
wiener cd: preiser 90498
symphoniker
edelmann

N 00681 R/recital of songs by french composers
sénéchal
bonneau

N 00682 R/choral music by venosa and hindemith
schmid
wiener
kammerchor

N 00683 R/traditional songs from england, ireland and scotland
recorded in the musikverein vienna on 9-13 april 1954
dickie further lp issue: NBR 6016
pritchard *excerpts*
 45 rpm issue: NBE 11070

N 00684 R/khachaturian violin concerto
moralt
wiener
symphoniker
magyar

N 00685 R/music by the strauss family
salmhofer further lp issues: SBR 6228/S06096R
wiener
symphoniker

N 00686 R/music for tenor and mandolin
recorded on 3-4 september 1953
dekker *excerpts*
cäcilie mandolin 45 rpm issues: ABE 10100/400 023AE
players
conrad

84

A 00687 R/dvorak cello concerto
moralt　　　　further lp issues: G05338R/LC 3083
wiener
symphoniker
de machula

A 00688 R/stallaert piano concerto
stallaert
orchestre
lamoureux
wayenberg

A 00689 R/grieg piano concerto
otterloo　　　further lp issues: ABR 4017/S06097R/GBL 5573/
residentie　　　G03061L/695 004KL/LC 3182
orkest
simon

A 00690 R/schubert piano quintet in a "trout"
amsterdam　　further lp issues: GBL 5543/G03041L/610 138VR/
piano quintet　　894 055ZKY/200 038WGL/700 106WGY/
　　　　　　　　695 056KL

A 00691 R/mozart violin sonatas k306 and k481
de klijn　　　　cd: GLO 6039 (k306 only)
heksch

N 00692 R/motets on texts by martin luther
voorberg
netherlands
madrigal and
motet choir

N 00693 R/bayer die puppenfee ballet music; lortzing zar und zimmermann ballet suite
loibner　　　further lp issue: LC 3102
wiener
symphoniker

N 00694 R/choral music by pergolesi, mozart, schubert and herbeck
brenn *excerpts*
wiener 45 rpm issues: NBE 10195/402 135NE
symphoniker
sängerknaben

N 00695 R/contemporary music for flute and harp
barwahser
berghout

A 00696 R/serenades by mozart
moralt **eine kleine nachtmusik**
wiener 45 rpm issues: ABE 10010/400 005AE
symphoniker further lp issues: ABR 4018/G03008L
serenata notturna
further lp issue: ABR 4018

N 00697 R/music by johann strauss
e.strauss further lp issues: NBR 6012/G05369R/200 018WGL
wiener *excerpts*
symphoniker 45 rpm issue: SBF 224
further lp issues: S06006R/G05336R/700 018WGY

A 00698 R/ *see 00369*

A 00699 R/ *see 00403*

A 00700 R/music for violin and piano by dohnanyi and bartok
magyar
hielkema

N 00701 R/chausson symphony in b flat
fournet further lp issue: NBR 6018
orchestre
pasdeloup

N 00702 R/orchestral works by liszt
otterloo **mazeppa**
residentie further lp issues: NBR 6014/GBL 5527/G03007L
orkest **les préludes** *see 00114*

N 00703 R/luigini ballet égyptien; saint-saens suite algérienne
recorded in the salle apollo paris between 14-24 september 1953 (luigini) and on 16 december 1953 (saint-saens)
fournet
orchestre
lamoureux

N 00704 R/ *see 00509*

N 00705 R/operatic arias by bellini, donizetti and rossini
recorded in the salle apollo paris in december 1953
dervaux   cd: 442 7502
orchestre
lamoureux
sciutti

N 00706 R/operatic scenes by massenet, bizet and offenbach
fournet
orchestre
lamoureux
brasseur choir
vroons

N 00707 R/operatic overtures by massenet, saint-saens, bizet, gounod and thomas
fournet   further lp issues: S06103R/LC 3079
orchestre
lamoureux

N 00708 R/ *see 00517*

A 00709 R/works by brahms and wagner
recorded in the concertgebouw amsterdam in 1954 (brahms) and in the jesus-christus-kirche berlin in june 1951 (wagner)
otterloo   **haydn variations**
residentie   further lp issue: ABR 4026
orkest
otterloo   **siegfried idyll**
berliner   further lp issue: ABR 4026
philharmon-
isches orchester

A 00710-00711 R / see 00405

N 00712 R / operatic arias by verdi
recorded in the musikverein vienna in 1951 (aida) and in 1954 (otello and un ballo in maschera)

loibner	**o patria mia / aida**
wiener	45 rpm issue: 402 017NE
symphoniker	further lp issues: G03147L/695 052KL
brouwenstijn	cd: 462 0712/preiser 89692
	ecco l'orrido campo; morro ma prima in grazia / un ballo in mascgera *see 00713*
kempen	**piangea cantando; ave maria / otello**
wiener	cd: 462 0712
symphoniker	
brouwenstijn	

N 00713 R / verdi scenes from un ballo in maschera
recorded in the musikverein vienna in 1954

loibner	further lp issue: NBR 6023
wiener	*excerpts*
symphoniker	45 rpm issue: 402 017NE
chor der wiener	further lp issues: G03147L/695 052KL/H72-AX 205
staatsoper	cd: 462 0712/preiser 89692
brouwenstijn	
vroons	

N 00714 R / orchestral works by ravel and de falla
recorded in the concertgebouw amsterdam on 5 january 1952 (pavane) and on 1-2 april 1954 (valses and sombrero)

otterloo	**pavane pour une infante défunte**
residentie	78 rpm issues: N12046H/N09036S
orkest	45 rpm issues: NBE 11023/402 064NE
	cd: challenge records CC 72142
	valses nobles et sentimentales
	further lp issues: SBR 6235/S06184R
	cd: challenge records CC 72142
	three dances from el sombrero de 3 picos
	cd: challenge records CC 72142

N 00715 R / saint-saens symphony no 3 "organ"

otterloo	further lp issues: NBR 6021/695 066KL/LC 3077
residentie	
orkest	
asma	

N 00716 R/grieg selection from the lyric pieces
hengeveld

N 00717 R/jugoslav folksongs
ljubljana
slovenski octet

A 00718 R/beethoven piano concerto no 4
otterloo further lp issues: ABR 4038/A06116R/G05305R/
wiener 695 041KL
symphoiker
de groot

A 00719 R/works by bach
sacher **brandenburg concerto no 6**
basel chamber further lp issues: S06106R/695 011KL/
orchestra 200 034WGY/LC 3167/SC 6008
sacher **concerto for violin and oboe**
basel chamber
orchestra
feliciani, shann

A 00720 R/beethoven symphony no 2
recorded in the concertgebouw amsterdam on 22 may 1954
beinum further lp issues: ABR 4036/GBL 5575/G03063L
concertgebouw
orkest

A 00721 R/schumann symphony no 3 "rhenish"
recorded in the concertgebouw amsterdam on 11 may 1954
zecchi further lp issue: LC 3092
concertgebouw
orkest

A 00722 R/debussy images pour orchestre
recordede in the concertgebouw amsterdam on 24-25 may 1954
beinum further lp issues: ABR 4032/6768 023/LC 3147
concertgebouw cd: 462 0692/475 6353/retrospective
orkest recordings RET 040

A 00723 R/brahms serenade no 2
recorded in the concertgebouw amsterdam on 14-17 may 1954
zecchi further lp issues: 642 110DXL/LC 3116
concertgebouw
orkest

A 00724 R/piano music by mozart
recorded in hilversum on 5-6 may 1954 (variations)
haskil **variations on a minuet by duport k573**
45 rpm issue: 400 052AE
further lp issues: 6733 002/6768 366/695 090KL
cd: 442 6352/442 6852/456 8292/475 7739
piano sonata k330 *see 00484*

N 00726 R/choral music by german and austrian composers
recorded in the musikverein vienna between 11-20 january 1954
kühbacher
wiener
sängerknaben

N 00727 R/gypsy melodies from hungary and the balkans
lendavi kalman
gypsy orchestra

A 00731 R/janacek diary of a man who disappeared
recorded at a concert in the bachzaal amsterdam on 14 july 1954
haefliger further lp issues: ABR 4041/LC 3121
canne-meyer
de nobel

A 00732 R/wagner scenes from lohengrin, der fliegende holländer, die meistersinger von nürnberg, rienzi and die walküre
moralt further lp issues: S06155R/G03185L
wiener cd: preiser 89695
symphoniker
hopf

N 00733 R/waltzes and polkas by johann strauss
salmhofer further lp issue: NBR 6022/200 018WGL
wiener
symphoniker

A 00734 R/ *see 00101*

N 00735 R/modern greek popular songs
recorded between 17-31 july 1954
tsitsanis typical
orchestra
ninou

N 00736 R/distler die weihnachtsgeschichte
voorberg
netherlands
madrigal and
motet choir

N 00737 R/fauré pelléas et mélisande suite; debussy petite suite
fournet further lp issue: S06118R
orchestre
lamoureux

N 00738 R/basler festmusik
h.münch
basler stadt-
orchester
and chorus
stader, gruber,
olsen

N 00739 R/chopin the four ballades
de groot further lp issues: NBR 6025/S06113R/G05393R
cd: 462 5272
excerpts
78 rpm issue: A11233G

A 00740 R/mozart arias from idomeneo, don giovanni, cosi fan tutte and la clemenza di tito
recorded in the musikverein vienna on 20-22 may 1954
paumgartner cd: 477 0222
wiener *excerpts*
symphoniker 45 rpm issue: 400 003AE
simoneau

A 00741 R/ *see 00465*

N 00742-00745 R/anthology of greek music

N 00746-00747 R/schubert winterreise
bogtman further lp issues: 695 084KL/LC 3154
de nobel

A 00748 R/roussel bacchus et ariane, ballet suites nos 1 and 2
martinon
orchestre
lamoureux

N 00749 R/honegger cantate de noel
sacher further lp issues: NBR 6026/LC 3153
orchestre
lamoureux
brasseur and
versailles choirs
roux, duruflé

A 00750 R/mendelssohn violin concerto
recorded in the musikverein vienna on 25-27 november 1953
moralt further lp issues: S04033L/S06112R/GBL 5582/
wiener G03001L/LC 3173
symphoniker cd: 473 1042
grumiaux *473 1042 gives recording date as september 1954*

A 00751 R/dvorak violin concerto
loibner further lp issues: G05453R/LC 3173
wiener
symphoniker
magyar

A 00752-00753 R/ *see 00315*

A 00754 R/marches, waltzes and polkas by johann strauss
salmhofer further lp issue: 200 018WGL
wiener
symphoniker

A 00756 R/rachmaninov piano concerto no 1
otterloo
residentie
orkest
de groot

A 00758 R/works for piano by mozart
henkemans   sonata k570; variations on unser dummer pöbel
                 cd: 462 7252
                 rondo in d k485
                 further lp issues: SBR 6200/S06100R
                 cd: 462 7252

N 00761 R/piano music by spanish composers
de groot   further lp issue: G05450R

A 00762-00763 R/mozart great mass in c minor
recorded in the musikverein vienna on 7-10 january 1955
paumgartner   further lp issues: ABR 4043-4044/A02033L/BC 6009
wiener   cd: retrospective recordings RET 042
symphoniker   *excerpts*
wiener   further lp issues: SBR 6200/S06100R
kammerchor
stich-randall,
rössl-majdan,
kmennt, raninger

N 00764 R/nielsen symphony no 3 "sinfonia espansiva"
recorded in copenhagen on 28 february-1 march 1955
frandsen   further lp issue: NBR 6034
danish radio   cd: retrospective recordings RET 043
orchestra

N 00766 R/ *see 00102*

N 00768 R/mozart symphonies nos 28 and 31 "paris"
paumgartner
camerata
academica

N 00771 R/mozart operatic and concert arias
recorded in the musikverein vienna in 1954
paumgartner   cd: preiser 89670
wiener
symphoniker
ilosvay

N 00773 R/vocal music by early italian composers
carbi, monterosso

N 00775 R/ *see 00372*

N 00776 R/debussy images pour piano
henkemans

A 00777 R/mozart piano concerto no 21 k467
paumgartner
wiener
symphoniker
heksch

A 00778 R/arias by mozart
paumgartner
wiener
symphoniker
schey

00779/ *see 00369*

S 00780 R/7 operatic overtures by mozart
moralt   further lp issues: SBR 6235/S06184R/
wiener   200 014WGL
symphoniker

N 00781 R/operatic arias by mozart
paumgartner
wiener
symphoniker
i.hollweg

N 00782 R/bach violin concerti bwv 1041 and bwv 1042
recorded in amsterdam in june 1955
guller   further lp issues: NBR 6032/G05326R/
chamber   695 032KL/LC 3342
orchestra
grumiaux

N 00783 R/schumann symphony no 4 (original 1841 version)
recorded in the town hall walthamstow on 20 october 1955
pope further lp issue: NBR 6004
royal
philharmonic

A 00785 R/chopin the 4 scherzi
uninsky further lp issue: LC 3430
excerpts
45 rpm issues: ABE 10114/400 063AE

N 00788 R/ *see 00603 and 00620*

N 00789 R/badings concerto for flute and orchestra
j.stotijn
sempre crescendo
orchestra
oordt

A 00790 R/ *see 00409*

N 00792 R/le compagnon de voyage
de froment
instrumental
ensemble

N 00793-00794 R/chansons polyphoniques francaises
blanchard

A 00795 R/string quartets by hemel and pijper
netherlands
string quartet

A 00796 R/836 177AZ/overtures by brahms
recorded in the musikverein vienna in january 1961 (academic festival overture)
and on 12-13 april 1961 (tragic overture)

sawallisch	**academic festival overture**
wiener	further lp issues: GL 5800/SGL 5800/140 182/
symphoniker	6752 001/6580 024
	cd: 438 7602
	tragic overture
	further lp issues: A02029L/835 082AY/GL 5801/
	SGL 5801/G03219L/140 165/6752 001
	cd: 438 7602

A 00995-00996 R/highlights from spanish zarzuelas
torroba
agrupacion
sinfonica

N 00998 R/piano music by russian composers
recorded in february 1953
boukoff

01100-01650/ *numbers in this sequence were allocated to publications under licence from the american columbia catalogue (certain recordings of european origin were included and are listed in a separate appendix at the end of the discography)*

02000-02006/ *these numbers were allocated to a series of sampler lps taken from complete opera recordings in the philips catalogue*

A 02007-02009 L/mendelssohn the complete string quartets
quatuor manolin

A 02010-02013 L/rimsky-korsakov sadko
basic
zagreb national
opera orchestra
and chorus

A 02014-02016 L/rimsky-korsakov the tale of tsar sultan
gebré
zagreb national
opera orchestra
and chorus

A 02017 L/ *see 00325*

A 02018-02020 L/835 010-012AY/operas by mascagni and leoncavallo
recorded in the teatro san carlo naples between 12-30 june 1958
rapalo	**cavalleria rusticana**
san carlo	further lp issue: SFL 14002-14004
orchestra	*excerpts*
and chorus	further lp issues: A02004L/H72-AX 205/G03071L/
mancini,	837 011GY/835 051AY/839 564VGY
lazzarini, cattelani,	
poggi, protti	
rapalo	**i pagliacci**
san carlo	further lp issue: SFL 14002-14004
orchestra	*excerpts*
and chorus	45 rpm issues: ABE 10151/409 109AE
beltrami, poggi,	further lp issues: A02004L/G03071L/
nobile, protti,	837 011GY/835 051AY/839 564VGY
monachesi	

A 02021-02022 L/835 052-053AY/verdi rigoletto
recorded in the teatro san carlo naples between 26 may-9 june 1958
molinari-	further lp issues: SFL 14005-14006/6747 407/
pradelli	american columbia M2L 404/M2S 901
san carlo	*excerpts*
orchestra	further lp issues: A02005L/H72-AX 205/
and chorus	G03072L/837 012GY/835 050AY/839 565VGY
d'angelo,	
pirazzini, tucker,	
capecchi, sardi	

A 02023 L/locatelli 4 concerti from op 1
recorded in rome on 28 april and 17 may 1960
i musici further lp issue: BC 1029

A 02024 L/835 035AY/symphonies by schubert and mendelssohn
*recorded in the musikverein vienna on 13-16 april 1959 (mendelssohn) and
on 30 october 1959 (schubert)*
sawallisch	**symphony no 8 "unfinished"**
wiener	further lp issues: ABL 3285/SABL 120/SDAL 501/
symphoniker	G05438R/610 102VR/836 214VZ/6701 005
	symphony no 4 "italian"
	further lp issues: ABL 3285/SABL 120/SDAL 501/
	610 101VR/836 215VZ/eterna 820 186

A 02025 L/835 036AY/orchestral works by brahms
recorded in the musikverein vienna between 30 october-6 november 1959
sawallisch **symphony no 2**
wiener further lp issues: ABL 3286/SABL 121/GL 5800/
symphoniker SGL 5800/140 128/6752 001
cd: 438 7572
haydn variations
further lp issues: ABL 3286/SABL 121/GL 5803/
SGL 5803/894 067ZKY/140 128/6752 001
cd: 438 7572

A 02026 L/835 067AY/orchestral works by beethoven
recorded in the concertgebouw amsterdam on 12-15 september 1960
sawallisch **symphony no 6 "pastoral"**
concertgebouw further lp issues: GL 5808/SGL 5808/SFM 23012/
orkest 610 800VL/838 600VY/LC 3785/BC 1134/
894 063ZKY
fidelio overture
45 rpm issues: 400 227AE/740 024AV
further lp issues: GL 5808/SGL 5808/894 058ZKY

A 02027 L/835 080AY/wagner rienzi and fliegende holländer overtures; tannhäuser venusberg music; siegfried idyll
recorded in the musikverein vienna on 5-6 november 1959 (rienzi and fliegende holländer), on 3-4 april 1960 (siegfried idyll) and on 16-19 january 1961 (tannhäuser venusberg)
sawallisch further lp issues: ABL 3404/SABL 210/SFM 23005/
wiener G05396R (holländer and siegfried idyll)/836 218VZ
symphoniker (holländer and siegfried idyll)/839 513VSY/6580 063/
6833 154 (rienzi)
cd: 422 4802/434 5462

A 02028 L/835 081AY/schubert symphony no 9 "great"
recorded in the musikverein vienna between 19-26 february 1961
sawallisch further lp issues: ABL 3405/SABL 211/
wiener 894 012XKY/6701 005
symphoniker

A 02029 L/835 082AY/orchestral works by brahms
recorded in the musikverein vienna on 16-19 january 1961 (symphony no 3)
sawallisch	**symphony no 3**
wiener	further lp issues: GL 5801/SGL 5801/G03219L/
symphoniker	140 165/6752 001
	cd: 438 7572
	tragic overture *see 00796*

A 02030 L/835 085AY/haydn   symphonies nos 94 "surprise" and 100 "military"/*recorded in the musikverein vienna on 13-17 april 1961*
sawallisch	further lp issues: 894 092ZKY (no 100)/6527 034
wiener	cd: 422 9732/432 2192
symphoniker	

A 02033 L/ *see 00762-00763*

A 02034 L/835 054AY/overtures by beethoven
recorded in the concertgebouw amsterdam between 6-10 june 1960
jochum	**leonore no 3; egmont; coriolan**
concertgebouw	further lp issues: ABL 3378/SABL 202/G05402R/
orkest	6770 028/6780 033
	namensfeier; die weihe des hauses
	further lp issues: ABL 3378/SABL 202

A 02037 L/835 028AY/works by bach, handel and mozart
recorded in may and october 1959
i musici	**bach violin concerto bwv 1043**
	see 00519
	handel concerto grosso op 6 no 4;
	mozart adagio and fugue k546

A 02038 L/concerti for one and two harpsichords by bach
fiala
amati orchestra
ahlgrimm
bretschneider

A 02039 L/mussorgsky pictures at an exhibition and other pieces
boukoff

A 02040 L/835 037AY/works by liszt and beethoven
recorded in the maison de la chimie paris on 2-5 february 1960
benzi	**les préludes; hungarian rhapsody no 2**
orchestre	further lp issue: G05391R/836 207VZ
lamoureux	**leonore no 3; coriolan; egmont**
	further lp issue: G05392R/836 208VZ

A 02041 L/835 038AY/haydn symphonies nos 103 "drum roll" and 104 "london"
recorded in the maison de la chimie paris between 10-23 december 1959
markevitch	further lp issues: SFM 23011/839 503VGY
orchestre	cd: 464 0942
lamoureux	

A 02042 L/835 039AY/bizet l'arlésienne suites nos 1 and 2; carmen suites nos 1 and 2
recorded in the maison de la chimie paris between 30 may-10 june 1960
markevitch	further lp issues: G03055L/837 036GY/875 024CY/
orchestre	SFL 14048/700 170WGY/6527 083/6570 107/
lamoureux	836 917DSY/894 043ZKY
	cd: 420 8632/450 0432/454 5312
	excerpts
	further lp issue: 6718 012
	cd: 422 2722

A 02043 L/835 040AY/beethoven piano concerto no 3
recorded in the maison de la chimie paris on 1 december 1959
markevitch	further lp issues: ABL 3330/SABL 172/A02347L/
orchestre	835 307AY/SFM 23006/839 508VG/894 019ZKY/
lamoureux	899 019/610 141VR/6500 324/6566 017/
haskil	6733 002/6747 055/LC 3726/BC 1097
	cd: 434 1682/442 6312/442 6852/475 7739

A 02047 L/contemporary dutch music
recorded in the kurhaus scheveningen in october 1959 (orthel) and in the concertgebouw amsterdam on 5 june 1951 (ricerare) and on 26 february 1952 (variations)
otterloo	**orthel symphony no 2 "piccola sinfonia"**
residentie	cd: challenge records CC 72142
orkest	**andriessen kuhnau variations**
	78 rpm issue: A11243G
	andriessen ricerare
	78 rpm issue: A11141G

A 02048 L/beethoven piano sonatas nos 21, 24 and 26
boukoff

A 02049 L/keyboard music by italian composers
particaroli

A 02050 L/chopin selection of mazurkas
recorded in amsterdam on 20-23 december 1961
uninsky cd: 442 5742

A 02051 L/835 055AY/violin concerti by tchaikovsky and mendelssohn
recorded in the concertgebouw amsterdam on 11-14 may 1960
haitink   **tchaikovsky**
concertgebouw   further lp issues: SAL 3671/SBAL 32/SC71-AX 403/
orkest   G05405R/610 132VR/836 247VZ
grumiaux   **mendelssohn**
further lp issues: A02821L/ABL 3337/SABL 176/
SAL 3671/SBAL 32/SC71-AX 403/G05469R/
610 103VR/836 201VZ/6580 022/LC 3762/BC 1120
cd: 442 2872/456 0742

A 02052 L/contemporary dutch music
recorded in the concertgebouw amsterdam on 11-14 may 1960 (andriessen)
haitink   **andriessen symphonic étude**
concertgebouw
orkest
alma musica   **escher le tombeau de ravel**
ensemble

A 02053 L/835 057AY/bizet scenes from carmen
recorded in the salle apollo paris between 7-14 april 1960
benzi   further lp issues: GL 5648/SGL 5648/6500 206
orchestre
lamoureux
rhodes, guiot,
lance, massard

A 02054 L/835 058AY/concerti by vivaldi
recorded in rome between 28 april-17 may 1960
i musici

A 02057 L/835 061AY/concerti by leo, durante, pergolesi and scarlatti
recorded in rome between 28 april-17 may 1960
i musici

A 02058 L/schumann dichterliebe and other lieder
recorded in the théatre de vevey between 16 june-1 july 1960
souzay further lp issues: ABL 3369/LC 3747/BC 1110
baldwin *excerpts from the recital*
45rpm issue: 400 219AE

A 02059 L/fauré la bonne chanson and other mélodies
recorded in the théatre de vevey between 16 june-1 july 1960
souzay further lp issues: ABL 3371/LC 3764/BC 1122
baldwin *excerpts from the recital*
cd: 420 7752

A 02060 L/835 066AY/orchestral works by richard strauss
recorded in the concertgebouw amsterdam on 10-11 june 1960 (don juan and till eulenspiegel) and in september 1960 (rosenkavalier)
jochum **don juan**
concertgebouw further lp issues: 894 119ZKY/6580 129
orkest cd: tahra TAH 257-258
till eulenspiegels lustige streiche
further lp issues: 610 127VR/836 239VZ/
894 119ZKY/6580 129
cd: tahra TAH 257-258
der rosenkavalier, waltz sequence
further lp issues: 610 127VR/836 239VZ/
894 119ZKY/6580 129

A 02061 L/schumann études symphoniques: haydn piano sonata no 30
recorded on 20-23 august 1960
magaloff

A 02062 L/der schalkhafte mozart: lieder, canons and trios
paumgartner *excerpts*
wiener further lp issue: SH71-AX 306
symphoniker
wiener
kammerchor
hollweg, brinck,
kmennt, christ,
uhl, berry

A 02063 L/835 068AY/sacred works by bach
recorded in the concertgebouw amsterdam in june and july 1960 (cantata 170)
goldberg   cantata no 170 "vergnügte ruh' beliebte seelenlust"
netherlands   further lp issues: ABL 3365/SABL 194
chamber   cd: 438 7722
orchestra
heynis
gillesberger   arias from cantatas 34 and 108 and weihnachts-
wiener   oratorium
symphoniker   further lp issues: ABL 3365/SABL 194/
heynis   6530 038 (weihnachtsoratorium)
                 cd: 426 1092/462 0842/462 1022

A 02064 L/dvorak string quartets nos 10 and 12 "american"
netherlands   further lp issue: 894 117ZKY
string quartet   cd: globe GLO 6036

A 02065 L/recital of piano music by liszt and prokofiev
uninsky

A 02066 L/835 047AY/haydn symphonies nos 44 "trauer" and 57
recorded in the concertgebouw amsterdam on 22-23 september 1958 (no 44)
and 13-15 october 1958 (no 57)
goldberg   further lp issues: SFL 14039/700 101WGY (no 57)
netherlands   cd: retrospective 93407
chamber
orchestra

A 02067 L/835 069AY/concerti for cello and orchestra
recorded in paris on 5-7 october 1960
casals   haydn concerto in d
orchestre   further lp issues: ABL 3355/SABL 188/6580 040/
lamoureux   LC 3817/BC 1152
gendron   **boccherini concerto in b flat**
                 further lp issues: ABL 3355/SABL 188/6747 103/
                 LC 3817/BC 1152
                 cd: 438 6062

A 02068 L/835 070AY/bartok concerto for orchestra; dance suite
recorded in the concertgebouw amsterdam on 21-23 september 1960
haitink   further lp issues: ABL 3407/SABL 213/
concertgebouw   6527 140/6580 036
orkest   cd: 438 8122 (concerto)/462 0802

A 02071 L/835 075AY/mozart piano concerti nos 20 k466 and 24 k491
recorded in the maison de la chimie paris on 14-18 november 1960
markevitch further lp issues: ABL 3406/SABL 212/SFM 23028/
orchestre 839 858VGY/610 108VR (no 20)/610 110VR (no 24)/
lamoureux 836 202VZ (no 20)/836 224VZ (no 24)/6500 265/
haskil 6530 036/6588 005/6733 002/6747 055/6768 366/
6833 065/6833 160/LC 3798/BC 1143
cd: 416 4432/420 7822/426 9642/442 6312/442 6852/
454 6962 (no 24)/456 8262/475 7739/
ermitage ERM 175 (no 24)

A 02072 L/835 071AY/schubert symphony no 4 "tragic"; schumann symphony no 4
recorded in the concertgebouw amsterdam on 5-7 september 1960 (schubert) and on 15-19 december 1960 (schumann)
jochum further lp issues: ABL 3402/SABL 208/836 921DSY
concertgebouw cd: tahra TAH 257-258
orkest

A 02073 L/835 098AY/beethoven piano sonatas nos 17 and 18
recorded in the théatre de vevey between 14-20 september 1960
haskil further lp issues: ABL 3358/6588 007/6733 002/
6747 055/PHC 9001/PHS 9001/LC 3831/BC 1168
cd: 420 0082/434 1682 (no 18)/442 6352/
442 6852/456 8292/475 7739

A 02074 L/piano music by schumann and mendelssohn
perticaroli

A 02075 L/835 072AY/chopin piano concerto no 2; de falla noches en los jardines de espana
recorded in the maison de la chimie paris on 3-4 october 1960
markevitch further lp issues: ABL 3340/SABL 173/SFM 23025/
orchestre 839 582VGY/610 104VR (chopin)/836 216VZ
lamoureux (chopin)/6500 263/6535 016/6540 065/6747 055/
haskil 500 034/900 034/894 051ZKY
cd: 416 4432/426 9642/432 8292 (de falla)/
434 2092 (de falla)/442 6312/442 6852/
454 6962 (chopin)/475 7739/ermitage ERM 175 (chopin)

A 02076 L/835 073AY/works by mozart, haydn and giordani
recorded in rome between 21 october-5 november 1960
i musici further lp issues: ABL 3323/SABL 127/
836 903DSY (mozart)/LC 3813/BC 1150

A 02077 L/835 074AY/concerti by bach
recorded in rome between 21 october-5 november 1960
i musici further lp issues: ABL 3380/SABL 204/
500 008/900 008
excerpts
further lp issue: 836 241VZ

A 02078 L/802 839LY/brahms violin sonata op 100; mozart violin sonata k481 *recorded in amsterdam in october 1959*
grumiaux cd: 476 7930
(violin and piano)

A 02079 L/835 235AY/works by albinoni
i musici *excerpts*
further lp issue: 836 903DSY

A 02080 L/835 076AY/works by rossini and respighi
recorded in paris between 28 november-10 december 1960
benzi **la boutique fantasque**
orchestre further lp issues: MG 50386/SR 90386
lamoureux **guillaume tell; la scala di seta; il barbiere di siviglia overtures**
further lp issues: 6870 585/6530 025/G03200L/
G05413R/837 034GY/836 204VZ/
MG 50386/SR 90386

A 02082 L/835 077AY/gregorian chant
benedictine monks of
saint-maurice and
saint-maur clervaux

A 02083 L/835 079AY/symphonies by mozart
recorded in the concertgebouw amsterdam on 15-19 december 1960
jochum **symphony no 35 "haffner"**
concertgebouw further lp issues: SFM 23013/839 522VGY/
orkest 500 004/900 004/PHS 900 186
symphony no 41 "jupiter"
further lp issues: GBL 5501/SFM 23013/839 522VGY/
G05427R/610 111VR/836 225VZ/500 004/900 004/
PHS 900 186

A 02084 L/ see 00315, 00484 and 00724

A 02085 L/835 078AY/works by mozart
recorded in the concertgebouw amsterdam in april 1958 (eine kleine nachtmusik)
and on 6-10 december 1960 (sinfonia concertante)

goldberg	**eine kleine nachtmusik**
netherlands	cd: retrospective 93407
chamber	
orchestra	
goldberg	**sinfonia concertante for 4 winds**
netherlands	further lp issues: SFL 14074/700 202WGY
chamber	cd: 462 5522/retrospective 93407
orchestra	
stotijn, de wilde,	
de klerk, bos	

A 02086 L/835 086AY/beethoven piano concerto no 5 "emperor"
recorded in the concertgebouw amsterdam on 3-4 february 1961

rosbaud	further lp issues: ABL 3379/SABL 203/6580 005/
concertgebouw	CC 7547/american columbia 3216 0326
orkest	cd: 477 0892
casadesus	

A 02087 L/ see 00108 and 00143

A 02090-02091 L/ see 00457-00458

A 02092 L/835 089AY/gregorian chant for christmas

A 02095-02096 L/verdi messa da requiem
recorded in moscow in 1960

markevitch	further lp issues: GL 5710-5711/G03096-03097L/
moscow	6768 215/TV 34210-34211
philharmonic	
state academy choir	
vishnevskaya	
isakova	
vanovsky	
petrov	

A 02098 L/835 095AY/works by mendelssohn and schubert
recorded in rome between 29 june-10 july 1961
i musici

A 02099 L/835 096AY/works by barber, bartok, britten and respighi
recorded in rome between 29 june-10 july 1961
i musici   further lp issues: ABL 3411/SABL 216/
                 500 001/900 001
                 excerpts
                 further lp issues: G05470R/836 265VZ/836 903DSY

N 02103 L/hungarian gypsy songs
recorded on 17-18 february 1955
lendavy   further lp issue: NBL 5011
gypsy orchestra
barabas

N 02104 L/suppé scenes from boccaccio
paulik   further lp issue: NBL 5026
volksoper
orchestra
and chorus
roon, kmennt,
berry, hermann,
szemere

02105-02199/ *numbers in this sequence were allocated to publications under licence from the american columbia catalogue*

A 02205-02207 L/835 198-200AY/bach the solo partitas and sonatas
recorded in berlin on 24-27 november 1960 and in february and march 1961
grumiaux   further lp issues: AL 3472-3474/SAL 3472-3474/
                 610 152VR (partita no 2)/6768 017/
                 PHM2-500/PHS2-900
                 cd: 416 8792/438 7362

A 02208 L/835 099AY/schubert string quintet in c
recorded at the prades festival between 7-23 july 1961
vegh, zoldy,   cd: 420 0772
janzer, szabo,
casals

A 02209 L/835 100AY/brahms piano quartet no 2
recorded at the prades festival between 7-23 july 1961
engel, vegh,
janzer, szado

**A 02210 L/835 101AY/beethoven cello sonata no 5; piano trio
no 4 "ghost"** *recorded at the prades festival between 7-23 july 1961*
vegh, casals,
engel

A 02211-02213 L/835 104-106AY/wagner der fliegende holländer
recorded at performances in the festspelhaus bayreuth between 31 july-18 august 1961
sawallisch   further lp issues: ABL 3412-3414/SABL 218-220/
bayreuth   6723 001/6747 248
festival   cd: 442 1032
orchestra   *excerpts*
and chorus   further lp issues: GL 5647/SGL 5647/G03092L/
silja, fischer,   837 010GY/6527 108/412 0241
uhl, crass,
greindl

A 02215 L/835 108AY/orchestral works by ravel
recorded in the concertgebouw amsterdam between 19-23 september 1961
haitink   **alborada del gracioso**
concertgebouw   further lp issues: 836 020DSY/6580 056/412 0101/
orkest   500 015/900 015
                      cd: 438 7452
                      daphnis et chloé, second suite
                      further lp issues: 6580 056/500 015/900 015
                      cd: 416 4952
                      pavane pour une infante défunte
                      further lp issues: 836 920DSY/6580 056/
                      6768 078/412 9341/500 015/900 015
                      cd: 416 4952/438 7452
                      rapsodie espagnole
                      further lp issues: 6580 031/6580 056/412 0101/
                      500 015/900 015
                      cd: 416 4952/438 7452

A 02216 L/highlights from viennese operetta
salmhofer   cagliostro in wien
wiener
symphoniker
chor der wiener
staatsoper
scheyrer, ludwig,
kmennt, wächter
e.strauss   der lustige krieg
wiener
symphoniker
chor der wiener
staatsoper
siebert, ludwig,
kmennt, wächter

A 02217-02218 L/church music from salzburg
recorded in the mozarteum salzburg on 4-5 march 1958
paumgartner   *excerpts*
camerata   further lp issues: SFL 14135/700 439WGY
academica

A 02220-02221 L/835 109-110AY/vivaldi   il cimento dell'
armonia e dell' invenzione
recorded in rome between 20-28 september 1961
i musici

A 02222 L/835 111AY/mozart symphonies nos 36 and 38
recorded in the concertgebouw amsterdam on 11-13 december 1961
jochum   further lp issues: AL 3541/SAL 3541/
concertgebouw   6580 023/PH32-991
orkest

A 02223 L/sweelinck psalms and cantiones
recorded in amsterdam in december 1961
de nobel
netherlands
chamber choir
de klerk

A 02224 L/835 112AY/mozart   violin concerti nos 3 and 5
recorded in the town hall walthamstow on 27-29 november 1961
davis   further lp issues: 610 130VR (no 3)/
london   610 128VR (no 5)/836 245VZ (no 3)/
symphony   836 240VZ (no 5)/6527 049/
grumiaux   500 012/900 012
                 cd: 412 2502/438 3232/438 5642/
                 438 5882/464 7222

A 02225 L/835 113AY/mozart symphonies nos 39 and 40
recorded in the town hall walthamstow on 27-29 november 1961
davis	further lp issues: 6580 029/500 036/900 036/
london	610 144VR
symphony	cd: 410 0462 (no 39)

A 02226-02227 L/835 114-115AY/choral works by brahms
recorded in the musikverein vienna in february 1962
sawallisch	**ein deutsches requiem**
wiener	further lp issues: SFL 14057-14058/700 198-199WGY/
symphoniker	6720 006/6780 018
wiener	cd: 438 7602
singverein	
lipp, crass	
sawallisch	**alto rhapsody**
wiener	further lp issues: SFL 14057-14058/700 198-199WGY/
symphoniker	GL 5803/SGL 5803/894 067ZKY/6780 018
wiener	cd: 438 7602
singverein	
heynis	
sawallisch	**schicksalslied**
wiener	further lp issues: SFL 14057-14058/700 198-199WGY/
symphoniker	GL 5803/SGL 5803/894 067ZKY/6780 018
wiener	cd: 438 7602
singverein	

A 02228 L/835 116AY/tchaikovsky symphony no 5
recorded in the concertgebouw amsterdam on 11-13 january 1962
sawallisch	further lp issues: 839 505VGY/
concertgebouw	500 020/900 020
orkest	

A 02229 L/835 117AY/haydn symphonies nos 55 and 85; leopold mozart toy symphony
recorded in paris between 8-12 january 1962
benzi	further lp issue: 894 056ZKY (toy symphony)
orchestre	
lamoureux	

A 02230-02231 L/835 118-119AY/mozart die entführung aus dem serail
recorded in the lukas-kirche dresden in october 1961
suitner further lp issues: 6720 005/eterna 820 297-299/
staatskapelle 825 297-299/turnabout TV 34320-34321
dresden cd: berlin classics BC 91162
dresden opera *excerpts*
chorus further lp issues: GL 5670/SGL 5670/G03098L/
vulpius, rönisch, 837 008GY/eterna 825 116/825 304/berlin
apreck, förster, classics BC 93432
van mill

02232/ *see 00559*

A 02233 L/835 121AY/oboe concerti by telemann, handel and dittersdorf
recorded in the mozarteum salzburg on 28-30 december 1961
paumgartner
camerata
academica
tright

A 02234 L/835 122AY/mozart the four horn concerti
recorded in the musikverein vienna between 4-11 december 1961
paumgartner 45 rpm issue: 400 250AE (no 2)
wiener further lp issues: MG 50409/SR 50409/
symphoniker 894 008ZKY/610 149VR (k417 and k447)
penzel

A 02236 L/835 123AY/violin sonatas by franck and grieg
recorded in amsterdam in december 1961
grumiaux further lp issues: AL 3738/SAL 3738/835 342AY
hajdu cd: 442 2962/476 7930

A 02237 L/835 124AY/beethoven symphony no 7; könig
stephan overture/*recorded in the concertgebouw amsterdam between 12-15 september 1960 (overture) and on 3-4 january 1962 (symphony)*
sawallisch 45 rpm issues: 400 227AE/740 024AV (overture)
concertgebouw further lp issues: GL 5809/SGL 5809/894 058ZKY/
orkest (symphony)/500 019/900 019

A 02239 L/835 126AY/tchaikovsky symphony no 6 "pathétique"
recorded in the town hall wembley on 9-12 january 1962
markevitch further lp issues: BAL 50/SBAL 50/6570 047/
london 6741 001/900 225
symphony cd: 438 3352/456 1872

A 02240 L/835 127AY/mahler symphony no 1
recorded in the concertgebouw amsterdam on 17-20 september 1962
haitink further lp issues: L09015L/802 883LY/
concertgebouw SC71-AX 602/6527 062/6768 021/
orkest 416 2431/500 017/900 017
cd: 442 0502

A 02241 L/835 128AY/concerti by durante, manfredini and vivaldi
recorded in may 1960 and in june and october 1962
i musici

02242/ *see 00219 and 00487*

A 02243 L/835 130AY/schumann cello concerto; tchaikovsky rococo variations and pezzo capriccioso
recorded in the musikverein vienna on 19-22 february 1962
dohnanyi further lp issue: 610 120VR (schumann)
wiener cd: 456 1872 (tchaikovsky)
symphoniker
gendron

A 02244 L/835 131AY/verdi scenes from aida/ *sung in french*
wagner further lp issues: G03424L/837 050GY
orchestra
jaumillot, kahn,
poncet, borthayre

A 02246 L/concerti by vivaldi, corelli, albinoni and manfredini
i musici

A 02247 L/835 132AY/beethoven symphony no 3 "eroica"
recorded in the concertgebouw amsterdam on 1-3 july 1962
monteux further lp issues: A02393L/6768 339/6856 003
concertgebouw cd: 420 8532/442 5442
orkest

A 02250 L/835 134AY/recital of songs by mussorgsky, tchaikovsky and prokofiev *recorded between 19-23 july 1961*
vishnevskaya
rostropovich

A 02251 L/835 133AY/beethoven symphony no 6 "pastoral"; die geschöpfe des prometheus overture
recorded in the town hall walthamstow on 13-17 april 1962
davis further lp issues: G05433R (symphony)/610 121VR
london (symphony)/836 231VZ (symphony)/836 929DSY
symphony (symphony)/6580 050

A 02252 L/835 135AY/schubert mass in e flat
recorded in the musikverein vienna between 3-7 may 1962
grossmann further lp issues: AL 3421/SAL 3421
wiener
symphoniker
sängerknaben
kmennt, berry

A 02253 L/835 136AY/mozart violin concerti nos 1 and 4
recorded in the town hall walthamstow on 11-12 april 1962
davis further lp issues: AL 3440/SAL 3440/6580 009/
london 610 142VR (no 1)/6527 049 (no 4)/500 236/900 236
symphony cd: 416 6322/432 3232/438 5642/438 5882/464 7222
grumiaux

A 02254-02255 L/835 137-138AY/schubert winterreise and schwanengesang
recorded in amsterdam between 28 december 1962-7 january 1963
souzay further lp issues: AL 3428-3429/SAL 3428-3429/
baldwin 500 510/900 510

A 02256 L/835 139AY/lieder by beethoven and brahms
recorded in amsterdam in may 1962
souzay further lp issues: AL 3422/SAL 3422
baldwin *excerpts from the recital*
further lp issue: 6580 011

A 02257 L/835 140AY/bach cantatas nos 11 and 65
recorded between 18-31 may 1961 and in march 1963
couraud
badische staatskapelle
stuttgart bach choir
schwaiger, litz,
altmeyer, crass

A 02258 L/835 141AY/waltzes by johann strauss
recorded in the musikverein vienna between 4 november-4 december 1961
sawallisch further lp issues: GL 5793/SGL 5793/G03116L/
wiener 837 021GY/SFL 14115/700 437WGY/
symphoniker 610 118VR/894 054ZKY/500 018/900 018
cd: 434 5422
excerpts
further lp issues: 6530 010/6747 041/6747 051

A 02259 L/beethoven piano sonatas nos 12, 13 and 14
recorded in the bachzaal amsterdam between 12-18 june 1962
arrau further lp issues: AL 3580/SAL 3580/6747 009/
6747 035/6747 199 (no 14)/6768 351/PHS 4914
cd: 420 1532 (no 14)/422 9702 (no 14)/
432 3012 (no 14)/462 3582

A 02260 L/beethoven piano sonatas nos 11, 15 and 28
recorded in the bachzaal amsterdam between 12-18 june 1962
arrau further lp issues: AL 3581/SAL 3581/6747 009/
6747 035/6768 351/PHS 3915
cd: 462 3582

A 02261 L/835 142AY/tchaikovsky selection from swan lake
recorded in the town hall walthamstow on 28-29 june 1962
monteux further lp issues: 6570 187/6580 020/6768 339
london cd: 420 8722/442 5442/442 5462
symphony *excerpts*
further lp issues: A02417L/835 287AY/
G03239L/837 046GY/610 812VL/839 512VSY
cd: 434 5442

A 02262 L/835 143AY/tchaikovsky selection from sleeping beauty
recorded in the town hall wembley on 10-11 january 1962
fistoulari further lp issues: AL 3415/SAL 3415
london *excerpts*
symphony further lp issues: A02417L/835 287AY/
G03239L/837 046GY/839 512VSY

A 02263 L/835 144AY/ballet music by stravinsky
recorded in the concertgebouw amsterdam on 19-23 september 1961 (oiseau de feu)
and on 4-6 july 1962 (petrushka)
haitink oiseau de feu suite
concertgebouw further lp issues: AL 3436/SAL 3436/
orkest 610 145VR/836 267VZ
rosbaud **petrushka**
concertgebouw further lp issues: AL 3436/SAL 3436/610 126VR
orkest cd: 477 0892

A 02264 L/835 174AY/violin sonatas by debussy, ravel and fauré
recorded in amsterdam in july 1962
grumiaux further lp issues: AL 3644/SAL 3644/802 770LY
hajdu cd: 442 6552 (debussy)/454 1342 (ravel)/473 1042

A 02265 L/835 145AY/massenet scenes from werther
recorded between 1-6 june 1962
couraud   further lp issues: GL 5667/SGL 5667/
badische   G03119L/837 048GY
staatskapelle
brazzi, berton,
gabriel

A 02266 L/835 147AY/chopin the 14 waltzes
recorded in paris in january 1963
cziffra   further lp issues: AL 3426/SAL 3426/
                      SDAL 504/894 042ZKY
                      cd: 434 5472

A 02267 L/835 148AY/chopin the 24 études
recorded in paris in january 1963
cziffra   further lp issues: AL 3427/SAL 3427
                      cd: 434 5472

A 02268 L/835 149AY/chopin the 6 polonaises
recorded in paris in january 1963
cziffra   further lp issues: AL 3425/SAL 3425/SDAL 504
                      cd: 434 5472

A 02269 L/835 150AY/beethoven violin sonatas nos 1 and 8
recorded in paris between 18 may-19 june 1962
oistrakh   further lp issues: AL 3416/SAL 3416/6768 036/
oborin   SC71-AX 405/eterna 826 951
                      also issued by philips usa, melodiya and chant du monde

A 02270 L/835 151AY/beethoven violin sonatas nos 2 and 10
recorded in paris between 18 may-19 june 1962
oistrakh   further lp issues: AL 3417/SAL 3417/6768 036/
oborin   SC71-AX 405/sterna 826 954 (no 10)
                      also issued by philips usa, melodiya and chant du monde

A 02271 L/835 152AY/beethoven violin sonatas nos 3 and 7
recorded in paris between 18 may-19 june 1962
oistrakh   further lp issues: AL 3418/SAL 3418/6768 036/
oborin   SC71-AX 405/826 954 (no 7)
                      also issued by philips usa, melodiya and chant du monde

A 02272 L/835 153AY/beethoven violin sonatas nos 4 and 9
recorded in paris between 18 may-19 june 1962
oistrakh   further lp issues: AL 3419/SAL 3419/6768 036/
oborin   SC71-AX 405/A02381L (no 9)/835 259AY (no 9)/
                      610 146VR (no 9)/836 268VZ (no 9)/
                      eterna 826 953 (no 9)
                      also issued by philips usa, melodiya and chant du monde

A 02273 L/835 154AY/beethoven violin sonatas nos 5 and 6
recorded in paris between 18 may-19 june 1962
oistrakh further lp issues: AL 3420/SAL 3420/6768 036/
oborin SC71-AX 405/A02381L (no 5)/835 259 (no 5)/
eterna 826 952 (no 5)
also issued by philips usa, melodiya and chant du monde

A 02274 L/835 155AY/works by mozart and giordani
recorded between 21 october-5 november 1960
i musici

A 02275 L/835 156AY/works by handel, bach and haydn
recorded between 21 october-5 november 1960
i musici

A 02276 L/835 157AY/bizet scenes from carmen
recorded between 16-21 june 1962
couraud further lp issues: G03241L/837 049GY
badische
staatskapelle
poncet, borthayre

A 02277-02279 L/835 162-164AY/vivaldi l'estro armonico
recorded in june, seotember and october 1962
i musici

A 02280 L/835 161AY/mélodies by duparc
recorded in amsterdam in june 1962
souzay further lp issues: AL 3434/SAL 3434/
baldwin 500 037/900 037

A 02281 L/concerti for 1 and 2 harpsichords by bach
fiala
amati orchestra
ahlgrimm, bretschneider

A 02282 L/835 158AY/offenbach scenes from les contes d'hoffmann
recorded between 5-14 september 1962
wagner further lp issues: GL 5617/SGL 5617/
orchestra G03145L/837 024GY
vivarelli, lorand,
poncet, rehfuss,
bianco

A 02283 L/835 159AY/gounod scenes from faust
recorded between 22 september-2 october 1962
couraud further lp issues: GL 5673/SGL 5673/
badische G03144L/837 023GY
staatskapelle
jaumillot, broudeur,
poncet, bianco

A 02284 L/835 160AY/rimsky-korsakov scheherazade and capriccio espagnol
recorded in the town hall wembley on 20-22 october 1962
markevitch further lp issues: AL 3437/SAL 3437/6580 025/
london 6570 148/6770 046 (capriccio)
symphony

A 02285 L/835 165AY/haydn symphony no 101 "clock"; schubert symphony no 5
recorded in the musikverein vienna in october 1962
sawallisch further lp issues: 894 092ZKY (haydn)/
wiener 6701 005 (schubert)/6747 057 (haydn)
symphoniker cd: 422 9732 (haydn)/432 2192 (haydn)

A 02286 L/835 166AY/mussorgskr-ravel pictures from an exhibition; berlioz carnaval romain overture; saint-saens danse macabre
recorded in the concertgebouw amsterdaqm on 10-12 september 1962
haitink further lp issues: 836 902DSY/
concertgebouw 610 134VR (mussorgsky)
orkest

A 02287 L/835 167AY/brahms symphony no 2; academic festival overture
recorded in the town hall walthamstow on 28 november-1 december 1962
monteux further lp issues: AL 3435/SAL 3435/6580 054/
london 6768 339/500 035/900 035
symphony cd: 442 5442/442 5472

A 02289 L/pergolesi scenes from lo frate innamorato
gerelli 78 rpm issue: angelicum SA 3027-3028
milan chamber further lp issue: S04014L
orchestra
and chorus
ribetti, borgonovo

A 02290 L/choral works by scarlatti and schubert
van der horst   scarlatti stabat mater
netherlands
bach society
grossmann   schubert deutsche messe
wiener
symphoniker
sängerknaben

A 02291 L/835 170AY/chopin piano sonata no 2 and other solo works
cziffra

A 02293 L/835 171AY/brahms symphony no 1
recorded in the musikverein vienna in december 1962
sawallisch   further lp issues: GL 5799/SGL 5799/140 127/
wiener   839 501VGY/6752 001
symphoniker   cd: 138 7572

A 02294 L/recital of short pieces for violin and piano
recorded in amsterdam in december 1962
grumiaux   cd: 442 8240/446 6502
hajdu   *excerpts*
                  further lp issue: 6570 177
                  cd: 454 1342/473 1042

A 02295 L/chopin piano sonatas nos 2 and 3
magaloff

A 02296 L/835 172AY/concerti by vivaldi
recorded in february 1963
barshai
moscow chamber
orchestra

A 02297 L/835 173AY/keyboard concerti by bach
recorded in february 1963
barshai   further lp issues: AL 3444/SAL 3444/
moscow chamber   839 507VGY/894 123ZKY
orchestra
devetzi

A 02299 L/835 175AY/works by handel
recorded in the concertgebouw amsterdam on 19-20 february 1963 (fireworks)
                  suite from the water music   *see 00491*
haitink   music for the royal fireworks
concertgebouw   further lp issue: G05119R
orkest

A 02301 L/835 177AY/chopin piano concerto no 1
recorded in paris in march 1963
rosenthal further lp issues: AL 3450/SAL 3450/
orchestre 802 745LY/894 004ZKY
national cd: 434 5472
cziffra

A 02303-02305 L/835 178-180AY/wagner tannhäuser
recorded at performances in the festspielhaus bayreuth in july and august 1962
sawallisch further lp issues: AL 3445-3447/SAL 3445-3447/
bayreuth festival 6723 001/6747 242/6747 249/6770 026
orchestra cd: 420 1222/434 4202/434 6072
and chorus *excerpts*
silja, bumbry, further lp issues: G03168L/837 025GY/6527 108/
windgassen, 412 0231
wächter, greindl cd: 446 5102/446 6202

A 02306 L/835 181AY/stravinsky l'histoire du soldat
recorded in théatre de vevey in october 1962
markevitch further lp issue: 6500 321
instrumental
ensemble
ustinov, cocteau

A 02307-02308 L/835 182-183AY/beethoven the 5 cello sonatas
recorded in london in july 1961 (no 3), in vienna between 25-31 march 1962
(nos 1 and 5) and in vienna on 4-9 june 1962 (nos 2 and 4)
rostropovich further lp issues: AL 3453-3454/SAL 3453-3454/
richter 839 602-603LY/6500 253-254/6700 027/
 6780 751
 cd: 412 2562/442 5652/464 6772
 also issued by philips usa and melodiya

A 02309 L/835 184AY/works for violin and orchestra by lalo and
saint-saens *recorded in paris on 1-5 april 1963*
rosenthal **symphonie espagnole**
orchestre further lp issues: AL 3587/SAL 3587/802 824AY/
lamoureux SBAL 32/SC71-AX 403/610 154VR/6570 192/
grumiaux 6768 304
 cd: 416 8862
 havanaise; introduction and rondo capriccioso
 further lp issues: 838 127DX/839 831GSY/
 894 100ZKY/6570 192/6768 304

A 02310 L/835 185AY/haydn symphony no 92 "oxford";
schubert symphony no 1
recorded in the musikverein vienna between 19-24 april 1963
sawallisch
wiener
symphoniker

A 02312 L/835 187AY/mozart coronation mass; spatzenmesse
grossmann　　further lp issue: 836 915DSY
wiener
symphoniker
sängerknaben

A 02313 L/835 188AY/berlioz symphonie fantastique
recorded in the town hall wembley on 16-18 april 1963
davis　　further lp issues: AL 3441/SAL 3441/836 904DSY/
london　　641 904DSL/6527 081/6570 031
symphony　　cd: 416 9592/422 2532/442 2902/
　　　　　　462 4702/468 1272

A 02314 L/835 189AY/piano concerti by grieg and schumann
recorded in the concertgebouw amsterdam on 24-28 may 1963
dohnanyi　　further lp issues: AL 3452/SAL 3452/610 139VR
concertgebouw　　(schumann)/6570 170/6580 108/6768 353
orkest　　　(schumann)/6833 020/500 047/900 047
arrau　　cd: 426 0792

A 02315 L/835 190AY/mozart violin concerto no 1; stravinsky
violin concerto
recorded in paris on 8-10 june 1963
haitink　　further lp issues: AL 3455/SAL 3455/610 153VR
orchestre　　(stravinsky)/6570 058 (mozart)/6585 003
lamoureux　　(stravinsky)/500 050/900 050
oistrakh　　cd: 434 1672
　　　　　　also issued by eterna, supraphon and melodiya

A 02316 L/835 191AY/recital of piano music by liszt
recorded in paris in march 1963
cziffra　　further lp issues: AL 3465/SAL 3465/SDAL 504
　　　　　cd: 434 5472

A 02317 L/835 192AY/saint-saens symphony no 3 "organ"
recorded in the concertgebouw amsterdaqm between 10-13 june 1963
benzi
residentie orkest

A 02318 L/835 193AY/dvorak symphony no 8; 3 slavonic dances
recorded in the concertgebouw amsterdam on 4-6 june 1963
haitink further lp issues: AL 3451/SAL 3451/894 102ZKY/
concertgebouw 6701 006 (symphony)
orkest cd: 462 0772

A 02319 L/835 194AY/prokofiev symphony no 1; shostakovich symphony no 1
horvat
zagreb
philharmonic

A 02320 L/835 195AY/bach brandenburg concerti nos 3, 4 and 5
i musici

A 02321 L/schubert the 8 impromptus
recorded in the concertgebouw amsterdam in may 1963
haebler further lp issue: 610 150 (op 90 only)
  cd: 456 3672

A 02322 L/mozart piano sonatas k310, k311 and k331
haebler

A 02323 L/835 205AY/debussy images; le martyre de st. sébastien
recorded in the town hall walthamstow between 18-21 may 1963
monteux further lp issues: AL 3459/SAL 3459/6768 339/
london 500 058/900 058
symphony cd: 420 3922/442 5442/442 5952

A 02324 L/835 201AY/recital of french mélodies
recorded in amsterdam on 7 july 1963
souzay further lp issues: AL 3480/SAL 3480/
baldwin 500 132/900 132

A 02325 L/835 202AY/beethoven piano sonatas nos 11, 19 and 20
recorded in paris in june 1963
richter further lp issues: AL 3456/SAL 3456/SFM 23014/
  839 524VGY/6580 095/500 076/900 076
  cd: 412 3792/438 6172/442 4642
  also published by melodiya

A 02326 L/835 203AY/beethoven piano sonatas nos 9 and 10
recorded in paris in june 1963
richter further lp issues: AL 3457/SAL 3457/SFM 23015/
839 525VGY/500 077/900 077
cd: 412 3792
also published by melodiya

A 02327 L/835 204AY/shostakovich selection from the preludes and fugues
recorded in paris in july 1963
richter further lp issues: AL 3458/SAL 3458/
6580 084/500 048/900 048
cd: 438 6272/442 4642
also published by melodiya

A 02330 L/835 208AY/beethoven piano sonata no 29 "hammerklavier"
recorded in amsterdam on 19 september 1963
arrau further lp issues: AL 3484/SAL 3484/802 732LY/
6570 055/6580 104/6747 009/6747 035/6768 351/
6780 020/6833 145/PHS 3915
cd: 462 3582

A 02331-02332 L/835 209-210AY/vivaldi la stravaganza
recorded between 26 may-3 june 1963
i musici

A 02333 L/835 211AY/concerti by venetian composers
recorded between 31 august-10 september 1963
i musici

A 02334 L/835 214AY/ballet suites from coppélia, sylvia and faust
benzi further lp issues: SFL 14068/700 177WGY
paris opéra
orchestra

A 02335 L/835 212AY/beethoven piano sonatas nos 8 and 21
recorded in amsterdam between 19-26 september 1963
arrau further lp issues: AL 3517/SAL 3517/CXL 15001
(no 8)/610 147VR (no 8)/836 269 (no 8)/
6570 190 (no 21)/6580 301 (no 21)/
6747 009/6747 035/6768 231 (no 8)/
6768 351/PHS 3907
cd: 422 9702 (no 8)/426 0682 (no 21)/
432 0412 (no 8)/462 3582

A 02336 L/835 213AY/halévy scenes from la juive
recorded between 17-21 september 1963
couraud further lp issues: GL 5756/SGL 5756/
badische G03198L/837 026GY
staatskapelle
rhodes, poncet,
serkoyan

A 02337 L/835 215AY/operatic arias by handel, rameau & lully
recorded in the bachzaal amsterdam in july 1963
leppard further lp issues: AL 3468/SAL 3468/
english chamber 500 051/900 051
orchestra
souzay

A 02338 L/835 216AY/mozart piano sonatas k282, k330 and k576; rondo k511
recorded in amsterdam in september 1963
haebler further lp issue: SC71-AX 601
cd: 456 1322 (sonatas only)

A 02339 L/835 217AY/bruckner symphony no 3
recorded in the concertgebouw amsterdam between 28 september-2 october 1963
haitink further lp issues: AL 3506/SAL 3506/6717 002
concertgebouw cd: 475 6740
orkest

A 02340-02341 L/835 218-219AY/chopin the 19 nocturnes
recorded in amsterdam between 13 april-5 may 1963
harasiewicz further lp issues: SFL 14019-14020/
894 072-894 073ZKY
cd: 442 2662/442 8746/brilliant 93529

A 02342-02346 L/835 220-224AY/wagner parsifal
recorded at performances in the festspielhaus bayreuth between 27 july-21 august 1962
knappertsbusch further lp issues: AL 3475-3479/SAL 3475-3479/
bayreuth festival 6723 001/6747 242/6747 250/PHM 5550/
orchestra PHS 5950
and chorus cd: 416 3902/464 7562
dalis, thomas,
london, hotter,
talvelva, neidlinger

**A 02347-02348 L/835 225-226AY/bruckner symphony no 5;
organ pieces by bruins, daquin and bach**
recorded at performances in the benedikter abtei ottobeuren on 30-31 may 1964
jochum further lp issues: AL 3532-3533/SAL 3532-3533/
concertgebouw 6700 028/PHS2-991 (bruckner)
orkest cd: 426 1072/464 6932
meier

**A 02349-02350 L/835 227-228AY/bach sonatas for violin and
harpsichord** *recorded in june 1963*
grumiaux further lp issues: AL 3487-3488/SAL 3487-3488/
sartori PHM2-597/PHS2-997

A 02351-02352 L/835 229-230AY/telemann markus-passion
recorded in lausanne in april 1964
redel further lp issues: AL 3494-3495/SAL 3494-3495
munich pro arte
orchestra
lausanne youth choir
giebel, malaniuk,
rehfuss

**A 02355 L/835 233AY/choral works by brahms, schubert and
michael haydn**
recorded between 29 october-3 november 1963
wiener
sängerknaben

A 02356 L/835 234AY/brahms violin concerto
recorded in the concertgebouw amsterdam on 3-4 july 1958
beinum   further lp issues: A02823L/L09007L/835 008AY/
concertgebouw   SABL 141/AL 3526/SAL 3526/SBAL 32/G05461R/
orkest   610 105VR/836 255VZ/SC71-AX 403/LC 3552
grumiaux   cd: 442 9788/retrospective RET 039

A 02357 L/835 236AY/works by telemann
grebe
hamburger
telemann-gesellschaft

A 02362 L/835 241AY/handel dettingen te deum
recorded at a concert in the janskerk gouda on 25 june 1958
van der horst further lp issues: 802 868DXY/698 012CL/
netherlands   875 015CY/CFL 1034/894 049ZKY
bach society   *excerpts*
bije, heynis,   45 rpm issue: 494 023EE
blanken, hollestelle

A 02363 L/835 242AY/stravinsky orpheus; symphony in three movements
recorded in the town hall walthamstow on 3-6 january 1964
davis   further lp issues: AL 3490/SAL 3490
london   cd: 442 5832 (symphony)/464 7442 (orpheus)
symphony

A 02364-02365 L/835 243-244AY/bach mass in b minor
recorded at concerts in the benedikter abtei ottobeuren in december 1957
jochum   further lp issues: 698 002-698 003CL/
bavarian radio   875 003-875 005CY/CFL 1028-1029/6768 214
orchestra   cd: 438 7392
and chorus   *excerpts*
marshall, töpper, 45 rpm issue: 495 002CE
pears, borg,   further lp issues: EFR 2023/663 009ER/
braun   697 022EL

A 02371 L/835 249AY/tchaikovsky symphony no 4
recorded in the town hall wembley on 19-21 october 1963
markevitch　　further lp issues:　AL 3481/SAL 3481/
london　　　　　6570 153/6741 001/900 206
symphony　　　　cd: 426 8482/438 3352

A 02372 L/835 250AY/tchaikovsky manfred symphony
recorded in the town hall wembley on 13-14 november 1963
markevitch　　further lp issues:　AL 3491/SAL 3491/6741 001
london　　　　　cd: 456 1872
symphony

A 02373 L/835 251AY/recital of lieder by richard strauss
recorded in the bachzaal amsterdam in december 1963
souzay　　　　　further lp issues:　AL 3483/SAL 3483/
baldwin　　　　　500 060/900 060

A 02374 L/835 252AY/stravinsky le sacre du printemps
recorded in the town hall walthamstow on 25-27 november 1963
davis　　　　further lp issues:　AL 3471/SAL 3471/6580 013
london
symphony

**A 02375 L/835 253AY/saint-saens violin concerto no 3;
vieuxtemps violin concerto no 5**
recorded in paris in december 1963
rosenthal　　further lp issues:　AL 3493/SAL 3493/836 931VZ
orchestre　　　　(saint-saens)/SBAL 32 (vieuxtemps)/SC71-AX 403
lamoureux　　　 (vieuxtemps)/6539 045 (vieuxtemps)/500 061/
grumiaux　　　　900 061
　　　　　　　　cd: 442 8561/468 8412 (vieuxtemps)

A 02376 L/835 254AY/violin concerti by bach and haydn
recorded between 24-27 june 1964
leppard　　　further lp issues:　AL 3489/SAL 3489/802 781DXY
english chamber　(haydn)/SBAL 32 (bach)/SC71-AX 403 (bach)/
orchestra　　　　SFM 23022/839 557VGY/6530 004/
grumiaux　　　　500 075/900 075

**A 02377 L/835 255AY/stravinsky apollon musagete; circus polka;
four norwegian moods; suites nos 1 and 2**
recorded in the town hall wembley between 17-30 october 1963
markevitch　　further lp issues:　AL 3485/SAL 3485
london　　　　　cd: 438 3502 (apollon)
symphony

A 02378 L/835 256AY/works for violin and viola by mozart
recorded in the town hall walthamstow on 19-22 may 1964

davis	**sinfonia concertante k364**
london	further lp issues: AL 3492/SAL 3492/500 130/
symphony	900 130
grumiaux,	cd: 412 2442/416 6322/422 9382/438 3232/
pellicia	PHCP 4919
davis	**violin concerto no 2**
london	further lp issues: AL 3492/SAL 3492/500 130/
symphony	900 130
grumiaux	cd: 416 6322/438 3232/438 5642/438 5882/
	464 7222/PHCP 4917/PHCP 4919

A 02379 L/835 257AY/works for flute and orchestra by mozart
recorded in the town hall walthamstow between 30 december 1963-1 january 1964

davis	further lp issues: AL 3499/SAL 3499/
london	836 922DSY/6570 091
symphony	cd: 412 2992
barwahser	

A 02380 L/835 258AY/ravel boléro; ma mere l'oye; la valse
recorded in the town hall wembley between 22-26 february 1964

monteux	further lp issues: AL 3500/SAL 3500/6527 036/
london	6570 092/6580 031 (la valse)/6768 399
symphony	cd: 412 5112/412 5182 (boléro)/415 5122/
	464 7332

02381/ *see 02272 and 02273*

A 02382 L/835 260AY/schubert die schöne müllerin
recorded in the théatre de vevey between 21-30 june 1964

souzay	further lp issues: AL 3501/SAL 3501/
baldwin	500 074/900 074

A 02383 L/835 261AY/contemporary polish music

rowicki	further lp issue: 839 261DSY
warsaw	
philharmonic	
woytowicz	

A 02384 L/835 262AY/mozart symphonies nos 25, 29 and 32
recorded in the town hall walthamstow on 26-29 november 1963

davis	further lp issues: AL 3502/SAL 3502/6570 207
london	
symphony	

A 02386 L/835 263AY/de falla el amor brujo; suite from
el sombrero de 3 picos
recorded in paris between 3-8 january 1964
benzi
paris opéra
orchestra
rivas

A 02387 L/835 264AY/orchestral works by hindemith
kondrashin symphonic metamorphoses on themes by weber
moscow
philharmonic
horvat   mathis der maler symphony
zagreb
philharmonic

A 02388 L/835 265AY/orchestral works by tadeusz baird
rowicki
warsaw
philharmonic
wilkomirska

A 02389 L/835 266AY/concerti by mozart and haydn
recorded in the musikverein vienna on 21-23 december 1961
paumgartner mozart oboe concerto; haydn oboe concerto
wiener
symphoniker
driehuys
paumgartner mozart bassoon concerto
wiener
symphoniker
de klerk

A 02390 L/835 267AY/beethoven piano sonatas nos 2 and 3
recorded in amsterdam between 27 march-4 april 1964
arrau   further lp issues: AL 3566/SAL 3566/6747 009/
     6747 035/6768 351/PHS 4914
     cd: 462 3582

A 02391 L/835 268AY/beethoven piano sonatas nos 1 and 4
recorded in amsterdam between 27 march-4 april 1964
arrau   further lp issues: AL 3568/SAL 3568/6747 009/
     6747 035/6768 351/PHS 3913
     cd: 462 3582

A 02392 L/835 269AY/franck symphony in d; les éolides
recorded in the concertgebouw amsterdam between 7-12 january 1964
otterloo
concertgebouw
orkest

A 02393 L/pierre monteux memorial album
recorded in the concertgebouw amsterdam on 1-3 july 1962 (eroica) and on 28-29 september 1963 (unfinished)
monteux **rehearsal extract from beethoven eroica sessions**
concertgebouw further lp issues: GL 5788/G03203L
orkest **schubert symphony no 8 "unfinished"**
further lp issues: A02455-02456L/835 325-326AY/
GL 5788/G03203L/894 068ZKY/
6747 057/6768 339
cd: 442 5442

A 02396 L/835 271AY/haydn nicolaimesse; kleine orgelmesse
recorded in vienna in october and november 1963 and in april and may 1964
wiener
sängerknaben

A 02397-02399 L/835 272-274AY/bach the 6 cello suites
recorded between 8-12 february 1964
gendron cd: 442 2932

A 02400 L/835 275AY/telemann magnificat in c; magnificat in g
recorded in lausanne in april 1964
redel further lp issues: AL 3546/SAL 3546
munich pro arte cd: 432 5002 (magnificat in c)
orchestra
lausanne
youth choir
giebel, malaniuk,
altmeyer, rehfuss

A 02401 L/835 276AY/schubert incidental music to rosamunde
recorded in the concertgebouw amsterdam between 31 may-4 june 1965
haitink further lp issues: AL 3534/SAL 3534
concertgebouw cd: 420 7152
orkest
netherlands
radio choir
heynis

A 02402 L/835 277AY/chopin the 24 préludes
recorded in amsterdam between 19-27 may 1962
harasiewicx further lp issues: 698 089CL/875 082CY
cd: 442 2662/442 8746/brilliant 93529

A 02404 L/835 270AY/stravinsky les noces and other choral works
simic
belgrade tv
orchestra
and chorus

A 02405 L/835 286AY/mélodies by fauré
recorded in the théatre de vevey on 7 july 1964
souzay firther lp issues: AL 3505/SAL 3505/
baldwin 500 191/900 191
excerpts
cd: 420 7752

A 02406 L/835 279AY/wind concerti by mozart
recorded in the town hall walthamstow on 2-3 january 1964 (flute and harp concerto) and on 5-6 may 1964 (clarinet concerto)
davis **flute and harp concerto**
london further lp issues: AL 3535/SAL 3535/6570 146
symphony cd: 442 2922
barwahser, ellis
davis **clarinet concerto**
london further lp issues: AL 3535/SAL 3535/6570 146
symphony cd: 420 7102/442 3902
brymer

A 02408 L/835 281AY/beethoven piano concerto no 1
recorded in the concertgebouw amsterdam between 9-13 june 1964
haitink further lp issues: 837 749LY/BAL 20/SBAL 20/
concertgebouw SC71-AX 501/SAL 3712/6570 167/6580 122/
orkest 6768 350/6770 014/PHS 5970
arrau cd: 462 3582/464 3162

A 02409 L/835 282AY/beethoven piano concerto no 2
recorded in the concertgebouw amsterdam on 22-23 september 1964
haitink further lp issues: 839 751LY/BAL 20/SBAL 20/
concertgebouw SC71-AX 501/SAL 3714/6570 173/6580 123/
orkest 6768 350/6770 014/PHS 5970
arrau cd: 462 3582

A 02410 L/835 283AY/beethoven piano concerto no 3
recorded in the concertgebouw amsterdam on 8-10 september 1964
haitink	further lp issues: BAL 20/SBAL 20/SC71-AX 501/
concertgebouw	SAL 3735/6570 104/6580 078/6768 350/
orkest	6770 014/PHS 5970
arrau	cd: 462 3582

A 02411 L/835 284AY/beethoven piano concerto no 4
recorded in the concertgebouw amsterdam on 12 april 1964
haitink	further lp issues: BAL 20/SBAL 20/SC71-AX 501/
concertgebouw	SAL 3736/6570 106/6580 060/6768 350/
orkest	6770 014/PHS 5970
arrau	cd: 462 3582/462 4552

A 02412 L/835 285AY/beethoven piano concerto no 5 "emperor"
recorded in the concertgebouw amsterdam between 9-13 june 1964
haitink	further lp issues: 640 600L/839 600LY/AL 3567/
concertgebouw	SAL 3567/SAL 3835/SC71-AX 501/BAL 20/
orkest	SBAL 20/6527 055/6570 086/6580 094/6768 231/
arrau	6768 350/6770 014/PHS 5970
	cd: 462 3582/462 4552

A 02413-02416 L/anthology of italian music
i musici

02417/ *see 02261 and 02262*

A 02418 L/835 288AY/contemporary british music
recorded in the town hall wembley on 15-16 august 1965
davis	**tippett concerto for orchestra**
london	further lp issues: AL 3497/SAL 3497/
symphony	6580 093/412 3781
	cd: 420 7812/470 1962
del mar	**goehr little symphony**
london	further lp issues: AL 3497/SAL 3497
symphony	

A 02419-02421 L/835 289-291AY/vivaldi la cetra
recorded between 26 may-5 june 1964 and in september 1964
i musici

A 02422-02425 L/835 292-295AY/beethoven the complete piano trios
beaux arts   further lp issue: 802 758LY (nos 5 and 7)
trio   cd: 412 8912 (nos 5 and 7)/464 6832 (nos 4, 5 and 7)/
              468 4112

A 02426 L/835 296AY/mozart piano concerti nos 15 and 16
recorded in the town hall walthamstow in september 1964 (16) and may 1965 (15)
davis   further lp issues: AL 3545/SAL 3545/BAL 30 (15)/
london   SBAL 30 (no 15)/6747 375
symphony   cd: 454 3522
haebler

A 02428 L/835 297AY/concerti by vivaldi, capuzzi and paisiello
recorded between 5-17 september 1964
i musici

A 02429 L/835 298AY/beethoven piano sonatas nos 5, 6 and 7
recorded in amsterdam on 12-14 september 1964
arrau   further lp issues: 839 749LY (no 6)/AL 3550/
            SAL 3550/SAL 3712 (no 6)/6580 122 (no 6)/
            6747 009/6747 035/6768 351/PHS 3915
            cd: 462 3582

A 02430 L/835 299AY/haydn symphonies no 96 "miracle" and 99
recorded in the concertgebouw amsterdam on 5-7 september 1964
haitink
concertgebouw
orkest

A 02431-02432 L/835 300-301AY/choral works by vivaldi
recorded between 17-29 october 1964
negri   further lp issues: AL 3536-3537/SAL 3536-3537
fenice orchestra
and chorus
giebel, höffgen

A 02433 L/835 302AY/orchestral music by russian composers
recorded in the concertgebouw amsterdam on 15-17 september 1964

markevitch	**borodin polovtsian dances/prince igor**
concertgebouw	further lp issues: 839 814LY/G03235L/837 045GY/
orkest	6527 057/140 185
netherlands	
radio chorus	
markevitch	**rimsky-korsakov russian easter festival overture**
concertgebouw	further lp issues: 839 814LY/G03235L/837 045GY/
orkest	6527 057/6539 067/140 185
	tchaikovsky romeo and juliet fantasy overture
	further lp issues: 839 814LY/6527 057/
	6768 167/140 185

A 02434 L/835 303AY/works by lutoslawski

rowicki	further lp issues: 839 261DSY/900 159
warsaw	
philharmonic	

A 02435 L/835 304AY/works by dvorak and tchaikovsky
recorded in the concertgebouw amsterdam between 19-23 september 1961 (capriccio italien), 27 september 1963 (dvorak) and 13 june 1964 (1812)

haitink	**scherzo capriccioso; romeo and juliet**
concertgebouw	further lp issues: AL 3462/SAL 3462/
orkest	G05426R/894 059ZKY (scherzo capriccioso)/6580 014
	cd: 462 0772 (scherzo capriccioso)
	capriccio italien
	further lp issues: AL 3492/SAL 3492/610 115VR/
	836 221VZ/G05426R/894 059ZKY/6580 014

A 02436 L/835 306AY/sibelius symphony no 2
recorded in the concertgebouw amsterdam between 30 november-2 december 1964

szell	further lp issues: AL 3515/SAL 3515/500 092/
concertgebouw	900 092/6580 051
orkest	cd: 420 7712/442 7272/475 6780

A 02437 L/835 307AY/works by beethoven
recorded in the musikverein vienna in june 1957 (choral fantasia)
                          piano concerto no 3 *see 02043*
böhm   choral fantasia
wiener   further lp issues: 663 000ER/695 064KL/
symphoniker   6833 188
chor der wiener   cd: 442 7322
staatsoper
richter-haaser
stich-randall
hellwig
rössl-majdan
dermota
majkut
schöffler

A 02438 L/835 308AY/mozart piano concerti nos 17 and 23
recorded in the town hall wembley on 4-6 january 1965
rowicki   further lp issues: AL 3537/SAL 3537/6747 375/
london   PHS 2906 (no 23)
symphony   cd: 454 3522
haebler

**A 02439 L/835 309AY/mendelssohn a midsummer night's dream
incidental music** *recorded in the concertgebouw amsterdam on 21-23 december 1964*
haitink   further lp issues: AL 3548/SAL 3548/
concertgebouw   641 908DSL/836 908DSY
orkest
netherlands
radio chorus
woodland, watts

A 02440 L/835 310AY/mozart piano sonatas k309, k332 and k570
recorded in amsterdam in december 1964
haebler   further lp issue: SC71-AX 601
                   cd: 456 1322

A 02443-02444 L/835 313-314AY/ravel the complete solo piano works
recorded in amsterdam between 11-16 may 1964 and in november 1964
haas   further lp issue: WS 2001
                   cd: 438 3532

A 02445 L/835 315AY/bach masses bwv 233 and bwv 234
recorded in lausanne in ocrober 1965
redel   cd: 438 7932 (bwv 233)
munich pro arte
orchestra
and chorus
giebel, litz, prey

A 02455-02456 L/835 325-326AY/symphonies by bruckner and schubert
recorded in the concertgebouw amsterdam on 10-12 may 1965 (bruckner)
         schubert symphony no 8 "unfinished"
         see 02393
haitink   **bruckner symphony no 4 "romantic"**
concertgebouw   further lp issues: 835 385AY/840 135WGY/
orkest   6717 002
         cd: 420 8812/475 6740

A 02473-02474 L/835 343-344AY/bach the 6 brandenburg concerti
recorded in berlin between 10 october-6 november 1965
maazel   further lp issues: AL 3551-3552/SAL 3551-3552
rso berlin   cd: 432 2162 (1-3)/432 2172 (4-6)

A 02475-02477 L/835 345-347AY/bach mass in b minor
recorded in berlin between 12-20 september 1965
maazel   further lp issues: AL 3553-3555/SAL 3553-3555
rso berlin
rias choir
donath, reynolds,
haefliger, shirley-quirk

A 02487 L/835 357AY/violin concerti by sibelius and prokofiev
recorded in the town hall wembley on 22-24 july 1965
rozhdestvensky further lp issues: AL 3571/SAL 3571
london   cd: 462 8562
symphony   *also issued in usa by mercury*
szeryng

A 02502-02505 L/835 372-375AY/bach matthäus-passion
recorded in the concertgebouw amsterdam between 20-30 november 1965
jochum further lp issues: AL 3562-3565/SAL 3562-3565/
concertgebouw 6747 019/6747 371/PHS4-999
orkest cd: 420 9002
netherlands *excerpts*
radio choir further lp issues: 802 786LY/6527 115/6701 012
giebel, höffgen,
haefliger, kesteren,
berry, crass

A 02507 L/835 377AY/recital of operatic arias
recorded in paris in october 1965
baudo further lp issues: AL 3574/SAL 3574/
orchestre 500 109/900 109
lamoureux
souzay
mono catalogue numbering in the 02500 series appears to have ceased as new recordings started to be published only in stereo format

03000/ *see 00101 and 00210*   **03001/** *see 00134 and 00750*

03002/ *see 00114 and 00200*   **03003/** *see 00179*

03004/ *see 00161, 00403 and 00635*

03005/ *see 00113 and 00429*   **03006/** *see 00373 and 00536*

03007/ *see 00114, 00702 and 06056*

03008/ *see 00111, 00307 and 00696*

03009/ *see 00120*   **03010/** *see 00228*

03011/ *see 00370*   **03012/** *see 00145-00146 and 00176*

03013/ *see 00177* **03014**/ *see 00318 and 00604*

03016/ *see 00160 and 00175* **03017**/ *see 00501 and 02038*

G 03018-03019 L/bach the 6 brandenburg concerti
recorded in the concertgebouw amsterdam between 20-22 april and 4-11 may 1958
goldberg further lp issues: GBL 5511-5512/835 046
netherlands (nos 4, 5 and 6)/894 014-015ZKY
chamber cd: 438 5082/438 5092/464 3552/
orchestra retrospective 93407

03020/ *see 00307* **03022**/ *see 00210*

03023/ *see 00323-00324, 00393-00394 and 00423-00425*

03024/ *see 00141* **03025**/ *see 00318 and 00319*

03026/ *see 00123* **03029**/ *see 00210 and 00636*

03030/ *see 00145-00146* **03031**/ *see 00102*

03032/ *see 00228, 00420 and 00750*

03034/ *see 00198* **03036**/ *see 00110*

03038/ *see 00183* **03040**/ *see 00191*

03041/ *see 00690* **03042**/ *see 00144*

03044/ *see 06133* **03045**/ *see 00139*

03046/ *see 00166* **03047**/ *see 04024*

03048/ *see 06150 and 835 009* **03050**/ *see 00180 and 05306*

03052/ *see 00102 and 00115* **03054**/ *see 00636 and 00674*

03055/ *see 02042* **03058**/ *see 00177*

03059/ *see 00518* **03061**/ *see 00689*

03062/ *see 00465* **03063**/ *see 00720*

03064/ *see 00319 and 00436* **03065**/ *see 835 062*

G 03066 L/ overtures by mendelssohn and schubert
recorded in the concertgebouw amsterdam on 23-25 september 1959 and between 11-14 may 1960 (hebrides)

dorati	**meeresstille glückliche fahrt overture**
concertgebouw	further lp issues: GBL 5581/G05398R/
orkest	LC 3723/BC 1094
	overture in the italian style d591
	further lp issues: GBL 5581/G05398R
haitink	**hebrides overture**
concertgebouw	further lp issues: GBL 5581/G05398R
orkest	*G03066L and GBL 5581 incorrectly named conductor of hebrides overture as antal dorati*

03067/ *see 00188-00189*   **03068**/ *see 00280-00282*

03069/ *see 00357-00359*   **03070**/ *see 00444-00445*

03071/ *see 02018-02020*   **03072**/ *see 02021-02022*

03073/ *see 00463-00464*

G 03074 L/7 overtures by rossini
recorded in the musikverein vienna on 1-4 october 1956

molinari-	further lp issue: GBL 5587/200 015WGL
pradelli	*excerpts*
wiener	further lp issues: S06189R/G05311R/
symphoniker	695 007KL/894 103ZKY

03082/ *see 00646*   **03084**/ *see 00128 and 00603*

03085/ *see 04021*   **03087**/ *see 00218*

03088/ *see 00435*   **03092**/ *see 02211-02213*

03093/ *see 06186*

G 03094 L/weber scenes from der freischütz
recorded in the musikverein vienna on 6-10 may 1957

hollreiser	further lp issue: GBL 5669
wiener	*excerpts*
symphoniker	45 rpm issue: ABE 10120/402 107AE
chor der wiener	cd: 462 0712
staatsoper	
brouwenstijn,	
schwaiger,	
kmennt, berry	

03096-03097/ *see 02095-02096*   **03098/** *see 02230-02231*

G 03099 L/837 009GY/verdi scenes from aida/ *sung in german*

wagner	further lp issue: 6593 013
orchestra	*excerpts*
zadek, litz,	45 rpm issues: 402 117NE/402 186NE
kozub, crass	further lp issues: G03120L/G03123L/837 038GY

03100/ *see 00413-00414*   **03101/** *see 00669*

03105/ *see 00606*

G 03107 L/837 015GY/bizet scenes from carmen/ *sung in german*

couraud	further lp issue: 6593 006
badische	*excerpts*
staatskapelle	45 rpm issues: 402 125NE/402 189NE
litz, schwaiger,	further lp issue: 837 082GY
kozub, crass	

03111/ *see 09905-09906 and 09910*

G 03113 L/837 016GY/offenbach scenes from les contes d'hoffmann/ *sung in german*

wagner	further lp issue: 6593 014
orchestra	*excerpts*
lorand, litz,	45 rpm issues: 402 121NE/402 188NE
kozub, crass	further lp issue: G03121L

03116/ *see 02258*

139

G 03117 L/837 019GY/gounod scenes from faust/*sung in german*
couraud *excerpts*
badische 45 rpm issues: 402 123NE/402 181NE
staatskapelle further lp issues: G03120L/G03203L/837 038GY
lorand,
kozub, crass

03118/*see 00360-00362* **03119/***see 02265*

G 03142 L/837 020GY/verdi scenes from la traviata/*sung in german*
wagner further lp issue: 6593 007
orchestra *excerpts*
streich, kozub, 45 rpm issue: 402 189NE
günter

03144/*see 02283* **03145/***see 02282*

G 03147 L/operatic arias by verdi, puccini and mascagni
recorded in the concertgebouw amsterdam on 6-7 march 1951 (vissi d'arte)),
13-14 april 1951 (miserere) and in the musikverein vienna between 1-4 february
1954 (d'amor sull'ali rosee)
kempen **vissi d'arte/tosca**
netherlands 78 rpm issue: N11169G
radio orchestra further lp issue: 695 052KL
brouwenstijn cd: 462 0712
kempen **miserere/il trovatore**
netherlands 78 rpm issue: N11176G
radio orchestra further lp issues: H72-AX 205/695 052KL
netherlands cd: 462 0712
opera chorus
brouwenstijn,
vroons
loibner **d'amor sull' ali rosee/il trovatore**
wiener further lp issue: 695 052KL
symphoniker cd: 462 0712
brouwenstijn **cavalleria rusticana** *see 00119*
 aida and otello *see 00712*

140

03148/ *see 00486*

03153/ *see 00154*

03161/ *see 00410-00411*

03168/ *see 02303-02304*

03177-03179/ *see 00417-00419*

03184/ *see 00393-00395*

03189/ *see 00375*

03198/ *see 02336*

03149/ *see 00203*

03156/ *see 00342*

03163/ *see 09007*

03171/ *see 00273*

03183/ *see 00266*

03185/ *see 00732*

03192/ *see 697 004*

G 03200 L/837 034GY/overtures by rossini
benzi semiramide; la gazza ladra; l'italiana in algeri;
orchestre il turco in italia
lamoureux further lp issues: 610 814VL/838 614CY/
6530 025/6870 585
guillaume tell *see 02080*

03202/ *see 02393*

G 03203 L/837 038GY/arias from german and italian opera
recorded in 1964
wagner
orchestra
kozub

G 03204 L/837 039GY/opera choruses
recorded in 1964
wagner
orchestra
and chorus

03215/ *see 00474*

03219/ *see 00796 and 02029*

03223/ *see 00547*

03226/ *see 00376*

03235/ *see 02433*

03239/ *see 02261 and 02262*

03241/ *see 02276*

03246/ *see 00188-00189*

03247/ *see 00545*

G 03400 L/837 499GY/rossini scenes from guillaume tell
couraud
badische
staatskapelle
jaumillot,
poncet,
borthayre

further lp issues: 835 496AY/GL 5650/ SGL 5650
excerpts
further lp issues: G03487L/837 493GY

G 03401 L/837 500GY/arias from german operas
wagner
orchestra
and chorus
van mill

further lp issues: GL 5651/SGL 5651

G 03482 L/837 488GY/recital of operatic arias
etcheverry
orchestre
lamoureux
poncet

excerpts
further lp issues: G03487L/837 493GY

G 03484 L/837 490GY/meyerbeer scenes from l'africaine
wagner
orchestra
monteil, esposito,
poncet, giband

G 03485 L/837 491GY/verdi scenes from rigoletto/ *sung in french*
wagner
orchestra
tavernier, kahn,
poncet, bianco

further lp issue: 835 495AY

G 03486 L/837 492GY/chopin the 14 valses
haas further lp issues: EFL 2517/697 104CL/
698 503CL/SFL 14060/700 162WGY/
839 802GSY

03487/ *see 03400, 03482 and 03498*

G 03489 L/837 495GY/ballet suites from faust and coppélia
etcheverry further lp issues: 698 502CL/894 032ZKY
orchestre
lamoureux

G 03490 L/837 496GY/waltzes by johann strauss
wagner further lp issue: 839 804GSY
orchestra

03493/ *see 00563*

G 03496 L/recital of piano music by chopin and liszt
reuchsel

03497/ *see 00583*

G 03498 L/837 497GY/leoncavallo scenes from i pagliacci/
sung in french
etcheverry further lp issue: 835 476AY
orchestre *excerpts*
lamoureux further lp issues: G03487L/837 493GY
boué, poncet,
giannotti,
legros, gui

G 03499 L/mozart symphonies nos 31, 32 and 33
martinon
orchestre
lamoureux

03500/ *numbers in this sequence were allocated to publications under licence from the american columbia and mercury catalogues*

03601/ *see 00506*

04000/ *see 00132*

04001/ *see 00114 and 00200*

04003/ *see 00642 and 00675*

04004/ *see 00201*

04005/ *see 00133*

04006/ *see 00198*

04007/ *see 00148 and 00627*

04008/ *see 00100-00111*

04010/ *see 00190*

04011/ *see 00144*

04012/ *see 00112 and 00614*

04013/ *see 00636 and 00674*

04014/ *see 02289*

S 04018-04019 L/cherubini il crescendo
gerelli
rai milano
orchestra
villa, vicentini,
spina, montarsolo

S 04020 L/cello concerti by haydn and boccherini
recorded in the musikverein vienna on 21-23 november 1955
paumgartner   45 rpm issue: 400 073AE (haydn)
wiener   further lp issues: 695 038KL/
symphoniker   698 093CL (boccherini)
de machula   cd: 462 8982/462 8952

S 04021 L/brahms violin concerto
recorded in the musikverein vienna on 21-23 december 1955
moralt   further lp issues: SBL 5232/GBL 5592/
wiener   G03085L
symphoniker
senofsky

S 04022 L/works for piano and orchestra
recorded in the concertgebouw amsterdam on 12-15 february 1955
otterloo   **dohnanyi variations on a nursery song**
residentie   further lp issue: SBL 5210
orkest   **rachmaninov paganini rhapsody**
simon   further lp issues: SBL 5210/LC 3182
              cd: challenge records CC 72142

S 04024 L/brahms piano concerto no 2
recorded in the concertgebouw amsterdam on 30-31 january 1956
otterloo further lp issues: SBL 5208/695 044KL/
residentie LC 3303/200 055WGL
orkest
uninsky

04027/ *see 00128 and 00603*   **04028/** *see 00371*

S 04031 L/zeller scenes from der vogelhändler
recorded in the musikverein vienna between 24-29 may 1956
moralt further lp issues: SBL 5215/P98485L/
wiener P14706L/695 100KL
symphoniker cd: retrospective RET 045
chor der wiener *excerpts*
staatsoper 45 rpm issues: ABE 10149/402 071NE
zadek, lipp,
majkut, patzak,
preger, wächter

S 04032 L/diepenbrock te deum
recorded at a concert in the concertgebouw amsterdam on 6 december 1956
beinum cd: donemus CVCD 7/BFO-A3
concertgebouw
orkest
toonkunst choir
spoorenberg,
merriman, haefliger,
bogtman

04040/ *see 00145-00146*

S 04042 L/orchestral works (twilight concert)
recorded in the concertgebouw amsterdam on 23 january 1951 (grieg and weber), 3 january 1952 (schumann), 21 december 1954 (saint-saens) and 4 may 1957 (liszt)

otterloo	**grieg 2 elegaic melodies** *see 06010*
residentie orkest	**weber-berlioz aufforderung zum tanz** *see 06002*
otterloo residentie orkest krebbers	**saint-saens havanaise for violin and orchestra** further lp issue: SBL 5236 cd: 462 5212
otterloo residentie orkest de groot	**liszt hungarian fantasia for piano and orchestra** further lp issues: SBL 5236/641 117LXL/ 835 700LXL/SFL 14047/700 169WGY cd: 462 8962
otterloo residentie orkest de machula	**schumann abendlied and träumerei, arranged for cello and orchestra** 78 rpm issues: N12015-12016G (abendlied)/ N12047G further lp issue: SBL 5236 cd: 462 0912

04100-04299/ *numbers in this sequence were allocated to publications under licence from the american vanguard catalogue*

S 04590 L/bach choruses and chorales from matthäus-passion
jansen further lp issue: 695 500KL
utrecht *excerpts*
philharmonic 45 rpm issues: 422 518NE/422 519NE
orchestra
and chorus

04600-04699/ *numbers in this sequence were allocated to publications under licence from the american columbia catalogue*

04900-04999/ *numbers in this sequence were allocated to publications under licence from the american mercury catalogue*

05300/ *see 00162*   **05301/** *see 00150-00153*

05302/ *see 00651*   **05303/** *see 00179*

146

05304/ *see 09002*

05305/ *see 00718*

05306/ *see 00145-00146*

05307/ *see 00325*

05308/ *see 00134*

05309/ *see 00437*

05310/ *see 00113 and 00124*

05311/ *see 03074*

05312/ *see 00101*

05313/ *see 00135*

05314/ *see 00318*

G 05317 R/mozart exsultate jubilate; ave verum corpus; laudate dominum from vesperae solennes k339
paumgartner   further lp issue: 695 072KL
camerata
academica
and chorus
boesch, cahnbley

05318/ *see 00256-00257*

05319/ *see 09007 and 00746-00747*

05320/ *see 00350-00351*

05321/ *see 00479*

05322/ *see 00350-00351*

05323/ *see 00474*

05324/ *see 00475*

05325/ *see 00674*

05326/ *see 00781*

05327/ *see 00465*

05328/ *see 00620*

05329/ *see 00436*

05330/ *see 00646*

05331/ *see 00475*

05332/ *see 00102*

05333/ *see 00440*

05334/ *see 00315*

05335/ *see 00315*

05336/ *see 00697*

05337/ *see 00369*

05338/ *see 00687*

05342/ *see 835 006*　　　05343/ *see 00199*

05344/ *see 00199*　　　05345/ *see 00258*

05347/ *see 00519*　　　05348/ *see 00228*

05349/ *see 835 009*　　　05351/ *see 00430*

05352/ *see 00166*　　　05353/ *see 00213*

05354/ *see 00420*　　　05356/ *see 835 065*

05359/ *see 00536*　　　05364/ *see 00505*

05365/ *see 00505*　　　05366/ *see 00604*

05369/ *see 00697*

G 05370 R/mozart clarinet quintet
members of wiener
symphoniker
schönhofer

G 05371 R/rachmaninov piano concerto no 2
recorded in the musikverein vienna in july 1958
fournet　　　further lp issues: L09009L/ABL 3278/
wiener　　　　610 100VR/894 010ZKY/6598 898/
symphoniker　　6833 156
boukoff

05374/ *see 835 064*　　　05375/ *see 00726*

05376/ *see 00116 and 06018*　　　05377/ *see 00635*

G 05378 R/j.c. bach sinfonias op 18 nos 2 and 4
recorded in the concertgebouw amsterdam on 6-7 october 1958
beinum　　　　45 rpm issues: 400 127AE (no 2)/
concertgebouw　400 128AE (no 4)
orkest　　　　　further lp issues: 698 096CL/6768 023/
　　　　　　　　LC 3749/BC 1112
　　　　　　　　cd: 462 5252

G 05379 R/mozart oboe quartet
members of   45 rpm issue: 400 014AE
netherlands   cd: globe GLO 6037
string quartet
j.stotijn

G 05381 R/836 213VZ/tchaikovsky piano concerto no 1
recorded in the musikverein vienna in july 1958
fournet   further lp issues: L09009L/ABL 3278/
wiener   610 107VR/894 010ZKY/SFL 14034/
symphoniker   700 156WGY/6598 898/6833 156
boukoff

05387/*see 835 062*   **05388**/*see 00150-00153*

05391/*see 02040*   **05392**/*see 02040*

05393/*see 00739*   **05396**/*see 02027*

05398/*see 03066*   **05401**/*see 00536*

05402/*see 02034*   **05405**/*see 02051*

G 05406 R/works for violin and orchestra
recorded in the concertgebouw amsterdam between 11-14 may 1960 (beethoven)
                    saint-saens havanaise *see 00420*
haitink   **beethoven the 2 violin romances**
concertgebouw   45 rpm issue: 400 211AE
orkest   further lp issue: 894 069ZKY
grumiaux

05407/*see 00373*   **05408**/*see 00544*

05412/*see 00516*   **05413**/*see 02080*

05414/*see 00547*

G 05418 R/recital of short piano pieces
richter-haaser   further lp issue: 200 025WGL

G 05420 R/recital of music for cello
gendron

G 05421 R/836 220VZ/music by scandinavian composers
      sibelius valse triste *see 835 003*
fjeldsted   **alfven swedish rhapsody no 1**
wiener
symphoniker

05423/*see 610 116*

G 05424 R/vivaldi le 4 stagioni
recorded in the liederhalle stuttgart in january 1962
couraud   further lp issues: 610 111VR/836 226VZ/
stuttgart   894 013ZLY/700 134WGY/WL 1138/
soloists   836 911DSY

05426/*see 610 115*   **05427/***see 02083*

05428/*see 610 119*

G 05431 R/prokofiev peter and the wolf
benzi   further lp issue: 894 056ZKY
orchestre
lamoureux

05433/*see 02251*

G 05435 R/836 238VZ/ballet music from verdi operas
loibner
wiener
symphoniker

05438/*see 02024*

G 05439 R/836 244VZ/chopin-douglas ballet suite from les sylphides
etcheverry   further lp issue: 695 039KL
orchestre
lamoureux

05440/*see 00318*

G 05441 R/concerti by haydn
recorded in the concertgebouw amsterdam on 22-24 september 1958
(horn concerto)
       trumpet concerto *see 05468*
goldberg   **horn concerto in d**
netherlands cd: retrospective 93407
chamber
orchestra
woudenburg

G 05442 R/works by mozart and haydn
recorded in the concertgebouw amsterdam in october 1955 (haydn)

goldberg	**eine kleine nachtmusik** *see 02085*
netherlands	**haydn symphony no 39**
chamber	45 rpm issue: 400 114AE
orchestra	cd: retrospective 93407

05443/ *see 00263*   **05444/** *see 00339*

05445/ *see 00339*   **05446/** *see 675 020*

G 05447 R/836 252VZ/waltzes by waldteufel
loibner   further lp issues: SFL 14049/700 171WGY
wiener
symphoniker

05449/ *see 00475 and 02299*   **05450/** *see 00761*

05453/ *see 00751*   **05461/** *see 09007*

05462/ *see 00140*   **05465/** *see 663012 and 698 024*

05466/ *see 00441*   **05467/** *see 698 048*

G 05468 R/836 263VZ/trumpet concerti by haydn, vivaldi and leopold mozart

paumgartner	**haydn**
wiener	further lp issues: G05441R/SFL 14029/
symphoniker	700 127WGY
sevenstern	
birnbaum	**vivaldi**
orchestra	
andré	
faerber	**leopold mozart**
württemberg	
chamber	
orchestra	
holy	

05469/ *see 02051*   **05470/** *see 02099 and 698 061*

05473/ see 698 022   05474/ see 02071

05476/ see 00474   05479/ see 697 103

05585/ see 839 800

05600/ *numbers in this sequence were allocated to publications under licence from the american columbia catalogue (10-inch lps)*

06000/ see 00140   06001/ see 00145-00146

06002/ see 00149   06003/ see 00119 and 00149

06004/ see 00113

S 06005 R/ ballet music by lortzing and helmesberger
recorded in the musikverein vienna on 17 september 1953
loibner   further lp issue: LC 3102
wiener
symphoniker

06006/ see 00139 and 00697   06007/ see 00139 and 00628

S 06008 R/ brahms academic festival and tragic overtures
recorded in the concertgebouw amsterdam between 4-12 december 1953
otterloo   cd: challenge records CC 72142 (tragic overture)
residentie
orkest

06009/ see 00183   06010/ see 894 126

06011/ see 00175 and 00536   06012/ see 00403 and 00631

S 06013 R/ russian folksongs
royal maastricht
choir

**S 06014 R/ viennese songs by zeller and gruber
and stolz** *recorded in the musikverein vienna on 21 july 1952*
sandauer   *excerpts*
wiener   78 rpm issue: N12044G
symphoniker
dotzer

S 06015 R/works by tchaikovsky, johann strauss and schubert
recorded in the concertgebouw amsterdam on 23 may 1951 (tchaikovsky) and on 3-5 december 1951

kempen concertgebouw orkest	**marche slave** 78 rpm issue: A11156G further lp issue: LC 3349 cd: 438 3102 **radetzky march** 78 rpm issues: N12048H/N09032S further lp issue: LC 3349 **marche militaire** 78 rpm issue: N09039S further lp issues: 6718 012/LC 3349 *6718 012 incorrectly named conductor as otterloo*

06017/ *see 00118*

S 06018 R/operatic choruses by verdi
recorded in the concertgebouw amsterdam on 7 march 1951 (nabucco)

        aida *see 00116*
        il trovatore and i lombardi *see 00634*

kempen netherlands radio orchestra netherlands opera chorus	**nabucco** 78 rpm issue: N11175G 45 rpm issues: NBE 11064/402 039NE further lp issue: G05376R

06019/ *see 00149*

S 06020 R/overtures and arias by beethoven
recorded in the concertgebouw amsterdam on 31 january 1956 (overtures)

        fidelio *see 00629*

otterloo residentie orkest	**weihe des hauses and leonore no 3** further lp issues: S06127R/675 008ER cd: challenge records CC 72142 (weihe des hauses)

S 06022 R/mussorgsky night on bare mountain; borodin in the steppes of central asia *recorded in the salle apollo paris on 18 june 1954*

fournet orchestre lamoureux	further lp issue: 200 024WGL

S 06023 R/christmas carols
hengeveld
orchestra and chorus

S 06024 R/favourite pieces for violin and piano
recorded in amsterdam on 16 may 1955
heksch, de klijn
the performers were described for this recording as bianca ritorno and ramon rubati

S 06025 R/arias from louise, faust and les contes d'hoffmann
recorded in the concertgebouw amsterdam on 6-7 march 1951 (avant de quitter and hoffmann) and in paris on 4-6 february 1953 (air des bijoux and louise)
fournet   depuis le jour; air des bijoux
orchestre
lamoureux
brumaire
kempen   **avant de quitter ces lieux; scintille diamant!**
netherlands   78 rpm issue: A11179G
radio orchestra
baylé
kempen   **belle nuit o nuit d'amour!**
netherlands   78 rpm issue: N11176G
radio orchestra   cd: 462 0712
netherland
opera chorus
browenstijn, van der veen

S 06026 R/choral works by miscellaneous composers
recorded in amsterdam on 10 february 1951 and in december 1952
de nobel
netherlands
chamber choir

S 06027 R/works for violin and piano by mozart
recorded in amsterdam on 20 june 1951
de klijn,   78 rpm issues: N11155G/A11246G
heksch

06028/ see 00103   06029/ see 00128

S 06031 R/ mozart wind divertimenti k213 and k240
recorded in the musikverein vienna between 10-13 december 1953
paumgartner
members of
wiener
symphoniker

S 06032-06033 R/ organ music by various composers
recorded in amsterdam on 1-3 september 1954
asma   *excerpts from the recital*
         cd: 441 9632

06034/ see 00161 and 00196   06035/ see 00611

S 06036 R/ works by contemporary dutch composers
recorded in the concertgebouw amsterdam in 1953 (anrooy) and on 3 april 1954 (wagenaar)

dorati	**anrooy piet hein rhapsody**
residentie	78 rpm issue: N12060G
orkest	further lp issue: 6530 044
	cd: 432 3902/462 1042
otterloo	**wagenaar overtures to cyrano de bergerac**
residentie	**and de getemde feeks**
orkest	further lp issue: 6530 044
	cd: challenge records CC 72142

06037/ see 00179

S 06038 R/ operetta arias by lehar and johann strauss
recorded in the musikverein vienna on 27-28 september 1954
sandauer
wiener symphoniker
dotzer

06040/ see 00155-00156, 00169-00171 and 00172-00174

S 06042 R/schumann cello concerto
recorded in the musikverein vienna on 13-14 september 1954
moralt   cd: 462 8982/462 8952
wiener
symphoniker
de machula

06043/ *see 00191*

S 06045 R/overtures by beethoven and schumann
recorded in the concertgebouw amsterdam on 23 october 1954
otterloo   **manfred**
residentie   cd: challenge records CC 72142
orkest   **leonore no 2**
                    further lp issue: 200 028WGL

S 06046 R/piano duets by bizet and schubert
recorded between 19-22 november 1954
schnabel
piano duo

S 06047 R/operetta arias by various composers
recorded in the musikverein vienna on 19-20 october 1955
sandauer   further lp issues: SBR 6203/S06137R
wiener
symphoniker
steingruber, dotzer

S 06049 R/works for violin and piano by spanish composers
recorded in amsterdam on 13 december 1954
magyar
hielkema

06050/ *see 00210*   **06051/** *see 00210*

S 06052 R/elgar serenade for strings; brahms selection from liebeslieder-walzer arranged by herrmann
dumont   45 rpm issues: NBE 11005 (elgar)/
boyd neel   400 029NE (elgar)
orchestra

06053/ *see 00620*

S 06054 R/overtures by mendelssohn
recorded in the jesus-christus-kirche berlin-dahlem between 26-28 may 1951 (hebrides) and in the salle apollo paris between 24-26 january 1955 (dream)

kempen berliner philharmonisches orchester	**the hebrides** 45 rpm issues: SBF 169/313 058SF cd: tahra TAH 512-513
kempen orchestre lamoureix	**a midsummer night's dream** further lp issue: 200 028WGL

S 06055 R/choral music by dutch composers
de nobel

S 06056 R/works by khachaturian, helmesberger and liszt
recorded in the musikverein vienna between 17-22 november 1954
loibner   further lp issues: GBL 5527/G03007L (liszt)
wiener
symphoniker

S 06057 R/kuhlau ballet music from the elf king
recorded in copenhagen on 28 february-1 march 1955
frandsen   further lp issue: SBR 6239
danish radio
orchestra

S 06058-06059 R/hungarian gypsy music

S 06060 R/gade ossian overture; hartmann hakon jarl overture
recorded in copenhagen on 28 february-1 march 1955
frandsen   further lp issue: SBR 6231
danish radio
orchestra

S 06061 R/liszt mephisto waltz no 1; funérailles
recorded in amsterdam between 3-7 january 1955
de groot

S 06062 R/zigeunerlieder by brahms and dvorak
recorded in the musikverein vienna between 3-6 april 1955
zadek, frid

06063/ *see 00183*

06067/ *see 00609*

S 06068 R/piano music by mozart
heksch

S 06069 R/schubert impromptus d899
recorded on 14-16 march 1955
engel   further lp issues: 695 069KL/LC 3232

06073/ *see 00436*

S 06074 R/piano music by bach
recorded in amsterdam on 29 june 1955
hengeveld

S 06075 R/arias from slavic operas
recorded in the musikverein vienna between 8-22 november 1954
loibner
wiener
symphoniker
kmennt

S 06076 R/arias from italian operas
recorded in the musikverein vienna between 14-18 february 1955
loibner
wiener
symphoniker
kmennt

06078/ *see 00603*   06081/ *see 00302*

S 06082 R/works for violin and piano by schubert
recorded in amsterdam between 14-15 july 1958
grumiaux   **sonata d385** *see 00499*
castagnone   **duo d574; rondo from sonata d408**
                further lp issues: SBR 6230/LC 3609
                cd: 438 5162

S 06083 R/cimarosa scenes from l'italiana in londra gerelli
rai milano orchestra
and chorus
villa, ligabue,
spina, montarsolo

06088/ *see 00178 and 00631*   **06089/** *see 00635*

06091/ *see 00638*   **06092/** *see 00639*

06094/ *see 00663*   **06095/** *see 00674*

06096/ *see 00685*

06100/ *see 00149, 00259, 00280-00282, 00375, 00758 and 00762-00763*

06101/ *see 00101*

S 06102 R/schubert impromptus d935
recorded between 14-16 march 1955
engel   further lp issue: LC 3232

06103/ *see 00707*

S 06104 R/operatic overtures by auber
recorded in the salle apollo paris on 10-12 november 1954
fournet   *excerpts*
orchestre   45 rpm issues: NBE 11021/402 023NE
lamoureux   further lp issues: 200 028WGL

06105/ *see 00668*   **06106/** *see 00214-00215 and 00719*

06107/ *see 00214-00215*   **06108/** *see 00214-00215*

06112/ *see 00750*

06113/ *see 00739* 06114/ *see 00135*

S 06115 R/beethoven piano concerto no 3
recorded in the musikverein vienna on 24-26 february 1956
otterloo further lp issue: 695 064KL
wiener
symphoniker
de groot

06118/ *see 00737* 06119/ *see 00145-00146*

06126/ *see 00114* 06127/ *see 06020*

06130/ *see 00433 and 00437*

S 06133 R/beethoven piano concerto no 1
recorded in the musikverein vienna on 24-26 february 1956
otterloo further lp issues: GBL 5523/G03044L/
wiener   695 047KL
symphoniker
de groot

S 06134 R/beethoven piano concerto no 2
recorded in the musikverein vienna on 24-26 february 1956
otterloo further lp issues: GBL 5523/G03044L/
wiener   695 047KL
symphoniker
de groot

06136/ *see 00119*

S 06140 R/overtures by rossini and verdi
recorded in the concertgebouw amsterdam on 17 may 1954 (verdi) and in the salle apollo paris between 24-26 january 1955 (rossini)
zecchi **i vespri siciliani**
concertgebouw
orkest
kempen **guillaume tell**
orchestre   further lp issues: S06189R/LC 3349/695 007KL/
lamoureux   894 103ZKY/200 015WGL
discography of paul van kempen by rené trémine does not include this recording, and discography of the concertgebouworkest by jan van bart states that the recording of vespri siciliani was coupled with guillaume tell also conducted by carlo zecchi

S 06141 R/strauss tod und verklärung
recorded in the concertgebouw amsterdam on 27 september 1955
böhm cd: 442 5342
concertgebouw
orkest

06149/ *see 00280-00282*

S 06150 R/brahms symphony no 3
recorded in the concertgebouw amsterdam on 24-25 september 1956
beinum further lp issues: GBL 5524/G03048L/
concertgebouw 200 073WGL
orkest cd: 462 5342

06155/ *see 00732* **06157**/ *see 00322-00324*

S 06159 R/orchestral music by french composers
recorded in the concertgebouw amsterdam on 1-2 april 1954 (lalo, ravel and satie)
otterloo **chabrier fete polonaise** *see 00161*
residentie **lalo le roi d'ys overture; ravel valses nobles**
orkest **et sentimentales; satie 2 gymnopédies**
further lp issue: SBR 6234

06160 **06161**

S 06162 R/overtures by suppé
boccacio; dichter und bauer *see 00631*
sandauer **leichte kavallerie; banditenstreiche**
wiener
tonkünstler-
orchester

06165/ *see 00437* **06177**/ *see 00354-00356*

06184/ *see 00780*

S 06186 R/flotow scenes from martha
salmhofer
wiener
symphoniker
stich-randall
rössel-majdan
kmennt, berry,
braun

further lp issues: SBR 6229/GL 5668/
G03093L
excerpts
45 rpm issues: ABE 10147/NBE 11019/
402 106AE/402 048NE
further lp issue: H72-AX 205

06187/ *see 00444-00445*   **06189**/ *see 03074 and 06140*

06190/ *see 00114 and 00603*

06191/ *see 00463-00464 and 02018-02020*

S 06192 R/recital of piano music
andriessen

06193/ *see 00393-00395*

S 06197 R/choruses for male voices by schubert
recorded in the musikverein vienna between 29 november-6 december 1954
etti
wiener männer-
gesangverein

06200/ *see 00323-00324, 00423-00425, 00444-00445, 02021-02022 and 09000*

06204/ *see 00610*

S 06206 R/recital of lieder by schubert
recorded in the musikverein vienna on 18-20 may 1958
kmennt
werba

06600-06700/ *numbers in these sequences were allocated to publications under licence from the american columbia catalogue*

L09000 L/puccini gianni schicchi
recorded in the teatro san carlo naples on 20-24 september 1956
molinari-   further lp issue: 6540 032
pradelli   cd: 442 1062
san carlo
orchestra
and chorus
rizzoli, lazzari,
capecchi

L 09002 L/symphonies by schubert
recorded in the concertgebouw amsterdam between 22-25 may 1957
beinum   **symphony no 8 "unfinished"**
concertgebouw   further lp issues: GBR 6502/G05304R/
orkest   6768 023/422 1771
   cd: 422 1772/462 7242/475 6353
   symphony no 6
   further lp issues: 6768 023/422 1771
   cd: 422 1772/462 7242/475 6353

L 09003-09004 L/orchestral works by smetana and dvorak
recorded in the concertgebouw amsterdam between 11-15 september 1956 and on 22 october 1957 (slavonic rhapsody no 2)
dorati   **ma vlast**
concertgebouw   further lp issue: SC 6026
orkest   cd: 476 8717
   excerpts
   45 rpm issues: ABE 10032/400 030AE
   further lp issues: ABL 3195/A00399L/G03135L
   slavonic rhapsodies nos 1 and 2
   further lp issues: 6701 008/SC 6026

L 09005 L/recital of piano music by chopin
uninsky   further lp issue: 700 173WGY

09006/ *see 00488*

L 09007 L/835 008AY/works by brahms
recorded in the concertgebouw amsterdam on 24 february 1958 (alto rhapsody)

beinum	**alto rhapsody**
concertgebouw	45 rpm issue: 400 057AE
orkest	further lp issues: GL 5686/610 123VR/G03163L/
apollo choir	G05319R/LC 3563
heynis	cd: 420 8542/442 9788/462 0842/
	retrospective RET 041
	violin concerto *see 02356*

09008/ *see 00519*   **09009/** *see 05371 and 05381*

09010/ *see 00369*   **09011/** *see 00390*

09015/ *see 02240*

L 09399 L/835 493AY/choral works by bach
recorded in may 1956

couraud	**magnificat**
stuttgart	further lp issues: A77410L/G05598R/836 398VZ
soloists	cd: vivace 625
and chorus	*excerpts*
sailer, bence,	cd: 477 5305
wunderlich,	**cantata no 31 "der himmel lacht"**
messthaler	further lp issues: A77410L/G05599R/836 399VZ
	excerpts
	cd: 477 5305

recordings originally published on the label discophiles francais; fritz wunderlich sang under the pseudonym of werner braun

09400/ *numbers in this sequence were allocated to publications under licence from the american columbia catalogue*

W 09900 L/symphonies by beethoven
recorded at concerts in the concertgebouw amsterdam on 14 april 1940 (symphony no 1) and 18 april 1940 (symphony no 8)

mengelberg   **symphony no 1**
concertgebouw   further lp issues: 6597 009/6767 003/pearl HE 301
orkest   cd: 416 2002/462 5262/music and arts CD 1006/
    dante LYS 222-226
    symphony no 8
    further lp issues: 6597 009/6767 003
    cd: 416 2042/462 5262/music and arts CD 1005/
    dante LYS 222-226

W 09901 L/beethoven symphony no 2
recorded at a concert in the concertgebouw amsterdam on 21 april 1940
mengelberg   further lp issues: 6597 009/6767 003
concertgebouw   cd: 416 2002/462 5262/music and arts CD 1005/
orkest   dante LYS 222-226

W 09902 L/beethoven symphony no 4
recorded at a concert in the concertgebouw amsterdam on 25 april 1940
mengelberg   further lp issues: GL 5806/6597 009/6767 003
concertgebouw   cd: 416 2022/462 5262/music and arts CD 1005/
orkest   dante LYS 222-226

W 09903 L/beethoven symphony no 6 "pastoral"
recorded at a concert in the concertgebouw amsterdam on 21 april 1940
mengelberg   further lp issues: 6597 013/6767 003/C73-AX 204
concertgebouw   cd: 416 2032/462 5262/music and arts CD 1005/
orkest   dante LYS 222-226

W 09904 L/beethoven symphony no 7
recorded at a concert in the concertgebouw amsterdam on 25 april 1940
mengelberg   further lp issues: 6597 014/6767 003/rococo 2056/
concertgebouw cd: 416 2032/462 5262/music and arts CD 1005/
orkest   dante LYS 222-226/history 205 253303

W 09905-09906 L/symphonies by beethoven
recorded at concerts in the concertgebouw amsterdam on 18 april 1940 (symphony no 5) and 2 may 1940 (symphony no 9)
mengelberg   **symphony no 5**
concertgebouw further lp issues: GL 5689/G03111L/6597 016/
orkest   6701 031/6767 003
              cd: 416 2202/462 5262/music and arts CD 1005/
              dante LYS 222-226
mengelberg   **symphony no 9 "choral"**
concertgebouw further lp issues: 6597 015/6701 031/6767 003/
orkest   cd: 416 2052/462 5262/music and arts CD 1005/
toonkunst   dante LYS 222-226
choir
sluys, luger,
tulder, ravelli

W 09907 L/brahms symphony no 1
recorded at a concert in the concertgebouw amsterdam on 13 october 1940
mengelberg   cd: 416 2102/dante LYS 075
concertgebouw *416 2102 was incorrectly dated december 1940*
orkest

W 09908 L/orchestral works by franck and richard strauss
recorded at concerts in the concertgebouw amsterdam on 3 october 1940 (symphony) and 12 december 1940 (don juan)
mengelberg   **symphony in d minor**
concertgebouw cd: 416 2142/468 0992/biddulph WHL 023/
orkest   archive documents ADCD 114/history 205 253303
              don juan
              further lp issues: 6866 044/rococo 2066
              cd: 416 2142/468 0992/history 295 253303

W 09909 L/schubert symphony no 9 "great"
recorded at a concert in the concertgebouw amsterdam on 19 december 1940
mengelberg further lp issue: PHM 500 041
concertgebouw cd: 416 2122/468 0992/dante LYS 077
orkest

W 09910 L/orchestral works by schubert
recorded at a concert in the concertgebouw amsterdam on 27 november 1939
mengelberg **symphony no 8 "unfinished"**
concertgebouw further lp issues: GL 5689/G03111L/6866 044
orkest cd: 416 2122/468 0992
 rosamunde overture
 further lp issue: pearl HE 301
 cd: 416 2102/462 1052
 entr'acte no 3 and ballet music no 2/rosamunde
 further lp issue: pearl HE 301
 cd: 416 2102/462 1052/
 archive documents ADCD 114

W 09911 L/mahler symphony no 4
recorded at a concert in the concertgebouw amsterdam on 9 november 1939
mengelberg further lp issues: A02847L/C73-AX 204/
concertgebouw PHM 500 040/discocorp RR 506/turnabout
orkest TV 4425/melodiya M10 44436 006
vincent cd: 416 2112/426 1082/462 9622/q-disc 97016/
 history 205 253303
 excerpts cd: 464 5222/belcanto BEL 6015

W 09912-09913 L/choral works by brahms and bach
recorded at a concert in the concertgebouw amsterdam on 7 november 1940
mengelberg **ein deutsches requiem**
concertgebouw further lp issue: turnabout TV 4445-4446
orkest cd: 416 2132/468 0992/dante LYS 099
toonkunst *excerpts*
choir cd: 464 5222/belcanto BEL 6015
vincent, kloos **choruses from the matthäus-passion**
 see 00150-00153

N 10721 L/orchestral works by malcolm arnold
recorded in the town hall walthamstow on 19 october 1955
arnold **symphony no 2; beckus the dandiprat**
royal **overture**
philharmonic further lp issue: NBL 5021
hollingsworth **tam o'shanter overture**
royal 45 rpm issue: NBE 11038
philharmonic further lp issue: NBL 5021
this recording was allocated a catalogue number in the non-classical sequence

200 001/ see 00325   200 002/ see 00133

200 004/ see 663 019 and 700 157

200 005/ see 00176   200 006/ see 698 031

200 007/ see 698 000   200 008/ see 00635 and 00674

200 009WGL/chopin the 14 valses
doyen

200 010/ see 00651   200 011/ see 00168

200 012/ see 697 005   200 013/ see 00114

200 014/ see 00780 and 697 011   200 015/ see 03074 and 06140

200 016WGL/waltzes by johann strauss
mehler
danube symphony
orchestra

200 017/ see 00135 and 00603

200 018/ see 00697, 00733 and 00754

200 020/ see 00183

200 023/ see 00271, 663 005 and 698 023

200 024WGL/orchestral works by russian composers
dourian   glinka kamarinskaya
orchestre   **borodin in the steppes of central asia and**
lamoureux   **rimsky-korsakov capriccio espagnol** see 06022
                   rimsky-korsakov russian easter overture
                        see 697 007

200 025/ see 05418   200 026/ see 838 611

200 027/ see 675 010 and 697 000

200 028WGL/famous overtures
dourian   smetana the bartered bride
orchestre   fra diavolo   see 06104
lamoureux   midsummer night's dream   see 06054
             oberon   see 00119
             egmont   see 00145-00146
             leonore no 2   see 06045

200 029/ see 00628, 697 004 and 698 009

200 030WGL/concert at schönbrunn
various artists

200 031WGL/works for violin and orchestra by tchaikovsky and beethoven
             beethoven the 2 violin romances   see 00140
westermann   tchaikovsky violin concerto
europa-orchester
laurane

200 032/ see 00378

200 033-200 034/ see 00214-00215 and 00719

200 035/ see 00620   200 036/ see 00646

200 037/ see 00114 and 00200   200 038/ see 00690

200 039WGL/orchestral works by dvorak
             slavonic rhapsody no 3   see 00620
korunsky   the 8 slavonic dances op 46
europa-orchester

200 042/ see 663 003

200 043WGL/music for christmas
             concerti by manfredini and corelli
             see 00668
             arrangements of christmas carols

200 044/ see 00111 and 00307   200 045/ see 00180

200 048WGL/famous marches
otterloo

200 049/ *see 697 012 and 697 016*

200 051/ *see 00210 and 697 004*

200 053/ *see 00198*

200 056/ *see 00367 and 00375*

200 062/ *see 697 007*

200 066/ *see 00134*

200 070/ *see 00109*

200 072/ *see 00435*

200 075/ *see 00235*

200 050/ *see 00399*

200 052/ *see 00141*

200 055/ *see 04024*

200 059/ *see 697 006*

200 064-200 065/ *see 00350-00351*

200 068/ *see 00318 and 00319*

200 071/ *see 00218*

200 073/ *see 06150*

400 000/ *the vast majority of philips 7-inch minigroove extended play records in this series were devoted to re-issues from existing philips 78 rpm and lp recordings; the following items on this page are some exceptions*

400 000AE/respighi suite from la boutique fantasque
recorded in the abbey road studios london on 11-12 october 1950
kurtz   78 rpm issues: columbia DX 1785-1787/
royal   american columbia M 981
philharmonic   further 45 rpm issue: ABE 10106
                 lp issue: american columbia ML 4367

400 007NE/elgar pomp and circumstance marches nos 1, 2, 4 and 5
recorded in the town hall walthamstow on 9 december 1954
pope   further 45 rpm issue: NBE 11002
royal
philharmonic

402 000NE/piano music by brahms, mendelssohn and mozart
barenboim   further 45 rpm issue: NBE 11013

402 000NE/piano music by kabalevsky and shostakovich
barenboim   further 45 rpm issue: NBE 11014
it is understood that these earliest recordings by daniel barenboim were issued in the uk only and without the artist's approval

402 029NE/tchaikovsky andante cantabile; bach air from the third suite; haydn serenade
dumont   further 45 rpm issue: NBE 11005
boyd neel
orchestra

402 030NE/tchaikovsky waltz from serenade for strings; dvorak nocturne; grieg popular song/norwegian melodies
dumont   further 45 rpm issue: NBE 11006
boyd neel
orchestra

422 520NE/bach arias from the matthäus-passion
jansen
utrecht philharmonic
de la bije, blanken

610 101/ see 02024   610 102/ see 02024

610 103/ see 02051   610 104/ see 02075

610 105/ see 09007   610 106/ see 00520

610 108/ see 02071   610 109/ see 00514

610 110/ see 02071   610 111/ see 02083

610 112/ see 00520   610 113/ see 00545

610 114/ see 00544

610 115VR/836 221VZ/orchestral works by smetana and tchaikovsky
recorded in the concertgebouw amsterdam between 19-23 september 1961
haitink   the moldau/ma vlast
concertgebouw   further lp issue: G05426R
orkest   **capriccio italien** see 02435

610 116VR/836 222VZ/beethoven piano concerto no 5 "emperor"
recorded in the musikverein vienna in december 1961
otterloo   further lp issues: G05423R/675 001ER/WL 1140/
wiener   SFL 14081/700 138WGY/894 002ZKY/DY 88431
symphoniker
magaloff

610 117/ see 05425   610 118/ see 02258

610 119VR/836 228VZ/chopin piano concerto no 1
benzi   further lp issues: G05428R/641 117/835 700/
orchestre   SGL 5637/837 018GY
lamoureux
magaloff

610 120/ see 02243   610 121/ see 02251

610 122/ see 05431   610 123/ see 00460 and 09007

610 124VR/836 234VZ/bruch violin concerto no 1
recorded in the concertgebouw amsterdam on 17-18 july 1962
haitink   further lp issues: AL 3526/SAL 3526/838 127HGY/
concertgebouw   894 100ZKY/6580 022
orkest
grumiaux

610 125VR/836 235VZ/beethoven symphony no 8
recorded in the concertgebouw amsterdam on 16 july 1962
haitink further lp issues: 04811HGL/838 120HGY/
concertgebouw GL 5660/SGL 5660
orkest

610 126/ *see 02263*   610 127/ *see 02060*

610 128/ *see 02224*   610 129/ *see 835 355-835 356*

610 130/ *see 02224*   610 132/ *see 02051*

610 133/ *see 00547*   610 134/ *see 02286*

610 138/ *see 00690*   610 139/ *see 02314*

610 141/ *see 02043*   610 142/ *see 02253*

610 143/ *see 00461*   610 144/ *see 02225*

610 145/ *see 02263*   610 146/ *see 02272*

610 147/ *see 02235 and 802 741*   610 149/ *see 02234*

610 150/ *see 02321*   610 152/ *see 02205-02207*

610 153/ *see 02315*   610 154/ *see 02309*

610 300/ *this was a series of 10-inch lps of publications under licence from the american columbia catalogue*

610 800/ *see 02026*   610 801/ *see 698 032*

610 802/ *see 698 081*

610 803VL/beethoven violin concerto
horvat further lp issue: 700 154WGY
zagreb
philharmonic
ozim

610 805/ *see 698 048*   610 806/ *see 00474*

610 807/ *see 836 901*   610 812/ *see 02261*

610 814/ *see 03200*

663 000/ *see 02437 and 698 000*

663 001ER/beethoven symphony no 5
recorded in the concertgebouw amsterdam on 23-26 february 1958
otterloo further lp issues: EFR 2004/675 016ER/
residentie 200 004WGY/695 005KL/697 011CL/
orkest 875 009CY

663 002ER/mussorgsky-ravel pictures from an exhibition
recorded in the concertgebouw amsterdam on 26-27 march 1957
otterloo further lp issues: EFR 2011/695 043KL
residentie cd: challenge records CC 72142
orkest

663 003ER/works by handel
recorded in the concertgebouw amsterdam between 1-4 may 1957
otterloo **suite from the water music**
residentie further lp issue: 695 021KL/EFR 2005/
orkest 698 008CL/200 042WGL
music for the royal fireworks
45 rpm issue: 495 000CE
further lp issue: 695 021KL/EFR 2005/
698 008CL/200 042WGL

663 004ER/invitation to the dance: works by weber-berlioz, brahms, grieg and smetana
moralt further lp issue: EFR 2006
wiener *excerpts*
symphoniker 45 rpm issue: CFE 15046/495 028CE
further lp issue: 697 016EL

663 005ER/orchestral works by mussorgsky and borodin
recorded in the musikverein vienna on 23-28 february 1958
otterloo **night on bare mountain**
wiener 45 rpm issues: CFE 15023/495 010CE
symphoniker further lp issues: EFR 2012/200 023WGL/
otterloo 894 065ZKY/6530 022
wiener **polovtsian dances/prince igor**
symphoniker 45 rpm issues: CFE 15025/495 008CE
wiener further lp issues: EFR 2012/894 065ZKY
singverein

663 006/ see 698 009   663 007/ see 698 015

663 008ER/beethoven symphony no 4
recorded in the concertgebouw amsterdam on 23-24 april 1957
otterloo   further lp issue: EFR 2004
residentie   cd: challenge records CC 72142
orkest

663 009/ see 02364-02365

663 010ER/grieg peer gynt, suites nos 1 and 2 from the
incidental music *recorded in the musikverein vienna in september 1958*
dorati   45 rpm issues: CFE 15037/495 017CE (suite no 1)
wiener   further lp issues: EFR 2009/CFL 1043 (suite no 1)/
symphoniker   SCFL 102 (suite no 1)/697 012EL (suite no 1)/
                       875 010CY (suite no 1)/SFL 14043/
                       700 126WGY/LC 3606
                       cd: 464 0962
                       excerpts
                       45 rpm issues: EFF 545/270 163EF (suite no 1)
                       further lp issues: CFL 1043 (suite no 2)/SCFL 102
                       (suite no 2)/697 012EL (suite no 2)/875 010CY
                       (suite no 2)

663 011/ see 697 005 and 698 023

663 012ER/dvorak slavonic dances op 46
recorded in the musikverein vienna between 8-11 february 1958
ancerl   further lp issues: CFL 1047/SCFL 111/698 024CL/
wiener   EFR 2022/SFL 14087/700 158WGY
symphoniker   *excerpts*
                       45 rpm issues: EFF 543
                       further lp issues: G05465R/836 264VZ

663 013/ see 697 000

663 014ER/operatic choruses
hollreiser   further lp issues: SFL 14091/700 210WGY
wiener   *excerpts*
symphoniker   45 rpm issue: CFE 15023
chor der wiener   further lp issue: 695 016KL
staatsoper

663 015ER/recital of piano music by chopin
harasiewicz further lp issues: EFR 2025/697 001EL
cd: 442 8746

663 016ER/4 overtures by suppé
recorded in the musikverein vienna on 30 june 1958
paul walter further lp issue: 700 027WGY
wiener
symphoniker

663 017ER/ *see 698 021*   **663 018ER/** *see 698 022*

663 019ER/beethoven overtures to egmont, coriolan and leonore 3
dohnanyi further lp issue: SFL 14086 (egmont)/
wiener 700 157WGY (egmont)
symphoniker

663 025ER/franck violin sonata
i.oistrakh
ginsburg

663 026/ *see 698 040*   **663 036/** *see 698 081*

663 038/ *see 698 026 and 698 059*

664 000/ *numbers in this series were allocated to publications under licence from the american columbia catalogue*

675 000/ *see 00132*   **675 001/** *see 610 116*

675 002/ *see 00135*   **675 003/** *see 00176*

675 004/ *see 00651*   **675 005/** *see 00114 and 697 005*

675 006/ *see 698 031*   **675 007/** *see 697 003*

675 008/ *see 00145-00146 and 06020*

675 010ER/works by johann strauss and suppé
recorded
lafosse   **strauss waltzes**
orchestra
paul walter   **overtures to boccaccio and banditenstreiche**
wiener   further lp issue: 200 027WGL
symphoniker

675 011/ *see 00140 and 06020*   **675 012/** *see 00107 and 697 011*

675 013/ *see 00210*   **675 016/** *see 663 001*

675 017/ *see 700 183*   **675 020/** *see 05446*

676 000/ *numbers in this series were allocated to publications under licence from the american columbia catalogue*

695 000/ *see 00145-00146*   **695 001/** *see 00177*

695 002/ *see 698 015*

695 003/ *see 00114 and 00135*   **695 004/** *see 00101 and 00689*

695 005/ *see 663 001 and 698 031*   **695 006/** *see 00120*

695 007/ *see 03074 and 06140*   **695 008/** *see 00139 and 00372*

695 009/ *see 663 010 and 697 012*   **695 010/** *see 00214*

695 011/ *see 00215 and 00719*   **695 012/** *see 697 005*

695 014/ *see 00111 and 00307*   **695 015/** *see 00674*

695 016/ *see 663 014*   **695 017/** *see 00200 and 835 065*

695 019/ *see 00636 and 00674*   **695 020/** *see 00145-00146*

695 021/ *see 663 003*   **695 022/** *see 00369 and 00527*

695 023/ *see 00782*   **695 025/** *see 00133*

695 026/ *see 00162*

695 027/ *see 00132 and 00140*

695 028/ *see 00378 and 700 127*

695 029/ *see 698 030*

695 031/ *see 700 137*

695 032/ *see 00463-00464*

695 034/ *see 00180*

695 035/ *see 00199 and 00313*

695 036/ *see 00239*

695 037/ *see 00144 and 00509*

695 038/ *see 04020*

695 039/ *see 05439 and 697 004*

695 041/ *see 00718*

695 042/ *see 700 130*

695 043/ *see 663 002*

695 044/ *see 04024*

695 047/ *see 06133 and 06134*

695 048/ *see 00199 and 00258*

695 049/ *see 00256-00257*

695 050/ *see 00675*

695 051/ *see 00376*

695 052/ *see 00712 and 00713*

695 054/ *see 00340*

695 056/ *see 00690*

695 057/ *see 00140 and 00299*

695 058/ *see 00280-00281*

695 064/ *see 02437 and 06115*

695 066/ *see 00715*

695 067/ *see 00313*

695 068/ *see 00259 and 00315*

695 070/ *see 00184*

695 071/ *see 00258*

695 072/ *see 00375*

695 073/ *see 00430*

695 075/ *see 00290*

695 078/ *see 00213*

695 079/ *see 00235*

695 081-695 082/ *see 00350-00351*

695 083/ *see 00658-00659*

695 084/ *see 00746-00747*

695 086/ *see 00318 and 00319*

695 088/ *see 00134*

695 089/ *see 00108 and 00372*

695 090/ *see 00143, 00484 and 00724*

695 091/ *see 00228 and 00420*   **695 092**/ *see 00420*

695 093/ *see 00103 and 00625*   **695 094**/ *see 00305 and 00339*

695 095/ *see 00131*   **695 100**/ *see 04031*

695 107/ *see 00633*   **695 500**/ *see 04590*

697 000EL/ waltzes by johann strauss
paul walter   further lp issue: 700 133WGY
wiener   *excerpts*
symphoniker   further lp issues: EFR 2024/663 013ER

697 001/ *see 663 015*

697 003EL/ orchestral works by liszt
recorded in the musikverein vienna between 15-21 november 1959
paul   **les préludes; hungarian rhapsody no 1**
wiener   further lp issues: EFL 2510/SFL 14047/700 169WGY
symphoniker   **hungarian rhapsody no 2**
    further lp issues: EFL 2510/675 007KR/SFL 14047/
    700 169WGY

697 004EL/ ballet suites by tchaikovsky
recorded in the musikverein vienna between 8-11 february 1958
ancerl   **swan lake**
wiener   further lp issues: GL 5746/G03192L/695 039KL/
symphoniker   200 051WGL/SFL 14054/700 169WGY/
    894 107ZKY/6870 584
    excerpts
    45 rpm issues: CFE 15032/CFE 15044/
    495 011CE/495 015CE
    further lp issue: 200 029WGL
    casse noisette
    further lp issues: GL 5746/G03192L/CFL 1025/
    SCFL 118/698 009CY/SFL 14071/700 189WGY/
    6870 584
    excerpts
    45 rpm issues: CFE 15032/CFE 15044/
    495 011CE/495 015CE
    further lp issue: 200 029WGL

697 005EL / orchestral works by dvorak and smetana
recorded in the musikverein vienna between 8-10 february 1958

ancerl	**symphony no 9 "new world"**
wiener	further lp issues: EFL 2519/695 012KL/
symphoniker	CFL 1024/SCFL 105/698 006CL/
	700 012WGY/6527 033
	the moldau/ma vlast
	further lp issues: EFL 2519/695 012KL/
	EFR 2013/663 011ER/CFL 1024/698 006CL/
	675 005KR/200 125WGL/700 012WGY/
	700 125WGY/6527 033

697 006EL / brahms violin concerto
otterloo   further lp issues: 200 059WGL/6554 031
wiener
symphoniker
auclair

697 007EL / 875 006CY / rimsky-korsakov scheherazade and russian easter festival overture
recorded in the musikverein vienna on 14-15 july 1958
fournet   further lp issues: SCFL 110/698 014CL/
wiener   200 024WGL (overture)/700 162WGY
symphoniker   (scheherazade)

697 008EL / programme of waltzes
paul walter   **waltzes by ivanovici and lehar**
wiener   further lp issues: SFL 14049/700 171WGY
symphoniker
loibner   **waltzes by waldteufel**
wiener   further lp issues: SFL 14049/700 171WGY
symphoniker

697 009EL / ballet music by chopin-douglas, luigini and meyerbeer
etcheverry   further lp issue: 894 107ZKY
orchestre   (chopin-douglas)
lamoureux

697 010EL / tchaikovsky symphony no 6 "pathétique"
recorded in the musikverein vienna between 14-18 october 1957
dorati   further lp issues: CFL 1019/698 001CL
wiener
symphoniker

697 011EL/875 009CY/works by mozart and beethoven
le roux   eine kleine nachtmusik
orchestre   further lp issues: 675 012KR/200 014WGL/
lamoureux   SFL 14029/700 127WGY
symphony no 5 *see 663 001*

697 012EL/875 010CY/works by grieg and mendelssohn
recorded in the musikverein vienna on 3-6 may 1958 and in september 1958
dorati   **peer gynt, suites nos 1 and 2** *see 663 010*
wiener   **overture, nocturne, wedding march and**
symphoniker   **scherzo/a midsummer night's dream**
further lp issues: CFL 1043/SCFL 102/695 009KL/
200 049WGL/SFL 14043/700 126WGY/
832 096PGY/6747 239/LC 3606/BC 1036
excerpts
45 rpm issues: CFE 15037/494 015EE/495 016CE
further lp issues: G03130L/6545 042/6747 050
stereo lps SCFL 102 and 875 010CY omitted the scherzo

697 014EL/overtures and ballet music from operas by verdi
loibner
wiener
symphoniker

697 016EL/ballet music by tchaikovsky, weber-berlioz and bayer
recorded in the musikverein vienna on 10-11 february 1958 (tchaikovsky)
ancerl   **ballet suite from the sleeping beauty**
wiener   further lp issues: CFL 1025/698 009CL/
symphoniker   200 049WGL/SFL 14054/700 190WGY
excerpts
further lp issue: 663 006ER
moralt   **aufforderung zum tanz** *see 663 004*
wiener
symphoniker
paul walter   **ballet suite from die puppenfee**
wiener   45 rpm issue: CFE 15052
symphoniker

697 018/ *see 698 018*   **697 019/** *see 698 000*

697 020/ *see 698 030*   **697 022/** *see 02364-02365*

697 023/ *see 698 047-698 048*

697 101-697 102EL/bach the 6 brandenburg concerti
couraud further lp issues: EFL 2513-2514/
stuttgart EFR 2028 (nos 3 & 4)/WL 1089-1090/
soloists 700 128-700 129WGY/american columbia
 M2L-259/M2S-605

697 103EL/chopin the complete études
haas further lp issues: EFL 2516/SFL 14061/700 163WGY/
 G05479R (op 10)/836 394VZ (op 10)

697 104/ see 03486

697 105EL/875 700EY/beethoven piano sonatas nos 8, 14 and 23
haas

697 200-697 300/ *numbers in these sequences were allocated to publications under licence from the american columbia catalogue*

698 000CL/beethoven symphony no 9 "choral"
recorded in the musikverein vienna between 20-26 june 1957
böhm further lp issues: CFL 1011/697 010EL/GL 5810/
wiener 894 001ZKY/200 007WGY/6527 027/6540 003/
symphoniker 6570 908/6701 026/6833 080
chor der wiener cd: 442 7322
staatsoper *choral movement*
stich-randall, 45 rpm issue: 494 022EE
rössl-majdan, further lp issues: 663 000ER/6833 188
dermota,
schöffler

698 001/ see 697 010   **698 002-698 003/** see 02364-02365

698 004CL/bartok divertimento for strings; weiner suite on hungarian folk dances
recorded in the musikverein vienna on 10-11 june 1958
dorati further lp issues: CFL 1022/LC 3513
philharmonia cd: 442 2722 (weiner)
hungarica

698 005CL/orchestral music by wagner
recorded in the herkulessaal munich on 9-10 december 1957
jochum	**der fliegende holländer and tannhäuser**
bavarian radio	**overtures; tristan prelude and liebestod**
orchestra	further lp issues: CFL 1023/LC 3485
	cd: tahra TAH 257-258
	die meistersinger von nürnberg overture
	further lp issues: CFL 1023/LC 3485

698 006/ *see 697 005* **698 008/** *see 663 003*

698 009CL/orchestral works by tchaikovsky
ancerl	**ballet suite from casse noisette** *see 697 004*
wiener	**waltz from sleeping beauty** *see 697 016*
symphoniker	**romeo and juliet**
	further lp issues: CFL 1025/SFL 14071/
	700 189WGY
	marche slave
	further lp issue: CFL 1025
	waltz from serenade for strings
	further lp issues: CFL 1025/663 006ER

698 011CL/recital of piano music by chopin
harasiewicz	further lp issues: 698 055CL/875 037CY/
	839 748LY
	cd: 442 8746

698 012/ *see 02362* **698 014/** *see 697 007*

698 015CL/beethoven piano sonatas nos 8, 14 and 23
recorded between 7-15 may 1958
del pueyo further lp issues: 663 013ER (nos 8 and 14)/
695 002KL

698 016CL/beethoven piano sonatas nos 26 and 29
recorded between 7-15 may 1958
del pueyo

698 018CL/875 007CY/beethoven symphony no 6 "pastoral"
recorded in the musikverein vienna between 20-26 september 1958
dorati further lp issues: SCFL 104/697 018EL
wiener LC 3611/BC 1038
symphoniker

698 021CL/875 012CY/works by chopin
hollreiser **piano concerto no 1**
wiener further lp issues: 838 123HGY/663 017ER/
symphoniker SCFL 101
harasiewicz cd: 442 8746

harasiewicz **polonaise no 1**
further lp issue: SCFL 101
cd: 442 8746

698 022CL/875 023CY/works by chopin
hollreiser **piano concerto no 2**
wiener further lp issues: CFL 1040/SCFL 116/G05473R/
symphoniker 663 018ER/836 278VZ/894 040ZKY/6527 100
harasiewicz cd: 442 8746

harasiewicz **scherzi nos 1 and 4**
further lp issues: CFL 1040/SCFL 116/
GL 5743/6527 100
cd: 442 8746/464 0252

698 023CL/875 011CY/orchestral works by tchaikovsky
recorded in the musikverein vienna in february 1958
ancerl **symphony no 4**
wiener further lp issues: CFL 1046/SCFL 103
symphoniker **ouverture solennelle 1812**
further lp issues: CFL 1046/EFR 2013/
663 011ER/200 023WGL
875 011 contained only the symphony

698 024CL / dances by dvorak and brahms
recorded in the musikverein vienna between 5-8 january 1959 (brahms)

paul wiener symphoniker	**dvorak slavonic dances op 46** *see 663 012* **brahms selection from the hungarian dances** further lp issues: SCFL 111/G05465R/ 894 065ZKY/200 039WGL/SFL 14087/ 700 158WGY

698 026CL / piano music by mozart and haydn
recorded in amsterdam in july 1960 (haydn)

haebler	**haydn variations in f minor** further lp issues: CFL 1048/663 038ER/ 802 737LY cd: 456 8232 **haydn piano sonata no 52** further lp issue: 802 737LY **mozart sonata and fantasia k475/k 457** further lp issue: 802 749LY

698 027 / *see 00376*

698 028CL / recital of piano music by chopin

harasiewicz	cd: 442 8746

698 029CL / 875 032CY / orchestral works by schubert

otterloo residentie orkest	**symphony no 5** further lp issue: eterna 820 186 **ballet music from rosamunde** 45 rpm issues: 495 050CE/CFE 15070/ SCFE 7006

698 030CL / 875 024CY / bizet suites from carmen and l'arlésienne
recorded in paris on 31 may-1 june 1959

dorati orchestre lamoureux	further lp issues: CFL 1061/SCFL 117/695 029KL/ 697 020EL/LC 3646/BC 1063 cd: 442 2722

698 031CL / symphonies by beethoven and schubert
recorded in the concertgebouw amsterdam in june 1959

otterloo residentie orkest	**beethoven symphony no 8** further lp issues: 200 006WGL/BC 1059 cd: challenge records CC 72142 **schubert symphony no 8 "unfinished"** further lp issues: 200 006WGL/700 135WGY/ 675 006ER/695 005KL/BC 1059 cd: challenge records CC 72142

698 032CL/875 025CY/berlioz symphonie fantastique
recorded in the concertgebouw amsterdam on 10-12 july 1959
otterloo further lp issues: CFL 1059/SCFL 125/
residentie 610 801VL/838 601VY/894 035ZKY/
orkest 200 046WGL/6870 573
cd: challenge records CC 72142

698 033CL/beethoven symphony no 2; prometheus overture
recorded in the bethanienkirche leipzig between 11-26 june 1959
konwitschny further lp issues: CFL 1056/SCFL 112/K71-BA 600/
gewandhaus- SFL 14038 (symphony)/700 100WGY (symphony)/
orchester eterna 820 104/820 417-418 (symphony)/
825 417-418 (symphony)
cd: berlin classics: BC 02172/BC 20052

698 034CL/beethoven symphony no 7
recorded in the bethanienkirche leipzig between 11-26 june 1959
konwitschny further lp issues: CFL 1053/SCFL 113/BWL 001/
gewandhaus- SFL 14084/K71-BA 600/SFL 14084/
orchester eterna 820 105/825 416
cd: berlin classics BC 02172/BC 20052

698 035-698 036CL/symphonies by beethoven
recorded in the bethanienkirche leipzig between 11-26 june 1959
konwitschny **symphony no 1**
gewandhaus- further lp issues: SCFL 114-115/K71-BA 600/
orchester SFL 14038/700 100WGY/eterna 820 106-107/
825 411
cd: berlin classics BC 02172/BC 20052

konwitschny **symphony no 9 "choral"**
gewandhaus- further lp issues: SCFL 114-115/K71-BA 600/
orchester SFL 14035-14036/eterna 820 106-107/
rundfunkchor 820 417-418/825 417-418
wenglor, cd: berlin classics BC 02172/BC 20052
zollenkopf,
rotzsch, adam

698 039CL/piano music by schumann and schubert
recorded in amsterdam in august 1959 (kinderszenen and papillons) and in april 1960 (deutsche tänze)
haebler **kinderszenen**
further lp issue: 802 738LY
cd: 456 8232
papillons
cd: 456 8232
deutsche tänze d783
further lp issue: 802 738LY
cd: 456 3672

698 040CL/875 034CY/piano concerti by mozart
recorded in the musikverein vienna on 9-11 may 1959
dohnanyi **piano concerto no 18 k456**
wiener further lp issues: SCFL 135/LC 3677
symphoniker **piano concerto no 27 k595**
haebler further lp issues: 663 026ER/SCFL 135/LC 3677

698 041CL/recital of piano music by chopin
harsiewicz cd: 442 8746

698 043CL/beethoven piano sonatas nos 18 and 21
del pueyo

698 044CL/875 027CY/kodaly hary janos suite; bartok two pictures *recorded in the musikverein vienna between 5-8 january 1959*
paul
wiener
symphoniker

698 047-698 048CL/organ concerti by handel
thomas further lp issues: 700 159-700 160WGY/
gewandhaus- eterna 820 179-820 180
orchester *excerpts*
köhler further lp issues: 697 023EL/G05467R/
610 805VL/836 262VZ

698 050CL/schubert piano sonata d894; moments musicaux
recorded in the bachzaal amsterdam in april 1960
haebler further lp issues: SAL 3604 (sonata)/SAL
3647 (moments musicaux)/802 738LY
(moments musicaux)
cd: 456 3672 (moments musicaux)

698 051-698 054CL/handel complete concerti grossi op 6
margraf further lp issues: 700 165-700 168WGY/
orchester der eterna 820 640-820 643/825 640-825 643
händel- *excerpts*
festspiele CFL 1068-1069/SCFL 122-123/894 074ZKY/
 894 070ZKY/eterna 720 087/720 088/720 089/
 720 138/720 139/720 140

698 055/ *see 698 011*

698 057CL/875 038CY/schumann symphony no 1 "spring"; manfred overture
recorded in the bethanienkirche leipzig between 20-23 august 1960
konwitschny further lp issues: GL 5794/SGL 5794/
gewandhaus- eterna 820 190/825 190
orchester cd: berlin classics BC 02172

698 058CL/875 039CY/schumann symphony no 3 "rhenish"; overture, scherzo and finale
recorded in the bethanienkirche leipzig between 22-29 august 1960
konwitschny further lp issues: GL 5796/SGL 5796/
gewandhaus- eterna 820 191/825 191
orchester cd: berlin classics BC 02172

698 059CL/875 040CY/works for piano and orchestra
recorded in the concertgebouw amsterdam between 1-7 july 1960
goldberg **mozart piano concerto no 12 k414; concert**
netherlands **rondo in d k386**
chamber further lp issue: 875 052CY
orchestra cd: retrospective 93407
haebler **haydn piano concerto in d**
 further lp issues: 875 052CY/802 737LY/
 MG 50414/SR 90414
 cd: 456 8232/473 7742/retrospective 93407

698 060CL/875 043CY/stravinsky firebird suite; khachaturian gayaneh suite
recorded in the concertgebouw amsterdam on 1-4 november 1960
rowicki
residentie
orkest

698 061CL/875 044CY/symphonies by prokofiev and shostakovich
recorded in the musikverein vienna on 28-30 october 1960
rowicki prokofiev symphony no 1 "classical"
wiener 45 rpm issue: 494 013EE
symphoniker further lp issues: G05470R/836 265VZ
shostakovich symphony no 1

698 062CL/string quartets by dvorak and tchaikovsky
borodin
quartet

698 068CL/875 051CY/chopin the complete études
recorded between 25 june-8 july 1959
harasiewicz further lp issue: 894 121ZKY
cd: 442 8746

698 069CL/875 053CY/works for piano duet by schubert
recorded in amsterdam between 10-14 may 1961
haebler, cd: 456 3672
hoffmann

698 073CL/875 056CY/recital of piano music by chopin
harasiewicz cd: 442 8746

698 076CL/875 059CY/schumann symphony no 4; konzertstück for 4 horns
recorded in the bethanienkirche leipzig on 24-25 august 1961
konwitschny further lp issues: GL 5797/SGL 5797/
gewandhaus- eterna 820 296/825 296
orchester cd: berlin classics BC 02172

698 077CL/875 060CY/schumann symphony no 2; genoveva overture
recorded in the bethanienkirche leipzig between 26-30 august 1961
konwitschny further lp issues: GL 5795/SGL 5795/
gewandhaus- eterna 820 289/825 289
orchester cd: berlin classics BC 02172

698 078/ *see 00367*

698 081CL/875 061CY/mozart piano concerti nos 19 and 26
recorded in the town hall wembley in december 1961
davis further lp issues: GL 5813/SGL 5813/
london 663 036ER (no 26)
symphony
haebler

698 083CL/875 064CY/handel-mozart acis and galathea
recorded in the mozarteum salzburg between 2-18 february 1959
paumgartner　　　further lp issue: 835 024AY
camerata academica
harvey, vrooman,
bruce

698 084/ *see 00392*

698 087CL/mozart violin concerti nos 4 and 5
recorded in the liederhalle stuttgart in 1961
couraud　　　further lp issue: 700 161WGY
stuttgarter　　　cd: sonia classics 74440
philharmoniker
auclair

698 089/ *see 02402*　　　**698 093/** *see 00602 and 04020*

698 094/ *see 00166 and 00213*　　　**698 096/** *see 05378*

698 502/ *see 03489*　　　**698 503/** *see 03486*

698 506CL/boieldieu ma tante aurore, opéra en 2 actes
couraud
rtf chamber
orchestra

698 507CL/prokofiev peter and the wolf; saint-saens carnaval des animaux
etcheverry　　　further lp issues: 839 803GSY/695 251KL
orchestre
lamoureux

698 509CL/concerti by albinoni, corelli, clarke, purcell and vivaldi
birnbaum
instrumentalists

698 511-516CL/836 806-836 811DSY/debussy the complete solo piano music
haas

699 000/ *numbers in this sequence were allocated to publications under licence from the american columbia catalogue*

700 100/ *see 698 033 and 698 035-698 036*

700 101/ *see 00459*   **700 105/** *see 836 000*

700 106/ *see 00690*   **700 125/** *see 697 005*

700 126/ *see 697 012*   **700 127/** *see 697 011*

700 128-700 129/ *see 697 101-697 102*

700 130WGY/works for violin and orchestra
jordans   **bruch violin concerto no 1**
brabants   further lp issues: SFL 14044/695 042KL/
orkest   WL 1137/6833 123
krebbers   cd: 162 0872
horvat   **beethoven the 2 violin romances**
zagreb   further lp issues: SFL 14044/695 042KL/WL 1137
philharmonic
ozim

700 131WGY/beethoven symphony no 3 "eroica"
recorded in the bethanienkirche leipzig between 11-26 june 1959
konwitschny   further lp issues: SFL 14045/K71-BA 600/
gewandhaus-   eterna 820 181/825 412
orchester   cd: berlin classics BC 02172/BC 20052

700 133/ *see 697 000*   **700 135/** *see 00107 and 698 031*

700 137WGY/brahms violin concerto
jordans   further lp issues: SFL 14033/695 031KL/
brabants   894 062ZKY/6599 435
orkest
krebbers

700 138/ *see 610 116*   **700 139/** *see 00474*

700 141WGY/beethoven symphonies nos 4 and 5
recorded in the bethanienkirche leipzig between 11-26 june 1959
konwitschny   further lp issues: SFL 14083/K71-BA 600/
gewandhaus-   eterna 820 182 (no 5)/820 413 (no 4)/ 825 413 (no 4)/
orchester   825 414 (no 5)
                 cd: berlin classics BC 02172/BC 20052

700 142WGY / symphonies by beethoven
recorded in the bethanienkirche leipzig between 11-26 june 1959
konwitschny **symphony no 7** *see 698 034*
gewandhaus- **symphony no 8**
orchester further lp issues: SFL 14084/K71-BA 600/
eterna 820 063/825 411
cd: berlin classics BC 02172/BC 20052

700 143-700 144WGY / symphonies by beethoven
recorded in the bethanienkirche leipzig between 11-26 june 1959
konwitschny **symphony no 9 "choral"** *see 698 035 036*
gewandhaus- **symphony no 6 "pastoral"**
orchester further lp issues: SFL 14035-SFL 14036/
K71-BA 600/eterna 825 415
cd: berlin classics BC 02172/BC 20052

700 154/ *see 610 803*   **700 155/** *see 836 901*

700 157WGY / overtures by beethoven
recorded in the bethanienkirche leipzig between 11-26 june 1959
konwitschny **leonore no 3; coriolan; fidelio**
gewandhaus- further lp issues: SFL 14086/200 004WGL
orchester (leonore no 3)/eterna 820 182 (coriolan)/
825 414 (coriolan)
cd: berlin classics BC 02172/BC 20052/
BC 31112
geschöpfe des prometheus *see 698 033*

700 159-700 160/ *see 698 047-698 048*

700 161/ *see 698 087*   **700 162/** *see 03486*

700 163/ *see 697 103*

700 165-700 168/ *see 698 051-698 054*

700 169WGY/works by liszt
               les préludes and hungarian rhapsodies 1 & 2
               see 697 003
benzi   **hungarian fantasy for piano and orchestra**
orchestre   further lp issues: SFL 14047/641 117LXL/
lamoureux   835 700LXL
magaloff

700 171/ *see 697 008*   **700 172/** *see 00544 and 835 065*

700 173/ *see 09005*   **700 177/** *see 02334*

700 182/ *see 00474*

700 183WGY/tchaikovsky symphony no 6 "pathétique"
westermann
europa-
orchester

700 185WGY/piano concerti by tchaikovsky and rachmaninov
               rachmaninov no 2 *see 00162*
jordans   **tchaikovsky no 1**
europa-   further lp issues: SFL 14033/SFL 14059/
orchester   700 211WGY
klein

700 189/ *see 697 004 and 698 009*   **700 190/** *see 697 004 and 697 016*

700 200WGY/tchaikovsky symphony no 4
horvat
zagreb
philharmonic

700 211/ *see 700 185 and 836 901*   **700 436/** *see 836 914*

700 437/ *see 02258*   **700 440/** *see 00642 and 00675*

700 472/ *see 00188-00189*

835 000/see 00502   835 001/see 00441

835 002/see 00476

835 003AY/works by sibelius, grieg, debussy and tchaikovsky
recorded in the concertgebouw amsterdam on 7-8 june 1957 (sibelius) and 1-3 may 1958 (grieg)

beinum
concertgebouw
orkest

finlandia
45 rpm issues: ABE 10162/400 034AE/SBF 186
further lp issues: ABL 3324/SABL 103/835 014AY/
894 126ZKY/6747 204/6768 023/LC 3477/
readers' digest RD 6997/RDS 6997
valse triste
45 rpm issues: ABE 10162/400 034AE
further lp issues: ABL 3324/SABL 103/835 014AY/
G05421R/836 220VZ/894 126ZKY/6768 023/
LC 3477
two elegaic melodies
45 rpm issue: 313 043SF
further lp issues: ABL 3324/SABL 103/
894 126ZKY/6768 023
berceuse héroique and marche écossaise
see 00441
valse des fleurs/casse noisette *see 835 006*

835 004/see 00491   835 005/see 00488

835 006AY/orchestral works by mendelssohn and tchaikovsky
recorded in the concertgebouw amsterdam on 30 april-1 may 1958

beinum
concertgebouw
orkest

suite from a midsummer night's dream
see 00475
ballet suite from casse noisette
further lp issues: SABL 143/GBR 6535/G05342R/
894 044ZKY/6570 183/LC 3585/BC 1027
excerpts
45 rpm issues: SABE 2001/740 008AV/SBF 104
further lp issues: ABL 3324/SABL 103/835 003

835 007/see 00519   835 008/see 09007

835 009/orchestral works by debussy and ravel
recorded in the concertgebouw amsterdam on 30 june 1958 (boléro) and on 25 september 1958 (la valse)

beinum	**berceuse héroique and marche écossaise**
concertgebouw	*see 00441*
orkest	**boléro**
	further lp issues: 835 014AY/G05349R/
	836 920DSY/894 011ZKY/6530 017/6570 183/
	LC 3585/BC 1027
	cd: retrospective RET 043
	la valse
	further lp issues: 835 014AY/G05349R/836 920DSY/
	6530 017/LC 3585/BC 1027
	cd: retrospective RET 043

835 010-835 012/ *see 02018-02020*

835 013AY/orchestral works by brahms
recorded in the concertgebouw amsterdam on 25-27 september 1958

beinum	**academic festival overture** *see 00502*
concertgebouw	**tragic overture**
orkest	cd: retrospective RET 039
	haydn variations
	further lp issues: GBL 5524/G03048L
	cd: 420 8542/retrospective RET 039

835 014/ *see 835 003 and 835 009*

835 015/ *see 00504*

835 016/ see 00514   835 017/ see 00516

835 018/ see 00520   835 019/ see 00505

835 020/ see 00506   835 021/ see 00495

835 022/ see 00528   835 023/ see 00529

835 024/ see 698 083

835 026/ see 00533   835 027/ see 00537

835 028/ see 02037   835 029/ see 00539

835 030/ see 00301   835 031/ see 00544

835 032/ see 00545   835 033/ see 00546

835 034/ see 00547   835 035/ see 02024

835 036/ see 02025   835 037/ see 02040

835 038/ see 02041   835 039/ see 02042

835 040/ see 02043   835 042/ see 00519

835 046/ see 03018-03019   835 047/ see 02066

835 050/ see 02021-02022   835 051/ see 02018-02020

835 052-835 053/ see 02021-02022

835 054/ see 02034   835 055/ see 02051

835 056/ see 02052   835 057/ see 02053

835 058/ see 02054   835 059/ see 02055

835 060/ see 02056   835 061/ see 02057

835 062AY / orchestral works by berlioz and weber
recorded in the concertgeboue amsterdam on 23-25 september 1959

dorati
concertgebouw
orkest

suite from la damnation de faust
further lp issues: LC 3723/BC 1094/6530 020
cd: 464 0922
excerpts
45 rpm issues: SBF 275/313 123SF
further lp issue: 6882 100
scene d'amour from roméo et juliette
further lp issues: LC 3723/BC 1094/
6530 020/6585 026
cd: 464 0922
der freischütz overture
further lp issues: GBL 5580/G03065L/G05387R/
839 516VGY/LC 3684/BC 1078/6527 071/
6530 020/6833 154
cd: 462 8682
overtures to oberon and euryanthe
further lp issues: GBL 5580/G03065L/G05387R/
839 516VGY/LC 3684/BC 1078/
6527 071/6530 020
cd: 462 8682

835 063/ *see 00474*

835 064AY / orchestral works by schubert and grieg
recorded in the concertgebouw amsterdam on 18-19 june 1959 (grieg)

fournet
concertgebouw
orkest
de la bije

incidental music from rosamunde *see 00475*
suites 1 and 2 from peer gynt
further lp issues: G05374R/836 212VZ

835 065AY / chopin piano concerto no 2; 2 polonaises

otterloo
residentie
orkest
uninsky

further lp issues: G05356R (concerto)/
SFL 14050 (concerto)/700 172WGY (concerto)/
WL 1134

835 066/ *see 02060*

835 067/ *see 02026* 835 068/ *see 02063*

835 069/ *see 02067* 835 070/ *see 02068*

835 071/ *see 02072* 835 072/ *see 02075*

835 073/ *see 02076* 835 074/ *see 02077*

835 075/ *see 02071* 835 076/ *see 02080*

835 077/ *see 02082* 835 078/ *see 02085*

835 079/ *see 02083* 835 080/ *see 02027*

835 081/ *see 02028* 835 082/ *see 02029*

835 085/ *see 02030* 835 086/ *see 02086*

835 087-835 088/ *see 00457-00458*

835 089/ *see 02092* 835 090/ *see 00456*

835 091-835 092/ *see 02090-02091* 835 093/ *see 00459 and 02085*

835 094/ *see 00460* 835 095/ *see 02098*

835 096/ *see 02099* 835 097/ *see 00461*

835 098/ *see 02073* 835 099/ *see 02208*

835 100/ *see 02209* 835 101/ *see 02210*

835 103/ *see 00432* 835 104-835 106/ *see 02211-02213*

835 107/ *see 02214* 835 108/ *see 02215*

835 109-835 110/ *see 02220 02221* 835 111/ *see 02222*

835 112/ *see 02224* 835 113/ *see 02225*

835 114-835 115/ *see 02226-02227*

835 116/ *see 02228* **835 117/** *see 02229*

835 118-835 119/ *see 02230-02231*

835 120/ *see 00559* **835 121/** *see 02233*

835 122/ *see 02234* **835 123/** *see 02236*

835 124/ *see 02237* **835 125/** *see 02238*

835 126/ *see 02239* **835 127/** *see 02240*

835 128/ *see 02241* **835 129/** *see 00488*

835 130/ *see 02243* **835 131/** *see 02244*

835 132/ *see 02247* **835 133/** *see 02251*

835 134/ *see 02250* **835 135/** *see 00559*

835 136/ *see 02253* **835 137-835 138/** *see 02254-02255*

835 139/ *see 02256* **835 140/** *see 02257*

835 141/ *see 02258* **835 142/** *see 02261*

835 143/ *see 02262* **835 144/** *see 02263*

835 145/ *see 02265* **835 146/** *see 02058*

835 147/ *see 02266* **835 148/** *see 02267*

835 149/ *see 02268* **835 150/** *see 02269*

835 151/ *see 02270* **835 152/** *see 02271*

835 153/ *see 02272*   835 154/ *see 02273*

835 155/ *see 02274*   835 156/ *see 02275*

835 157/ *see 02276*   835 158/ *see 02282*

835 159/ *see 02283*   835 160/ *see 02284*

835 161/ *see 02080*   835 162-835 164/ *see 02277-02279*

835 165/ *see 02285*   835 166/ *see 02286*

835 167/ *see 02287*   835 170/ *see 02291*

835 171/ *see 02293*   835 172/ *see 02296*

835 173/ *see 02297*   835 174/ *see 02264*

835 175/ *see 02299*   835 176/ *see 02300*

835 177/ *see 02301*   835 178-835 180/ *see 02303-02305*

835 181/ *see 02306*   835 182-835 183/ *see 02307-02308*

835 184/ *see 02309*   835 185/ *see 02310*

835 186/ *see 02311*   835 187/ *see 02312*

835 188/ *see 02313*   835 189/ *see 02314*

835 190/ *see 02315*   835 191/ *see 02316*

835 192/ *see 02317*   835 193/ *see 02318*

835 194/*see 02319*   **835 195**/*see 02320*

835 198-835 200/*see 02205-02207*   **835 201**/*see 02324*

835 205/*see 02323*   **835 206-835 207**/*see 00457-00458*

835 208/*see 02330*   **835 209-835 210**/*see 02331-02332*

835 211/*see 02333*   **835 212**/*see 02335*

835 213/*see 02336*   **835 214**/*see 02334*

835 215/*see 02337*   **835 216**/*see 02338*

835 217/*see 02339*

835 218-835 219/*see 02340-02341*

835 220-835 224/*see 02342-02346*

835 225-835 226/*see 02347-02348*

835 227-835 228/*see 02349-02350*

835 229-835 230/*see 02351-02352*

835 231/*see 02353*   **835 232**/*see 02354*

835 233/*see 02355*   **835 234**/*see 02356*

835 235/*see 02079*

835 241/ *see 02362* **835 242**/ *see 02363*

835 243-835 244/ *see 02364-02365*

835 249/ *see 02371* **835 250**/ *see 02372*

835 251/ *see 02373* **835 252**/ *see 02374*

835 253/ *see 02375* **835 254**/ *see 02376*

835 255/ *see 02377* **835 256**/ *see 02378*

835 257/ *see 02379* **835 258**/ *see 02380*

835 259/ *see 02381* **835 260**/ *see 02382*

835 261/ *see 02383* **835 262**/ *see 02384*

835 263/ *see 02386* **835 264**/ *see 02387*

835 265/ *see 02388* **835 266**/ *see 02389*

835 267/ *see 02390* **835 268**/ *see 02391*

835 269/ *see 02392* **835 270**/ *see 02404*

835 271/ *see 02396* **835 272-835 274**/ *see 02397-02399*

835 275/ *see 02400* **835 276**/ *see 02401*

835 277/ *see 02402* **835 279**/ *see 02406*

835 280/ *see 02407* **835 281-835 285**/ *see 02408-02412*

835 287/ see 02261 and 02262   835 288/ see 02418

835 289-835 291/ see 02419-02421   835 292-835 295/ see 02422-02425

835 296/ see 02426   835 297/ see 02428

835 298/ see 02429   835 299/ see 02430

835 300/ see 02431   835 301/ see 02432

835 302/ see 02433   835 303/ see 02434

835 304/ see 02435   835 306/ see 02436

835 307/ see 02043 and 02437   835 308/ see 02438

835 309/ see 02439   835 310/ see 02440

835 313-835 314/ see 02443-02444   835 315/ see 02445

835 316AY/works for cello and piano by french composers
gendron
francaix

835 317AY/elgar enigma variations; cockaigne overture
recorded in the town hall walthamstow on 16-17 january 1965
davis   further lp issues: SAL 3516/6570 188/
london   6570 763 (cockaigne)/6580 265
symphony   cd: 442 6522

835 318AY/shostakovich symphony no 9; piano concerto no 2
horvat
zagreb
philharmonic
radic

835 323AY/dvorak symphony no 6
recorded in the town hall wembley on 7-9 january 1965
rowicki   further lp issues: SAL 3570/6770 045/WS 9008
london   cd: 446 5302
symphony

835 324AY/bizet symphony in c; jeux d'enfants; la jolie fille de perth suite
recorded in the town hall wembley on 12-14 april 1965
benzi further lp issues: SGL 5851/6527 180/WS 9086
london cd: 442 2722
symphony

835 325-835 326/ *see 02455-02466*

835 327AY/tchaikovsky symphony no 3 "polish"
recorded in the town hall wembley on 3-6 march 1965
markevitch further lp issues: SAL 3549/6741 001/
london 6799 002/900 224
symphony cd: 446 1482/456 1872

835 330AY/beethoven violin concerto
recorded in the town hall wembley on 8-10 july 1965
schmidt- further lp issues: SAL 3538
isserstedt cd: 467 8922
london *also published by mercury in the usa*
symphony
szeryng

835 331AY/bach the concerti for one and two violins
recorded on 27-28 may 1965
szeryng further lp issues: SAL 3540
collegium
musicum
winterthur
szeryng, rybar

835 342/ *see 02236*   **835 343-835 344/** *see 02473-02474*

835 345-835 347/ *see 02475-02476*

835 348-835 349AY/bach the 4 orchestral suites
recorded between 10 october-6 november 1965
maazel further lp issues: SAL 3556-3557/SFL 14136-14137/
rso berlin 700 433-700 434WGY/6738 009

835 351AY/mozart piano concerti nos 5 k175 and 8 k246
recorded in the town hall wembley on 13-14 july 1965
galliera further lp issues: SAL 3592/6747 375
london cd: 454 3522
symphony
haebler

835 355-835 356AY/bach the 6 brandenburg concerti
recorded between 3-15 june 1965 and between 16-30 september 1965
i musici further lp issues: PHS 2912/610 129VR (nos 3 & 4)/
 cd: 412 7902/438 3172/438 5622/438 5862

835 357/ *see 02487*

835 358AY/cello concerti by haydn and boccherini
recorded in the town hall wembley on 15-16 july 1965
leppard further lp issues: SAL 3636/6580 068
london cd: 422 4812
symphony
gendron

835 359-835 360AY/telemann matthäus-passion
recorded in lausanne on 28 august-1 september 1965
redel further lp issue: SAL 3560-3561
lucerne festival cd: 432 5002
orchestra
and chorus
jurinac, altmeyer,
günter, crass

835 361AY/string quartets by debussy and ravel
recorded between 11-14 august 1965
quartetto further lp issues: SAL 3643/900 154
italiano cd: 464 6992

835 363AY/schubert piano sonatas d664 and d894
haebler

835 364AY/mozart piano concerti nos 14 k449 and 24 k491
recorded in the town hall wembley on 3-4 may 1965
davis further lp issues: SAL 3642/6747 375
london cd: 454 3522/468 1712 (no 24)
symphony
haebler

835 365AY/stravinsky symphony in c; jeu de cartes ballet
recorded in the town hall walthamstow on 17-19 september 1965
davis further lp issues: SAL 3572/900 113
london cd: 442 5832 (symphony)
symphony

835 367AY/overtures by berlioz
recorded in the town hall walthamstow on 8-10 october 1965
davis further lp issues: SAL 3573/836 923DSY/
london 6527 179/900 138
symphony cd: 416 4302/456 1432/462 4702 (carnaval romain)/
470 5432

835 370AY/haydn string quartets nos 17, 67 and 77
recorded between 15-24 august 1965
quartetto further lp issue: SAL 3591
italiano

835 371AY/beethoven septet
recorded in the kongresshalle leipzig in july 1966
members of the further lp issues: SAL 3595/eterna 825 549
gewandhaus-
orchester

835 372-835 375/*see 02502-02505*   **835 377/***see 02507*

835 378AY/mozart piano sonatas k280, k281, k283 and k545
recorded in amsterdam in november 1965
haebler further lp issue: SC71-AX 601
cd: 456 1322

835 379AY/telemann pimpione
koch further lp issues: WS 9066/eterna 820 459
staatskapelle
berlin
roscher, süss

835 380AY/beethoven piano sonatas nos 22, 23 and 27
recorded in the concertgebouw amsterdam on 24-25 september 1965 (no 23),
between 23-28 october 1965 (no 22) and between 8-12 april 1966 (no 27)
arrau further lp issues: SAL 3605/6747 009/
6747 035/6768 351/PHS 3907
cd: 422 9702 (no 23)/426 3142 (no 27)/
432 0412 (no 23)/432 1732 (no 22)/
432 3012 (no 23)/446 8592 (no 22)/462 3582

835 381AY/bruckner symphony no 9
recorded in the concertgebouw amsterdam between 20-24 december 1965
haitink further lp issues: SAL 3575/6717 002/900 162
concertgebouw cd: 475 6740
orkest

835 382AY/beethoven piano sonatas nos 31 and 32
recorded in the concertgebouw amsterdam between 23-28 october 1965
arrau further lp issues: SAL 3576/6747 009/
6747 035/6768 351/6780 022/
PHS 3913 (no 31)/PHS 4914 (no 32)
cd: 462 3582

835 383AY/beethoven piano sonatas nos 28 and 30
recorded in the concertgebouw amsterdam between 7-10 november 1965
arrau further lp issues: SAL 3577/6747 009/
6747 035/6768 351/6780 020 (no 30)/
6780 022 (no 30)/PHS 3907 (no 30)/
PHS 3915 (no 28)
cd: 462 3582

835 384AY/handel music for the royal fireworks; suite from the water music
recorded between 17-22 january 1965
maazel further lp issues: SAL 3583/900 142
rso berlin

835 385/ *see 02455-02456*

835 387AY/violin concerti by vivaldi
i musici

835 388AY/bruckner symphony no 6
recorded in the kongresshalle leipzig on 14-16 december 1964
bongartz further lp issues: PHC 9048/eterna 820 540-541
gewandhaus-
orchester

835 389AY/handel violin sonatas
recorded in amsterdam between 2-5 january 1966
grumiaux further lp issues: SAL 3687/9502 023
veyron-lacroix

835 390AY/tchaikovsky symphony no 2 "little russian"
recorded in the town hall wembley between 6-12 march 1965
markevitch further lp issues: SAL 3601/6741 001/
london 900 205
symphony cd: 446 1482

835 392AY/mozart piano concerti nos 11 k413 and 13 k415
recorded in the town hall walthamstow on 4-5 october 1965
davis further lp issues: BAL 30/SBAL 30/6747 375
london cd: 454 3522
symphony
haebler

835 393-835 394AY/schubert the piano trios
recorded in february 1966
beaux arts further lp issues: SAL 3607-3608/WS 2003
trio cd: 438 7002/475 7571

835 395AY/piano trios by schumann and ravel
recorded in february 1966
beaux arts further lp issue: SAL 3619
trio

835 396AY/choral works by mozart
wiener
sängerknaben

835 397AY/schubert string quartet no 14; quartettsatz
recorded between 12-17 december 1965
quartetto further lp issues: SAL 3618/900 139
italiano cd: 446 1632

835 474/ *see 00576*   **835 476/** *see 03498*

835 478/ *see 00555*   **835 479/** *see 00556*

835 480-835 481/ *see 00557-00558*   **835 482/** *see 00559*

835 483/ *see 00563*   **835 484/** *see 00564*

835 485-835 486/ *see 00565-00566*

835 487/ *see 00567*   **835 488/** *see 00568*

835 489/ *see 00569*   **835 490**/ *see 00570*

835 491/ *see 00571*   **835 492**/ *see 00572*

835 493/ *see 09399*

835 494AY / prodromides les perses, dramatic oratorio
girard
orchestre national
and chorus

835 495/ *see 03485*   **835 496**/ *see 03400*

835 497AY / operatic duets by puccini *sung in french*
recorded in paris between 18-21 april 1961
etcheverry
orchestre
lamoureux
poncet, jaumillot

835 498AY / bach osteroratorium
recorded in stuttgart in may 1956 for the label discophile francais
couraud   further lp issues: A77412L
stuttgart   *excerpts*
soloists   cd: 477 5305
and chorus   *fritz wunderlich sang under the pseudonym of*
sailer, bence,   *werner braun*
wunderlich,
messthaler

835 500/ *numbers in this sequence were allocated to publications under licence from the american columbia catalogue*

835 700AY/ *see 00651 and 700 169*

836 200/ *see 610 100 and 610 800 series*

836 600AY / recital of organ music
recorded in the martinikerk bolsward
jansen

836 750AY / wöldike springtime in funen
wöldike further lp issue: SAL 3620
danish radio *also published in usa on the mercury label*
orchestra
and chorus
hermann, hansen,
westi

836 811-836 816 / *see 698 511-698 516*

836 900DSY / chopin the 14 valses
harasiewicz cd: 442 8746

836 901DSY / violin concerti by mendelssohn and tchaikovsky
recorded between 17-20 february 1963
wagner further lp issues: GL 5815/SGL 5815/
innsbruck 894 037ZKY/SFL 14059 (tchaikovsky)/
symphony 700 155WGY/700 211WGY (tchaikovsky)
auclair

836 902 / *see 00536 and 02286* **836 903** / *see 02076, 02079 and 02099*

836 904 / *see 02313* **836 908** / *see 02439*

836 909DSY / ballet music from rameau castor et pollux and gluck orfeo ed euridice
recorded in the town hall walthamstow between 19-23 july 1961
mackerras further lp issue: WS 9002
london
symphony

836 911 / *see 05424*

836 912DSY / concerti by telemann
grebe
hamburger
telemann-gesellschaft

836 914DSY / tchaikovsky piano concerto no 2
recorded in the town hall walthamstow between 20-23 september 1965
davis further lp issue: SGL 5873/SFL 14114/
london 700 436WGY/WS 9007
symphony cd: 438 6972
magaloff

836 915/ *see 02312*   836 916/ *see 00441*

836 917/ *see 02042*   836 918/ *see 00457-00458*

836 919DSY/mozart violin concerti nos 5 and 7
recorded in the town hall watford on 18-19 april 1966
gibson   further lp issues: SAL 3588/6747 376/
new   6707 011/802 709LY
philharmonia
szeryng

836 920/ *see 02215 and 835 009*   836 921/ *see 02072*

836 922/ *see 02379*   836 923/ *see 835 367*

836 924DSY/recital of piano music by fauré
doyen

836 925/ *see 00447*   836 926/ *see 00246*

836 927DSY/berlioz harold en italie
horvat
zagreb
philharmonic

836 928/ *see 00547 and 02090-02091*

836 929/ *see 02251*   836 930/ *see 00121*

836 948/ *see 894 041*

837 000/ *see 03000 series*

838 120HGY / symphonies by mendelssohn and beethoven
recorded in the concertgebouw amsterdam on 18 february 1963 (mendelssohn)

haitink	**symphony no 4 "italian"**
concertgebouw	further lp issues: 04811HGL/GL 5660/SGL 5660/
orkest	894 068ZKY/6747 057
	symphony no 8 *see 610 125*

838 123/ *see 698 021*   **838 127/** *see 610 124*

838 400/ *numbers in this sequence were allocated to publications under licence from the american mercury catalogue*

838 601/ *see 698 032*

838 611AY / beethoven symphony no 3 "eroica"
jordans   further lp issues: 200 026WGL/894 000ZKY
brabants
orkest

838 700AY / organ music by bach, buxtehude and reger
recorded in the liederhalle stuttgart
förstemann

838 704AY / piano music by brahms
kraus

838 705AY / organ music by reger
recorded in the liederhalle stuttgart
förstemann

802 700-802 701LY / liszt a faust symphony; 2 episodes from lenau's faust
benzi
bucharest
philharmonic
orchestra and chorus
spiess

802 702LY/tchaikovsky symphony no 1 "winter dreams"
recorded in the town hall wembley on 16-18 february 1966
markevitch   further lp issues: SAL 3578/6570 160/6741 001/
london   900 223
symphony   cd: 446 1482/456 1872

802 703LY/tchaikovsky symphony no 5
recorded in the town hall wembley between 19-25 february 1966
markevitch   further lp issues: SAL 3579/6799 002/6741 001/
london   900 207
symphony   cd: 456 1872

802 706LY/beethoven piano sonatas nos 16 and 17
recorded in the concertgebouw amsterdam between 28-31 may 1965
arrau   further lp issues: SAL 3603/6570 190 (no 17)/
                 6747 009/6747 035/6768 351/
                 PHS 3913 (no 17)/PHS 4914 (no 16)
                 cd: 462 3582

802 707LY/brahms string sextet no 1
recorded in the johannesstift berlin between 25-29 january 1966
philharmon-   further lp issue: SAL 3599/WS 9050
isches oktett
berlin

802 708LY/vieuxtemps violin concerto no 4; chausson poeme pour violon et orchestre
recorded in paris in march 1966
rosenthal   further lp issues: SAL 3587/SBAL 32 (chausson)/
orchestre   6539 045 (vieuxtemps)/6768 304 (chausson)/
lamoureux   PHS 900 195
grumiaux   cd: 416 8862 (chausson)/442 8561 (vieuxtemps)/
                 468 8412 (vieuxtemps)

802 709/ *see 836 918*

802 710LY/trumpet concerti by leopold mozart, telemann, albinoni and vivaldi
beaucamp further lp issue: SAL 3662
rouen chamber
orchestra
andré

802 711-802 712LY/mahler symphony no 3
recorded in the concertgebouw amsterdam between 10-14 may 1966
haitink further lp issues: SAL 3593-3594/SC71-AX 602/
concertgebouw 6768 021/PHS 2996
orkest cd: 420 1132/412 0502
ladies' and
childrens' choirs
forrester

802 713-802 714LY/haydn die schöpfung
recorded in the herkulessaal munich between 9-16 july 1966
jochum further lp issues: SAL 3596-3597/SC71-AX 201/
bavarian radio 6700 002/PHS2-903
orchestra cd: 446 1752
and chorus *excerpts*
giebel, kmennt, cd: 464 0142
frick

802 715LY/concerti by albinoni, bonporti and geminiani
i musici

802 716-802 717LY/anthology of spanish zarzuelas
recorded between 29 october-22 november 1967
markevitch
spanish radio
orchestra
and chorus

802 718LY/mendelssohn symphonies nos 4 and 5
recorded in the town hall walthamstow on 22-24 june 1966
sawallisch further lp issues: SAL 3727/AXS 4004/
new SC71-AX 404/6707 005/412 0081
philharmonia cd: 432 5982/434 5362

802 719LY/beethoven violin concerto
recorded in the town hall wembley on 3-5 july 1966
galliera further lp issues: SAL 3616/802 822LY/
new SC71-AX 403/SBAL 32/PHS 900 222
philharmonia cd: 420 3482/426 0642
grumiaux

802 720LY/schumann liederkreis op 39 and other lieder
recorded in amsterdam in july 1966
souzay further lp issues: SAL 3606/PHS 900 180
baldwin

802 721-802 723LY/handel messiah
recorded in the town hall watford between 24 june-10 july 1966
davis further lp issues: SAL 3584-3586/6703 001/
london PHS 3992
symphony cd: 420 8652/438 3562/464 7032
lso chorus *excerpts*
harper, watts, further lp issues: 802 795LY/SAL 3623/
wakefield, 6833 050/6833 200
shirley-quirk

802 724LY/bruckner symphony no 0
recorded in the concertgebouw amsterdam on 4-6 july 1966
haitink further lp issues: SAL 3602/6717 002
concertgebouw cd: 475 6740
orkest

802 725LY/chamber music by mendelssohn, wolf and rossini
i musici

802 726LY/clarinet concerti by stamitz, pokorny and molter
beaucamp
rouen chamber
orchestra
lancelot

802 727LY/music for violin and piano by debussy, prokofiev, ravel and ysaye *recorded in paris on 2 february 1966*
oistrakh further lp issues: SAL 3589/6570 206/
bauer PHS 900 112
cd: 420 7772
also issued by melodïya and chant du monde

802 728LY/mozart piano concerti nos 20 k466 and 27 k595
recorded in the town hall wembley between 31 december 1965-2 january 1966
galliera further lp issues: SAL 3626/SBAL 30/
london SC75-AX 200/6747 375
symphony cd: 422 9752 (no 27)/454 3522/
haebler 461 5792 (no 20)

802 729LY/beethoven piano sonatas nos 9, 10, 19 and 20
recorded in the concertgebouw amsterdam between 8-12 april 1966
arrau further lp issues: SAL 3611/6747 009/6747 035/
6768 351/PHS 3913 (nos 9 and 10)/
PHS 3915 (nos 19 and 20)
cd: 462 3582

802 730LY/beethoven piano sonatas nos 18, 24 and 26
recorded in the concertgebouw amsterdam between 28-31 may 1965 (no 18),
between 7-10 november 1965 (no 24) and between 8-12 april 1966 (no 26)
arrau further lp issues: SAL 3600/6570 055 (no 24)/
6570 167 (no 26)/6580 104 (no 24)/6747 009/
6747 035/6768 351/6833 245 (no 24)/PHS
3907 (no 24)/PHS 3913 (no 18)/PHS 4914 (no 26)
cd: 426 0682 (no 26)/462 3582

802 731LY/bach osteroratoriun
recorded in berlin on 11-14 september 1966
maazel further lp issues: SAL 3612/900 176
rso berlin
rias choir
donath, reynolds,
haefliger, talvela

802 732/ *see 02330*

802 733-802 736LY/masters of the baroque anthology
i musici

802 737/ *see 698 026 and 698 059*   **802 738/** *see 698 039 and 698 050*

802 741LY/beethoven piano sonatas nos 12, 13 and 14
recorded in the bachzaal ansterdan between 12-18 june 1962
arrau further lp issues: SAL 3580/6747 009/6747 035/
6747 199 (no 14)/6768 231 (no 14)/6768 351/
PHS 4914/610 147VR (no 14)/836 269VZ (no 14)
cd: 420 1532 (no 14)/422 9702 (no 14)/
432 3012 (no 14)/462 3582

802 742/ *see 02260*

802 743LY/pergolesi stabat mater
recorded in berlin between 15-18 may 1966
maazel further lp issues: SAL 3590
rso berlin
rias choir
lear, ludwig

802 744   **802 745/** *see 02301*

802 746LY/schumann carnaval; fantasy in c
recorded in amsterdam between 15-18 september 1966
arrau further lp issues: SAL 3630/6570 319 (carnaval)/
6768 084/6768 353
cd: 420 8712 (carnaval)/432 3082

802 747-802 748LY/brahms the 4 piano trios
beaux arts further lp issues: SAL 3626-3627
trio cd: 438 3652/454 0172

802 749LY/works for piano by mozart
recorded in amsterdam in august 1966 (k397 and k533/k494)
haebler **piano sonata and fantasy k475/k457** *see 698 026*
fantasy in d minor k397; sonata k533/k494
further lp issue: SC71-AX 601
cd: 456 1322

802 750-802 751LY/bach concerti for 2, 3 and 4 harpsichords
recorded in the lukaskirche dresden in december 1965
redel further lp issues: eterna 820 681/825 681/
staatskapelle cd: berlin classics BC 31792/BC 31282/
dresden BC 18662/BC 18682
ahlgrimm, *excerpts*
pischner further lp issues: 6580 089/6799 001
veyron-lacroix
ruzickova

802 752-802 754LY / mozart the 6 quartets dedicated to haydn
recorded between 14-22 august 1966
quartetto further lp issues: SAL 3632-3634/6747 097/
italiano 839 604-839 606LY
cd: 416 4192

802 755LY / mozart symphonies nos 38 "prague" and 39
recorded in berlin between 23 august-1 september 1966
maazel further lp issues: SAL 3609/H71-AX 222
rso berlin

802 756LY / mozart symphonies nos 40 and 41 "jupiter"
recorded in berlin between 23 august-1 september 1966
maazel further lp issues: SAL 3610/H71-AX 222
rso berlin

802 757LY / schubert piano quintet "the trout"
recorded in amsterdam between 23-26 august 1966
haebler further lp issues: SAL 3621/6570 115
grumiaux
janzer, czako,
cazauran

802 758/ *see 02422-02425*

802 759-802 760LY / works by bruckner
recorded in the concertgebouw amsterdam on 19-20 september 1966 (te deum)
and on 1-3 november 1966 (synphony no 7)
haitink **symphony no 7**
concertgebouw further lp issues: SAL 3624-3625/6717 002
orkest PHS 2998
cd: 420 8052/473 3012/475 6740

haitink **te deum**
concertgebouw further lp issues: SAL 3624-3625/PHS 2998
orkest
dutch radio
chorus
ameling, reynolds,
hoffmann, hoekman

802 761-802 763LY / corelli concerti grossi op 6
recorded between 4-20 november 1966
i musici further lp issue: 6707 002

802 764LY / mozart piano concerti nos 18 k456 and 22 k482
recorded in the town hall wembley between 22-25 september 1966
davis further lp issues: 802 878LY/SAL 3740/
london SC75-AX 200/6747 375
symphony cd: 454 3522/456 8232 (no 22)
haebler

802 765LY / mélodies by poulenc
recorded in amsterdam in september 1966
souzay further lp issues: SAL 3635/PHS 900 148
baldwin

802 766-802 768LY / handel concerti grossi op 6
recorded between 14-22 december 1966
leppard further lp issues: SBAL 21/6747 036
english chamber *also published in usa on the mercury label*
orchestra

802 769LY / symphonies by mozart and beethoven
recorded in the concertgebouw amsterdam on 28-30 november 1966
szell **symphony no 34**
concertgebouw further lp issues: SAL 3667/PHS 900 169/
orkest cd: 438 5242/442 7272/475 6780
symphony no 5
further lp issues: SAL 3667/PHS 900 169/
6833 102/6566 004
cd: 420 7712/442 7272/475 6780

802 770LY / *see 02264*

802 771-802 772LY / penderecki saint luke passion
recorded at a concert in the domkirche münster on 30 march 1966
czyz   further lp issue: PHS 2901
cracow
philharmonic
orchestra
and chorus
woytowicz,
hiolski, ladysz,
heidiger

802 776 / *see 00509*

802 779LY / choral works by halffter, ramoneda, espla and victoria
recorded between 11-24 october 1966
markevitch
spanish radio
orchestra
and chorus

802 781 / *see 02376*

802 783LY / falla el amor brujo; chabrier espana; ravel boléro
recorded between 11-24 october 1966
markevitch
spanish radio
orchestra

802 785LY / works by berg and stravinsky
recorded in the concertgebouw amsterdam on 19-21 december 1966 (stravinsky)
and on 23-25 january 1967 (berg)
markevitch   **berg violin concerto**
concertgebouw   further lp issues: SAL 3650/6555 078/PHS 900 194
orkest   cd: 412 1362
grumiaux
bour   **stravinsky violin concerto**
concertgebouw   further lp issues: SAL 3650/6527 160/PHS 900 194
orkest   cd: 412 1362
grumiaux

802 787LY/dvorak symphony no 9 "new world"
recorded in berlin between 27-31 december 1966
maazel further lp issues: SAL 3622/900 161
rso berlin

802 793LY/schumann piano sonata no 1; fantasiestücke op 111
recorded in amsterdam between 23-27 october 1967 (sonata) and on 13-14 april 1968 (fantasiestücke)
arrau further lp issues: SAL 3663/6768 084/6768 353
cd: 432 3082

802 795/ *see 802 721-802 723*

802 796LY/mendelssohn octet; string symphony no 9
i musici further lp issues: SAL 3640/6580 103

802 797LY/schubert symphonies nos 1 and 2
recorded in the lukaskirche dresden in may 1966
sawallisch further lp issues: SBAL 40/SC71-AX 500/6729 001/
staatskapelle 6747 491/eterna 826 287
dresden cd: 446 5362

802 798LY/schubert symphonies nos 3 and 4 "tragic"
recorded in the lukaskirche dresden in may 1966
sawallisch further lp issues: SBAL 40/SC71-AX 500/
staatskapelle 6539 015 (no 4)/6729 001/6747 491/eterna
dresden 820 805/825 805/826 288 (no 3)/826 290 (no 4)
cd: 422 9772 (no 4)/446 5362

802 799LY/schubert symphonies no 5 and 6
recorded in the lukaskirche dresden in may 1966
sawallisch further lp issues: SAL 3679/SBAL 40/SC71-AX 500/
staatskapelle 6527 050 (no 5)/6580 010 (no 5)/6729 001/6747 491/
dresden eterna 820 806/825 806/826 285 (no 6)/826 289 (no 6)
cd: 446 5392/459 3902 (no 5)

802 800LY / schubert symphony no 8 "unfinished"; overtures in the italian style in c and in d
recorded in the lukaskirche dresden in may 1966

sawallisch	further lp issues: SAL 3672/SBAL 40/SC71-AX 500/
staatskapelle	6527 050 (symphony)/6539 015 (symphony)/
dresden	6580 010 (symphony)/6729 001/6747 491/
	eterna 826 289 (overtures)/826 290 (symphony)
	cd: 422 9772 (symphony)/446 6362 (overtures)/
	446 5392 (symphony)

802 801LY / schubert symphony no 9 "great"
recorded in the lukaskirche dresden in may 1966

sawallisch	further lp issues: SAL 3702/SBAL 40/SC71-AX 500/
staatskapelle	6527 156/6570 054/6580 207/6729 001/6747 491/
dresden	eterna 820 807/825 807/826 291
	cd: 446 5392

802 802LY / mendelssohn the piano trios

beaux arts	further lp issues: SAL 3646/WS 9082
trio	cd: 416 2972 (no 1)/475 1712

802 803LY / mozart divertimento k563
recorded in amsterdam between 2-6 june 1967

grumiaux	further lp issues: SAL 3664/900 173
janzer	cd: 416 4852/422 5132/426 8872/
czako	454 0232/470 9502

802 805LY / works for cello and piano by schubert and beethoven
recorded between 26-28 november 1966
gendron
francaix

802 806LY / beethoven string quartet no 15
recorded between 18-30 august 1967

quartetto	further lp issues: SAL 3638/6707 008/6747 272
italiano	cd: 416 6382/454 0622/454 7122/464 6842

802 807-802 809LY / mahler symphonies nos 5 and 6
recorded in the kongresshalle leipzig between 6-10 june 1966

neumann	further lp issues: eterna 820 761-820 762 (no 6)/
gewandhaus-	825 602-825 603 (no 5)
orchester	cd: berlin classics BC 20742 (no 5)/
	BC 90452 (no 6)
	symphony no 5 also published in usa by vanguard

802 810-802 812LY/bach johannes-passion
recorded in the concertgebouw amsterdam between 3-8 june 1967
jochum further lp issues: SAL 3652-3654/SC71-AX 303/
concertgebouw 6747 019
orkest cd: 426 6452/462 1732
netherlands *excerpts*
radio chorus further lp issue: 6701 012
giebel, höffgen,
haefliger, berry, crass

802 813LY/russian liturgical music
spassky further lp issue: 894 118ZKY
russian orthodox
choir

802 816LY/telemann works for chamber ensemble
recorded in october 1963 and november 1966
grebe
hamburger
telemann-gesellschaft

802 818LY/vivaldi cello sonatas
recorded between 25-30 january 1967
gendron
sibinga

802 820LY/dvorak symphony no 5; carnival overture
recorded in the town hall wembley between 3-6 february 1967
rowicki further lp issues: SAL 3631/6770 045
london cd: 432 6022/446 5302
symphony

802 822/ *see 802 719*

802 825-802 826LY/bach 6 flute sonatas bwv 1020-1025
larrieu further lp issues: SAL 3656-3657
puyana *also published in usa on the mercury label*

802 827LY/mozart piano sonatas k279, k284 and k333
recorded in amsterdam in june 1967
haebler further lp issues: SAL 3666/SC71-AX 601
cd: 456 1322

802 831LY/recital of schubert lieder
recorded in the concertgebouw amsterdam between 1-7 july 1967
souzay further lp issues: SAL 3651
baldwin *excerpts*
cd: 422 4182

802 833-802 834LY/mozart the 6 piano trios
beaux arts further lp issues: SAL 3681-3682/SC71-AX 202
trio cd: 448 1542

802 839/ *see 02078*

802 840LY/tchaikovsky francesca da rimini; hamlet overture
recorded in the town hall wembley between 6-9 june 1967
markevitch further lp issues: PHS 900 234
new
philharmonia

802 848LY/works for violin and orchestra by haydn, schubert and mozart
recorded in the town hall wembley between 5-11 april 1967
leppard further lp issues: SAL 3660
new cd: 438 3232 (mozart)/438 5642 (mozart)/
philharmonia 438 5882 (mozart)/442 8294 (haydn and
grumiaux mozart)

802 850LY/orchestral works by dvorak
recorded in the concertgebouw amsterdam on 14 may 1966 (slavonic dance op 46 no 5)
haitink **slavonic dance op 46 no 5**
concertgebouw cd: 462 0772
orkest **scherzo capriccioso** *see 02435*
slavonic dances op 46 nos 1-4 and 6-8
see 00546 and 02318

802 851LY/dvorak string quintet op 77; waltzes
recorded in the johannesstift berlin
philharmon-
isches oktett
berlin

802 856-802 857LY / mendelssohn symphonies nos 1 and 2
recorded in the town hall walthamstow between 14-23 june 1967
sawallisch further lp issues: AXS 4004/SC71-AX 404/
new 6700 023/6707 005/PHS 2904
philharmonia cd: 432 5982
orchestra
and chorus
donath, hansmann,
kmennt

802 858LY / mendelssohn symphony no 3 "scotch"; ruy blas overture *recorded in the town hall walthamstow between 14-23 june 1967*
sawallisch further lp issues: SAL 3739/AXS 4004/
new SC71-AX 404/6707 005
philharmonia cd: 432 5982 (symphony)

802 862LY / mozart requiem mass
recorded in the town hall watford between 19-23 september 1967
davis further lp issues: SAL 3649/6598 694/6747 384/
bbc symphony 900 160
alldis choir cd: 420 3532/422 5192/438 8002
donath, minton,
davies, nienstedt

802 863LY / chamber music by spohr, weber and wagner
recorded in the johannesstift berlin
philharmon- further lp issue: SAL 3692
isches oktett
berlin

802 864LY / concerti by telemann
recorded between 1-12 november 1967
i musici

802 866LY / concerti by vivaldi and albinoni
i musici

802 870LY / wolf selection from the italienisches liederbuch
recorded in amsterdam in september 1967
souzay further lp issues: SAL 3661/6700 041
baldwin

802 872LY/mozart piano concerti nos 6 k238 and 9 k271
recorded in the town hall wembley in january 1966 (no 6) and on 9-11 january 1968 (no 9)
rowicki further lp issues: SC75-AX 200/6747 375/
london 6580 083 (no 9)
symphony cd: 454 3522
haebler

802 874LY/mozart piano concerti nos 12 k414 and 26 k537
recorded in the town hall wembley between 6-11 november 1967
rowicki further lp issues: SC75-AX 200/6747 375/
london PHS 2906 (no 26)
symphony cd: 454 3522
haebler

802 878/ *see 802 764*

802 879LY/mozart piano concerti nos 19 k459 and 21 k467
recorded in the town hall wembley on 7 january 1966 (no 19) and on 9-11 january 1968 (no 21)
rowicki further lp issues: SC75-AX 200/6500 267 (no 21)/
london 6570 077 (no 19)/6747 375/PHS 2906 (no 21)
symphony cd: 454 3522
haebler

802 881LY/mozart piano concerto no 25 k503; concert rondos k382 and k386
recorded in the town hall wembley in january 1966 (rondos) and in november 1967 (no 25)
galliera further lp issues: SC75-AX 200/6747 375
london cd: 454 3522
symphony
haebler

802 882LY/mozart the concerti for 2 and 3 pianos
recorded in the town hall wembley on 21 january 1968 (double concerto) and 4-5 july 1968 (triple concerto)
galliera further lp issues: SCX75-AX 200/6580 144 (triple)/
london 6747 375
symphony cd: 454 3522
haebler
hoffmann
bunge

802 883/ *see 02240*

802 884-802 885LY/mahler symphony no 2 "resurrection"
recorded in the concertgebouw amsterdam between 26-29 may 1968
haitink further lp issues: SC71-AX 602/6700 024/
concertgebouw 6768 021
orkest cd: 420 2342/442 0502
dutch radio
chorus
ameling, heynis

802 888LY/mahler symphony no 4
recorded in the concertgebouw amsterdam on 20-22 december 1967
haitink further lp issues: SAL 3729/6768 021/900 190
concertgebouw cd: 420 3502/442 0502
orkest
ameling

802 889-802 891LY/mendelssohn elias
recorded in the kongresshalle leipzig in june 1968
sawallisch further lp issues: eterna 826 048-826 050
gewandhaus- cd: 420 1062/438 3682
orchester *excerpts*
rundfunkchor further lp issue: 6527 146
leipzig
ameling, burmeister,
schreier, rotzsch,
adam

802 892LY / works for cello and orchestra by dvorak
recorded in the town hall wembley on 14-15 november 1967

haitink	**cello concerto; rondo in g minor**
london	further lp issues: SAL 3675/6527 186/6570 112/
philharmonic	6570 112/6580 149/PHS 900 189
gendron	cd: 422 4672
	waldesruhe
	further lp issues: SAL 3675/6527 186/
	6570 112/6580 149/PHS 900 189

802 893LY / overtures by eighteenth century composers volume 1
recorded in the town hall wembley on 5-6 december 1967

leppard further lp issue: SAL 3674
new
philharmonia

802 894LY / handel concerti a due cori
recorded in the town hall wembley on 8-9 december 1967

leppard further lp issue: 6570 114/6747 036
english chamber
orchestra

802 895LY / beethoven string trios op 9 nos 1 and 3
recorded in amsterdam in september 1968

grumiaux	further lp issues: SC71-AX 309/6500 168
janzer	(no 1)/6768 034/PHS 900 226 (no 1)
czako	cd: 456 3172

802 898LY / harpsichord music by italian composers
recorded between 24-28 november 1967
puyana

802 901LY / overtures by eighteenth century composers volume 2
recorded in the town hall wembley on 14-15 january 1969

leppard further lp issues: SAL 3760/412 4061/900 235
new
philharmonia

802 902LY/dvorak symphony no 8
recorded in the town hall wembley on 19-21 january 1969
rowicki further lp issues: 6527 199/6770 045
london cd: 456 3272
symphony

802 903LY/dvorak symphony no 9 "new world"
recorded in the town hall wembley on 18-19 january 1969
rowicki further lp issues: 6580 259/6770 045
london cd: 456 3272
symphony

802 904LY/music from the time of boccaccio's decameron
recorded on 18-19 january 1969
beckett
musica
reservata

802 905LY/string trios by haydn and schubert
recorded in amsterdam in february 1969
grumiaux further lp issue: SAL 3782
janzer cd: 422 8362 (schubert)/438 7002 (schubert)
czako

802 906LY/piano music by liszt
recorded in amsterdam on 7-8 march 1969
arrau further lp issues: SAL 3783
cd: 432 3052

802 907LY/mozart wind serenades k375 and k388
recorded in amsterdam between 7-16 august 1969
de waart
netherlands
wind ensemble

802 908LY/schumann kreisleriana; piano sonata no 2
recorded between 11-15 may 1969
varsi

802 909LY/chamber music by hasenöhrl, mozart and rossini
recorded in the johannesstift berlin between 22-26 june 1969
philharmon-
isches oktett
berlin

802 912LY/bruckner symphony no 2
recorded in the concertgebouw amsterdam on 14-16 may 1969
haitink   further lp issues: SAL 3785/6717 002
concertgebouw   cd: 475 6740
orkest

802 913LY/works by berlioz
recorded in the town hall watford between 3-8 may 1969
davis   **prelude to les troyens; marche funebre**
london   **pour hamlet**
symphony   further lp issues: SAL 3788/6747 271
       cd: 416 4312/456 1432
davis   **symphonie funebre et triomphale**
london   further lp issues: SAL 3788/6747 271
symphony   cd: 416 2832/442 2902/456 1432
alldis choir

802 914LY/debussy la mer; trois nocturnes
recorded in the concertgebouw amsterdam on 22-23 september 1969
inbal   further lp issue: SAL 3798
concertgebouw
orkest
dutch radio choir

802 915LY/beethoven string quartet no 14
recorded between 26 july-3 august 1969
quartetto   further lp issues: 6707 008/6747 272
italiano   cd: 416 6382/454 0622/454 7122/464 6842

802 916-802 918LY/dvorak the piano trios
beaux arts   further lp issue: 6703 015
trio   cd: 416 2922 (op 90)/454 2592

802 919LY/wolf selection from the italienisches liederbuch
recorded in amsterdam between 9-13 june 1969
ameling   further lp issue: 6700 041
baldwin

802 920LY/bach sinfonias from the cantatas
recorded in the johannesstift berlin
winschermann
deutsche bach-
solisten

839 240DSY/music for violin and piano by grieg
tellefsen
levin

839 241DSY/string quartets by grieg
hindar quartet
of oslo

839 259DSY/orchestral works by svendsen
grüner-hegge
oslo philharmonic
fjeldsted
oslo philharmonic

839 260/ *see 02383* **839 261/** *see 02434*

839 308/ *see 00167* **839 501/** *see 02293*

839 503/ *see 02041* **839 505/** *see 02228*

839 507/ *see 02297* **839 512/** *see 02261 and 02262*

839 513/ *see 02027* **839 525/** *see 02326*

839 575DSY/overtures and preludes to operas by verdi
recorded in the town hall wembley on 16-18 october 1967
markevitch   further lp issues: SFM 23023/6580 073
new
philharmonia

839 600/ *see 02412*   **839 602-839 603/** *see 02307-02308*

839 604-839 606/ *see 802 752-802 754*

839 700LY/schubert piano sonatas d784 and d960
recorded in eindhoven in october 1967
haebler   further lp issues:
                cd: 456 3672

839 701LY/penderecki auschwitz oratorio; polymorphia for strings
czyz   further lp issue: 900 184
warsaw
philharmonic
orchestra
and chorus
woytowicz,
ochman, ladysz

839 702LY/beethoven diabelli variations
recorded on 14-16 february 1968
bishop-   further lp issues: SAL 3676/900 220
kovacevich

839 706LY/dvorak serenade for strings; symphonic variations
recorded in the town hall wembley on 1-2 march 1968
davis   further lp issues: SAL 3706/900 196
london   cd: 420 3492 (variations)/438 3472
symphony

839 707LY/mozart divertimenti k334 and k407
recorded in the johannesstift berlin between 12-18 march 1968
philharmon-
isches oktett
berlin

839 708LY/mozart divertimento k287; eine kleine nachtmusik
recorded in the johannesstift berlin between 12-18 march 1968
philharmon-
isches oktett
berlin

839 709LY/schumann faschingsschwank aus wien; arabeske; humoreske
recorded in amsterdam between 23-27 october 1967 (arabeske) and on 13-14 april 1968 (faschingsschwank)
arrau   further lp issues: SAL 3690/6570 320 (arabeske)/
                 6768 084/6768 353/900 181
                 cd: 432 3082

839 713LY/sinfonias by johann christian bach
recorded in the town hall wembley on 20-21 march 1968
leppard further lp issue: SAL 3685
new
philharmonia

839 715LY/chamber music by beethoven and spohr
philharmon-
isches oktett
berlin

839 716-839 717LY/berlioz roméo et juliette
recorded in the town hall wembley between 26-29 february 1968 and on 13-14 april 1968
davis further lp issues: SAL 3695-3696/6700 032/
london 6747 271/PHS 2909
symphony cd: 416 9622/462 2522
alldis choir *excerpts*
kern, tear, further lp issues: 6580 052/6833 062
shirley-quirk cd: 416 8712/438 3072/446 2022/456 1432

839 718LY/piano works by franck, ravel and schumann
recorded between 27-30 april 1968
varsi

839 719-839 721LY/haydn die jahreszeiten
recorded in the town hall wembley in june and july 1968
davis further lp issues: SAL 3698-3700/6703 023/
bbc symphony 6770 035/PHS 3911
bbc chorus cd: 434 1692/464 0342
harper, davies *excerpts*
shirley-quirk further lp issue: 6580 015

839 722LY/piano music by brahms
bishop- further lp issue: SAL 3758
kovacevich

839 726LY / vivaldi the flute concerti op 10
recorded between 20-28 june 1968
i musici further lp issue: SAL 3705
gazzeloni

839 727LY / brahms string sextet no 2
recorded in the johannesstift berlin between 23 october-3 november 1965
philharmon- further lp issue: SAL 3763
isches oktett
berlin

839 728-839 730LY / bartok the 6 string quartets
nowak cd: 442 2842
quartet

839 731LY / organ works by bach
köbler furrher lp issue: eterna 820 561

839 732LY / harpsichord suites by handel
ahlgrimm

839 733LY / works for voice and chamber ensemble by ravel
recorded in the théatre musica le-chaux-de-fonds in may 1968
souzay further lp issue: SAL 3704
baldwin
larrieu, degenne

839 734LY / mozart serenade for 13 wind
recorded in amsterdam between 10-13 november 1968
de waart
netherlands
wind ensemble

839 735-839 736LY / haydn 7 sonatas for fortepiano
recorded between 20-28 august 1968
haebler

839 737-839 739LY / schoenberg the 4 string quartets; verklärte nacht
neues wiener cd: 464 0462 (quartet no 2)
streichquartett
lear

839 740LY/albinoni 4 oboe concerti from op 9
i musici
holliger, bourge

839 741-839 742LY/sinfonias by carl philipp emmanuel bach
recorded in april 1968
leppard further lp issue: SAL 3689-SAL 3690
english chamber
orchestra

839 743LY/piano variations by beethoven
recorded in amsterdam between 10-13 november 1968
arrau further lp issues: SAL 3764/6580 300/6768 351
cd: 432 3012/462 3582

839 745LY/beethoven string quartets nos 12 and 16
recorded between 11-18 june 1968
quartetto further lp issues: 6707 008/6747 242
italiano cd: 416 6382/454 0622/454 7112/464 6842

839 747LY/duos for violin and viola by mozart and hoffmeister
recorded in amsterdam between 21-25 june 1968
grumiaux further lp issue: 412 0591 (mozart)
pelluccia cd: 422 5132 (mozart)/426 8872 (mozart)/
454 0232 (mozart)

839 748/ *see 698 011*   **839 749/** *see 02408*

839 751/ *see 02409*

839 752LY/misa criola
ramirez

839 754LY/chamber music by dvorak
recorded in the johannesstift berlin between 23 october-2 november 1968
philharmon- cd: 462 2842
isches oktett
berlin

839 755LY/ravel the 2 piano concerti
recorded in the salle de l'alcazar monaco in november and december 1968
galliera cd: 438 3632
monte carlo opera
orchestra
haas

839 756LY/concerti by j.c. bach, fiala and hummel
recorded on 24-26 november 1968
leppard further lp issues: SAL 3723/6833 097 (fiala)
english chamber
orchestra
holliger

839 757LY/violin concerti by viotti and michael haydn
recorded in the concertgebouw amsterdam in october 1969
de waart further lp issues: SAL 3804/6515 002/
concertgebouw PHCP 4916
orkest cd: 442 8294 (michael haydn)/
grumiaux 476 8477 (viotti)

839 758-839 760LY/mozart idomeneo
recorded in the town hall wembley between 21-27 september 1968
davis further lp issues: SAL 3747-3749/6598 710/
bbc symphony 6703 024/6747 386
bbc chorus cd: 420 1302
rinaldi, tinsley,
davies, tear,
shirley-quirk

839 761LY/bartok piano concerto no 2; stravinsky concerto for piano and wind *recorded in the town hall wembley on 16-19 december 1968 (bartok) and on 29-30 april 1969 (stravinsky)*
davis further lp issues: SAL 3779/6542 206 (bartok)/
london 6768 053 (bartok)
symphony cd: 426 6602 (bartok)/438 8122 (bartok)
bishop-
kovacevich

839 762LY/bach cantatas nos 56 and 82
recorded in the johannesstift berlin in december 1968
winschermann further lp issue: SAL 3767
deutsche bach- cd: 454 3462
solisten
souzay

839 769LY/schubert piano sonata d959
recorded in the johannesstift berlin in november 1968
haebler cd: 456 3672

839 770LY/schubert piano sonatas d575 and d568
recorded in the johannesstift berlin in november 1968
haebler cd: 456 3672

839 772LY/schubert piano sonatas d664 and d 894
recorded in the mozarteum salzburg in february 1969
haebler cd: 456 3672

839 773LY/schubert piano sonata d850
recorded in the mozarteum salzburg in february 1969
haebler cd: 456 3672

839 775LY/works by de falla, halffter and granados
recorded between 18 october-2 november 1968
markevitch
spanish radio
orchestra

839 776LY/sacred works by mompou, victoria and ferrer
recorded between 18 october-2 november 1968
markevitch
spanish radio
orchestra
and chorus

839 777LY / beethoven symphonies nos 1 and 8
recorded in the concertgebouw amsterdam on 13-14 march 1967 (no 1) and on 28-29 may 1969 (no 8)

jochum	further lp issues: SC71-AX 900/AXS 9000/
concertgebouw	6500 087/6580 148
orkest	cd: 422 9662 (no 1)/422 4742 (no 8)/
	450 0582 (no 8)/475 8147

839 778LY / beethoven symphony no 2; leonore no 2 overture
recorded in the concertgebouw amsterdam between 21-24 march 1969 (symphony) and on 28-29 may 1969 (overture)

jochum	further lp issues: SC71-AX 900/AXS 9000/
concertgebouw	6500 088/6580 146 (overture)/6580 175
orkest	(symphony)/6700 040 (overture)
	cd: 422 9662 (symphony)/426 0612 (overture)/
	475 8147

839 779LY / beethoven symphony no 3 "eroica"
recorded in the concertgebouw amsterdam on 20-21 may 1969

jochum	further lp issues: SC71-AX 900/AXS 9000/
concertgebouw	6580 137
orkest	cd: 426 0662/434 5282/475 8147

839 780LY / beethoven symphony no 4; leonore overtures nos 1 and 3
recorded in the concertgebouw amsterdam on 13-14 june 1968 (symphony), between 29 november-4 december 1968 (leonore no 3) and between 21-24 march 1969 (leonore no 1)

jochum	further lp issues: SC71-AX 900/AXS 9000/
concertgebouw	6500 089/6580 146 (symphony and leonore 1)/
orkest	6580 175 (leonore 3)/6700 040 (leonore 3)
	cd: 422 9662 (leonore 1)/422 9672 (symphony)/
	426 0662 (leonore 3)/434 5282 (leonore 3)/
	475 8147

839 781LY / beethoven symphony no 5; fidelio overture
recorded in the concertgebouw amsterdam between 29 november-4 december 1968

jochum	further lp issues: SC71-AX 900/AXS 9000/
concertgebouw	6580 145
orkest	cd: 422 4742 (symphony)/426 0662 (overture)/
	434 5282 (overture)/475 8147

839 782LY/beethoven symphony no 6 "pastoral"
recorded in the concertgebouw amsterdam between 29 november-4 december 1968
jochum further lp issues: SC71-AX 900/AXS 9000/
concertgebouw 6527 045/6580 139
orkest cd: 426 0612/450 0582/475 8147

839 783LY/beethoven symphony no 7
recorded in the concertgebouw amsterdam on 19-20 september 1967
jochum further lp issues: SC71-AX 900/AXS 9000/
concertgebouw 6500 090/6580 176
orkest cd: 422 9672/438 8392/475 8147

839 784-839 785LY/works by beethoven
recorded in the concertgebouw amsterdam on 4-7 june 1969 (symphony)
jochum **symphony no 9 "choral"**
concertgebouw further lp issues: SC71-AX 900/AXS 9000/
orkest 6700 040/6780 033
dutch radio cd: 422 4642/432 2252/475 8147
chorus **leonore no 2 overture** *see 839 778*
rebmann, **leonore no 3 overture** *see 839 780*
reynolds,
de ridder, feldhoff

839 786LY/works for flute, harpsichord and cello
recorded between 16-23 december 1968
holliger
picht-axenfeld
ververa

839 787LY/works for oboe, harpsichord and cello
recorded between 16-23 december 1968
h.holliger
u.holliger
jucker

839 788LY/liszt les préludes; tasso; orpheus
recorded in the town hall wembley on 20-21 november 1968
haitink further lp issues: SAL 3750/6527 201/6570 056/
london 6709 005/6833 227 (les préludes)
philharmonic cd: 426 6362 (les préludes and tasso)/438 7512

839 789LY / gesualdo responses and madrigals
recorded between 3-6 march 1969
voorberg
dutch radio
ensemble

839 790LY / berlioz te deum
recorded in the town hall watford on 5-6 january 1969
davis further lp issues: SAL 3724/6768 002
london cd: 416 6602/456 5222/464 6892
symphony
lso chorus
wandsworth
school choir
tagliavini

839 791LY / operatic arias by verdi, bellini and donizetti
recorded in rome between 14-19 march 1969
franci
rome symphony
deutekom

839 792-839 793LY / bach the 4 orchestral suites
recorded between 5-13 december 1968
leppard further lp issues: 6500 067-6500 068
english chamber
orchestra

839 795LY / beethoven string quartet no 13; grosse fuge
recorded
quartetto further lp issues: SAL 3780/6707 008/6747 242
italiano cd: 416 6382/454 0622/454 7112/464 6842

839 796LY / haydn symphonies nos 22, 39 and 47
recorded between 1-4 december 1968
leppard further lp issue: SAL 3776
english chamber
orchestra

839 797-839 798LY/mahler symphony no 6
recorded in the concertgebouw amsterdam between 29 january-2 february 1969
haitink   further lp issue: 6768 021
concertgebouw   cd: 420 1382/442 0502
orkest

839 799LY/bach missae breves bwv 235 and bwv 236
recorded in the johannesstift berlin between 3-7 march 1969 and on 12 september 1969
winschermann
deutsche bach-
solisten
westfälische
kantorei
ameling, finnilä,
altmeyer, reimer

839 800GSY/music by ketelby
recorded in thr liederhalle stuttgart in 1962
mareczek   further lp issues: G05585R/6599 258
stuttgarter
philharmoniker

839 801GSY/gershwin rhapsody in blue; an american in paris
legrand
orchestra

839 802/ *see 03486* **839 803/** *see 698 507*

839 804/ *see 03490* **894 000/** *see 838 611*

894 001/ *see 698 000* **894 002/** *see 610 116*

894 003/ *see 00502* **894 004/** *see 02301*

894 005/ *see 00441* **894 006/** *see 00545*

894 007/ *see 00491* **894 008/** *see 02334*

894 009/ *see 00544* **894 010/** *see 05371 and 05381*

894 011/ *see 00536 and 835 009* **894 012/** *see 02028*

894 013/ *see 05424*

894 014-894 015/ *see 03018-03019*   **894 016**/ *see 00547*

894 017/ *see 00465*   **894 018**/ *see 00440*

894 019/ *see 02043*   **894 032**/ *see 03489*

894 035/ *see 698 032*   **894 036**/ *see 00504*

894 037/ *see 836 901*   **894 038**/ *see 00518*

894 040/ *see 698 022*

894 041ZKY / orchestral works by mozart
recorded in the lukaskirche dresden in september 1960 (symphony) and in november 1960

suitner **symphony no 29**
staatskapelle further lp issues: eterna 820 222/825 222/826 681
dresden cd: berlin classics CC 00422/BC 02612/BC 94732
    eine kleine nachtmusik; serenata notturna
    further lp issues: 836 948DSY/eterna 820 222/
    825 222/826 477
    cd: berlin classics CC 00422/BC 02612

894 042/ *see 02266*   **894 043**/ *see 02042*

894 044/ *see 00475 and 835 006*

894 045ZKY / concerti by pergolesi
koch further lp issue: eterna 820 702
kammerorchester
berlin

894 046ZKY / concerti by mozart and haydn
recorded in the lukaskirche dresden in august 1963 (mozart)
suitner   **piano concerto no 21**
staatskapelle   further lp issues: eterna 820 464/825 464
dresden
schmidt
suitner   **violin concerto in d**
staatskapelle   further lp issue: eterna 820 560
berlin
suske

894 048/ *see 00434*   **894 049/** *see 02362*

894 050/ *see 00390*   **894 051/** *see 02075*

894 053/ *see 00527*   **894 054/** *see 02258*

894 055/ *see 00690*   **894 056/** *see 02229 and 05431*

894 058/ *see 02026 and 02237*   **894 059/** *see 02435 and 610 115*

894 061/ *see 00460*   **894 062/** *see 700 137*

894 063/ *see 02026*   **894 064/** *see 00461*

894 065/ *see 663 005 and 698 024*   **894 067/** *see 02025 and 02226-02227*

894 068/ *see 02393 and 838 120*   **894 069/** *see 00475 and 05406*

894 070/ *see 698 051-698 054*

894 072-894 073/ *see 02340-02341*

894 074/ *see 698 051-698 054*   **894 092/** *see 02030 and 02285*

894 093/ *see 698 009*   **894 100/** *see 02309 and 610 124*

894 102/ *see 02318*   **894 103/** *see 03074 and 06104*

894 105/ *see 00199 and 00313*   **894 107/** *see 697 004 and 697 009*

894 108ZKY / grieg peer gynt, incidental music
recorded in the kongresshalle leipzig
neumann   further lp issues: eterna 820 667/825 667
gewandhaus-
orchester
stolte

894 117/ *see 02064*   **894 118**/ *see 802 813*

894 119/ *see 02060*   **894 120**/ *see 00410-00411*

894 121/ *see 698 068*   **894 123**/ *see 02297*

894 125ZKY / organ music by bach
albrecht   further lp issue: eterna 825 759

894 126ZKY / works by debussy, sibelius, grieg and alfven
recorded in the concertgebouw amsterdam in july 1960 (norwegian dances) and in 1961 (norwegian rhapsody)
	berceuse héroique *see 00441*
	finlandia; valse triste *see 835 003*
	2 elegaic melodies *see 835 003*
otterloo	4 norwegian dances
residentie	cd: challenge records CC 72142
orkest	**norwegian rhapsody**

appendix a: recordings made or issued by philips in europe for american columbia

these recordings are not included in the philips numerical index

A 01106 L/brahms violin concerto
recorded in abbey road studios london between 5-9 november 1951
beecham further lp issues: ABL 3023/A06694R/GBL 5638/
royal G05612R/699 027CL/american columbia ML 4530
philharmonic cd: sony SM3K 45952/SMK 87799
stern

A 01107 L/schubert piano trio in e flat
recorded in the église saint pierre prades on 5-6 july 1952
schneider further lp issues: ABL 3009/american
casals columbia ML 4706
horszowski cd: sony SMK 58998
also published on cd by music and arts and pearl

A 01109-01111 L/organ works by bach and mendelssohn
recorded in günsbach
schweitzer further lp issues: columbia 33CX 1074/33CX 1081/
33CX 1084/american columbia SL 223
excerpts
45 rpm issues: ABE 10000/409 000AE
further lp issues: GBL 5509/G03515L/
american columbia ML 4602

A 01127 L/berlioz te deum
recorded in the parish church hornsey in december 1953
beecham further lp issues: ABL 3006/GL 5637/G03619L/
royal american columbia ML 4897/3216 0206/77395
philharmonic cd: sony SMK 87964

A 01130 L/tchaikovsky symphony no 2 "little russian"
recorded in the town hall walthamstow in december 1953
beecham further lp issues: ABL 3015/GL 5636/G03618L/
royal american columbia ML 4872
philharmonic cd: sony SMK 87875

A 01132 L/works for viola and orchestra
recorded in the town hall walthamstow in december 1953 (walton) and on 8-9 december 1953 (hindemith)

sargent royal philharmonic primrose	**walton viola concerto** further lp issues: ABL 3045/american columbia ML 4905/Y-35922
pritchard royal philharmonic primrose	**hindemith der schwanenderher** further lp issues: ABL 3045/american columbia ML 4905

A 01136 L/schubert symphonies nos 1 and 2
recorded in the town hall walthamstow in december 1953 (no 1) and on 28 april 1954 (no 2)

beecham
royal
philharmonic

further lp issues: ABL 3001/GL 5634/G03616L/
american columbia ML 4903
cd: sony SMK 87876

A 01137 L/stravinsky oedipus rex
recorded in the sendersaal cologne on 8 october 1951

stravinsky
wdr orchestra
and chorus
mödl, pears,
krebs, rehfuss
cocteau

further lp issues: ABL 3054/american
columbia ML 4644/61131
cd: music and arts CD 1184

A 01164 L/dvorak symphonic variations; balakirev thamar
recorded in the town hall walthamstow in december 1953 (dvorak) and on 16 april 1954 (balakirev)

beecham
royal
philharmonic

further lp issues: ABL 3047/GL 5717/
G03629L/american columbia ML 4974
cd: sony SMK 91171

A 01170 L/brahms string sextet no 1
recorded in the église saint pierre prades between 23 june-3 july 1952

stern, schneider,
katims, thomas,
casals, foley

further lp issues: ABL 3085/GBL 5623/
G03599L/american columbia ML 4703
cd: sony SMK 58994
also published on cd by music and arts and pearl

A 01180 L/orchestral works by elgar
recorded in the town hall walthamstow on 26-27 november 1954
beecham   **enigma variations**
royal   further lp issues: ABL 3053/SBR 6224/
philharmonic   S06686R/GBL 5646/G03623L/
                  american columbia ML 5031/61660
                  cd: sony SMK 89405
                  excerpts
                  45 rpm issues: SBF 122/313 413F
                  further lp issue: GL 5678
                  serenade for strings
                  45 rpm issues: ABE 10188/409 153AE
                  further lp issues: ABL 3053/SBR 6225/
                  S06687R/GBL 5646/G03623L/
                  american columbia ML 5031/61660
                  cd: sony SMK 89405
                  cockaigne overture
                  45 rpm issues: ABE 10041/409 073AE
                  further lp issues: ABL 3053/SBR 6224/
                  S06686R/GBL 5646/G03623L/american
                  columbia ML 5031/ML 5247/
                  61660/30055
                  cd: sony SMK 89405
recordings of enigma and cockaigne were completed on 13-14 december 1954

A 01188 L/schubert string quintet in c d956
recorded in the église saint pierre on 1-2 july 1952
stern, schneider,   further lp issues: ABL 3100/GBL 5624/
katims, casals,   G03600L/american columbia ML 4714
tortelier   cd: sony MPK 44853/SMK 58992
                  also piblished on cd by music and arts and pearl

A 01208-01209 L/organ works by bach
recorded in günsbach
schweitzer   further lp issues: ABL 3092/ABL 3134/
                  american columbia SL 223
                  excerpts
                  further lp issues: GBL 5519/G03505L

A 01215 L/beethoven piano concerto no 5 "emperor"
recorded in the maison de la mutualité paris on 19 september 1955
mitropoulos   further lp issues: ABL 3142/GBL 5613/
new york   american columbia ML 5100/P 14201/72312
philharmonic   cd: sony 5033 952
casadesus

A 01216 L/symphonies by mozart
recorded in the town hall walthamstow between 30 april-1 may 1954 (no 35) and in november and december 1955 (no 36)

beecham royal philharmonic	**symphony no 35 "haffner"** further lp issues: ABL 3067/S06685R/GL 5742/ GBR 6525/G03643L/G05610R/EFL 2503/ 697 206EL/699 023CL/american columbia ML 5001/3236 0009 cd: sony SMK 89809 **symphony no 36 "linz"** further lp issues: ABL 3067/S06636R/699 035CL/ american columbia ML 5001/3236 0009/54001 cd: sony SMK 87963

A 01218 L/overtures by berlioz
recorded in the town hall walthamstow on 2-3 december 1954

beecham royal philharmonic	further lp issues: ABL 3083/GL 5633/G03015L/ american columbia ML 5064/Y-33287/77395 cd: sony SMK 89807 *excerpts* 45 rpm issues: ABE 10016/ABE 10040/ ABE 10190/409 016AE/409 019AE/ 409 155AE further lp issues: SBR 6243/SBR 6244/ S06706R/S06707R/699 031CL/ american columbia XSM 15811

A 01229 L/works by delius
recorded in the town hall walthamstow on 28 april 1954 (sea drift) and in november and december 1955 (paris)

beecham royal philharmonic bbc chorus boyce	**sea drift** further lp issues: ABL 3088/american columbia ML 5079/61224 cd: sony SMK 89430/SX5K 87342 *recording completed in december 1954*
beecham royal philharmonic	**paris** further lp issues: ABL 3088/american columbia ML 5079/Y-33284/61271 cd: sony SMK 89430/SX5K 87342

A 01230 L/symphonies by mozart
recorded in the town hall walthamstow on 27 april 1954 (no 40) and in november and december 1955 (no 39)

beecham	**symphony no 39**
royal	further lp issues: ABL 3094/GL 5742/EFL 2503/
philharmonic	697 203EL/699 035CL/american columbia
	ML 5194/3236 0009/54048
	cd: sony SMK 87963
	symphony no 40
	further lp issues: ABL 3094/GL 5747/EFL 2516/
	697 209EL/american columbia ML 5194/
	3236 0009/54048
	cd: sony SMK 89089

A 01240 L/orff scenes from antigonae
recorded in the musikverein vienna in 1955

hollreiser	further lp issues: ABL 3116/american
wiener	columbia ML 5038
symphoniker	
chor der wiener	
staatsoper	
goltz, rössl-majdan,	
uhde, greindl	

A 01243 L/prokofiev suite from lieutenant kijé
recorded in the abbey road studios london on 25-26 july 1951

kurtz	further lp issues: ABL 3117/S06601R/
royal	american columbia ML 4683
philharmonic	

philips editions A01243L and ABL 3117 were coupled with an american columbia recording of shostakovich symphony no 9 conducted by efrem kurtz with the new york philharmonic orchestra

A 01250 L/sibelius violin concerto
recorded in abbey road studios london on 7-8 november 1951

beecham	78rpm issue: columbia LX 8947-8950
royal	further lp issues: NBL 5030/GL 5718/G03630L/
philharmonic	664 017ER/699 040CL/columbia 33C 1008/
stern	FC 1022/QC 5003/american columbia
	ML 4550/Y-35200
	cd: sony SMK 87799

A 01326-0327 L/works for organ and strings
recorded in the mozarteum salzburg
paumgartner camerata academica power biggs further lp issue: american columbia K3L-231
excerpts
further lp issue: A01342L

A 01329 L/symphonies by beethoven and mendelssohn
recorded in the kingsway hall london on 18 may 1951 and in abbey road studios london between october-december 1951 (beethoven) and in the abbey road studios on 19 december 1951 and in may and june 1952 (mendelssohn)
beecham royal philharmonic
beethoven symphony no 8
further lp issues: GL 5730/G03638L/CFL 1004/ 699 030CL/EFL 2507/697 205EL/EFR 2020/ 664 012ER/699 008CL/699 038CL/columbia 33CX 1039/QCX 10040/WCX 1039/VCX 517/ american columbia ML 4681/CB 21
cd: sony SMK 89888/emi CDM 763 3982
mendelssohn symphony no 4 "italian"
further lp issues: GL 5745/G03642L/CFL 1008/ 699 007CL/EFL 2507/697 205EL/EFR 2021/ 664 015ER/699 038CL/columbia 33C 1006/ QC 5002/FCX 236/american columbia ML 4681
cd: sony SMK 87965/emi CDM 763 3982

A 01335 L/delius appalachia
recorded in the abbey road studios london between 29 october-7 november 1952 and in december 1952
beecham royal philharmonic orchestra and chorus
further lp issues: GL 5690/G03634L/CFL 1009/ 699 009CL/columbia 33CX 1112/american columbia ML 4915/Y-33283/61354
cd: sony SMK 89429/SX5K 87342

A 01351 L/works by mozart and beethoven
recorded in the théatre municipal perpignan on 6-7 july 1951 (mozart) and on 31 july 1951 (beethoven)

casals	**mozart piano concerto no 9 k271**
perpignan	further lp issues: columbia 33CX 1091/FCX 225/
festival	american columbia ML 4568
orchestra	cd: sony SMK 58984
hess	*also published on cd by music and arts and pearl*
casals	**beethoven variations on mozart's bei männern**
serkin	**welche liebe fühlen**
	further lp issues: columbia 33CX 1093/american columbia ML 4572/ML 4877/SL 201/K3L-233/ 3236 0016
	cd: sony MPK 46724/SM2K 58985/5153 042
	also published on cd by music and arts and pearl

A 01352 L/works by mozart and beethoven
recorded in the théatre municipal perpignan on 26 july 1951 (mozart) and on 31 july 1951 (beethoven)

casals	**mozart piano concerto no 22 k482**
perpignan	further lp issues: columbia 33CX 1092/
festival	american columbia ML 4569
orchestra	cd: sony SMK 66570
serkin	*also published on cd by music and arts and pearl*
casals	**beethoven variations on mozart's ein mädchen**
serkin	**oder weibchen**
	further lp issues: columbia 33CX 1093/american columbia ML 4572/ML 4877/SL 201/3236 0016
	cd: sony MPK 46724/SM2K 58985/5153 042
	also published on cd by music and arts and pearl

A 01369 L/works by schumann
recorded in the éhlise saint pierre prades on 4 july 1952 (piano trio) and on 28-29 may 1953 (cello concerto)

ormandy	**cello concerto**
prades festival	further lp issues: ABR 4035/S01617R/G05621R/
orchestra	american columbia ML 4926
casals	cd: sony SMK 58993
	also published on cd by music and arts and pearl

horszowski	**piano trio no 1**
schneider	further lp issue: american columbia ML 4708
casals	cd: sony SMK 58993
	also published on cd by music and arts and pearl

A 01381 L/bach preludes and fugues
recorded in the netherlands

power biggs	further lp issue: american columbia KL 5262

A 01392 L/orchestral works by tchaikovsky, boccherini, beethoven and brahms
recorded in the town hall walthamstow in december 1953

beecham	**tchaikovsky suite from casse noisette**
royal	further lp issues: ABL 3247/SBR 6213/
philharmonic	S06649R/699 016CL/american columbia ML 5171
	cd: sony SMK 87875
	excerpts
	further lp issues: american columbia
	ML 4872/PE 17
	recording completed in december 1954
	boccherini overture in d
	further lp issues: ABL 3247/SBR 6218/SBR 6244/
	S06656R.S06707R/GL 5714/G03626L/699 037CL/
	american columbia ML 5029
	brahms tragic overture
	further lp issues: ABL 3247/SBR 6218/S06656R/
	GL 5714/G03626L/699 037CL/american
	columbia ML 5029/ML 5247
	beethoven coriolan overture
	45 rpm issue: 313 358SF
	further lp issues: ABL 3247/SBR 6216/SBR 6244/
	S06656R/S06707R/GL 5714/G03626L/699 037CL
	american columbia: ML 5029/ML 5247
	cd: sony SMK 89887

A 01397-01398 L/835 530-835 531AY/handel organ concerti op 4
recorded in saint james church great packington between 22-28 july 1957
boult	further lp issues: ABL 3260-3261/SABL 148-149/
london	american columbia K2L-258/K2S-602/
philharmonic	D3S-777/77358
power biggs	cd: sony M3YK 45825

excerpts
45 rpm issues: ABE 10227/SABE 2007/
409 159AE/740 104AV
further lp issues: G05648R/610 310VR/836 413VZ/
american columbia ML 5839/MS 6439

A 01407 L/bach sonatas for cello and harpsichord
recorded in the église saint pierre prades between 31 may-6 june 1950
casals	further lp issue: american columbia ML 4349
baumgartner	cd: sony MPK 46445

also published on cd by music and arts and pearl

A 01424 L/835 526AY/piano concerti by beethoven
recorded in the concertgebouw amsterdam on 1-2 march 1959
beinum
concertgebouw
orkest
casadesus

piano concerto no 1
further lp issues: ABL 3299/L09423L/american columbia ML 5437/MS 6111/3216 0056/
BRG 72200/SBRG 72200
cd: sony 5033 872

piano concerto no 4
further lp issues: ABL 3299/L09423L/G05656R/
610 303VR/american columbia ML 5437/
MS 6111/3216 0056/BRG 72200/
SBRG 72200/10002
cd: sony 5033 872

A 01430-01431 L/835 533-835 534AY/handel organ concerti op 7
recorded in saint james church great packington between 22-28 july 1957
boult	further lp issues: ABL 3326-3327/american
london	columbia M2L-261/M2S-604/D3S-778/77358
philharmonic	cd: sony M3YK 45825
power biggs	

A 01496-01498 L/berg lulu/ *original unfinished version*
recorded in vienna by austrian radio in 1949
häfner　　　　further lp issues: ABL 3394-3396/
wiener　　　　　american columbia SL 121
symphoniker
steingruber,
cerny, libert,
kmentt, sieger,
wiener

A 01501 L./835 574AY/weill happy end
recorded in the musikhalle hamburg on 9-10 july 1960
brückner-　　　further lp issues: ABL 3364/SABL 193/
ruggeberg　　　american columbia 73463
orchestra　　　　cd: sony MK 45886
lenya

A 01505-01506 L/schoenberg moses und aron
recorded at a concert in the musikhalle hamburg on 12 march 1954
rosbaud　　　　further lp issues: ABL 3398-3399/
ndr-orchester　　american columbia K3L-241/78213
choirs　　　　　cd: stradivarius STR 10022
steingruber,
krebs, kretschmar,
fiedler

A 01511 L/concerti by bach
recorded in the église saint pierre prades on 5 june 1950 (piano concerto) and on 15 june 1950 (violin concerto)
casals　　　　**piano concerto bwv 1056**
prades festival　further lp issues: columbia 33CX 1109/american
orchestra　　　columbia ML 4353/76082
haskil　　　　　cd: sony SMK 58982
　　　　　　　　also published on cd by music and arts and pearl

casals　　　　**violin concerto bwv 1041**
prades festival　further lp issues: columbia 33CX 1109/american
orchestra　　　columbia ML 4353/SL 169/SL 170/76082
stern　　　　　cd: sony SMK 58982
　　　　　　　　also published on cd by music and arts and pearl

A 01513 L/orchestral works by bach
recorded in the église saint pierre prades on 20-21 may 1950 (suite) and on 27 may 1950 (musikalisches opfer)

casals orchestral suite no 2
prades festival further lp issue: american columbia ML 4348
orchestra *published on cd by music and arts and pearl*
  selection from musikalisches opfer
  further lp issue: american columbia ML 4347
  published on cd by music and arts and pearl

A 01644 R/overtures by méhul
recorded in the town hall walthamstow in december 1953

beecham **timoléon**
royal further lp issues: ABR 4056/SBR 6244/SBR 6263/
philharmonic S06707R/S06710R/G03626L/american
  columbia ML 5029
  cd: sony SMK 91167
  le trésor supposé
  further lp issues: ABR 4056/SBR 6263/S06710R/
  american columbia ML 5029
  cd: sony SMK 91167
  la chasse du jeune henri
  45 rpm issues: ABE 10042/409 079AE
  further lp issues: ABR 4056/G03625L/
  american columbia ML 5029

A 01645 R/schubert piano trio no 1
recorded in the théatre municipal perpignan between 20-22 august 1951

istomin further lp issues: ABR 4059/american
schneider columbia ML 4715
casals cd: sony SMK 58989
  also published on cd by music and arts and pearl

N 02113 L/orchestral music by wagner

recorded in the town hall walthamstow in december 1953 (karfeitagszauber and trauermarsch), on 16 april 1954 (holländer), on 17 april 1954 (meistersinger) and on 20 april 1954 (rheinfahrt)

beecham
royal
philharmonic

karfreitagszauber/parsifal
45 rpm issues: ABE 10184/409 107AE
further lp issues: ABL 3039/GL 5635/G03617L/
american columbia ML 4962
cd: sony SMK 89889

siegfrieds trauermarsch/götterdämmerung
45 rpm issues: ABE 10016/409 019AE
further lp issues: ABL 3039/GL 5635/G03617L/
american columbia ML 4962
cd: sony SMK 89889

der fliegende holländer overture
further lp issues: ABL 3039/GL 5635/G03617L/
american columbia ML 4962
cd: sony SMK 89889

act three suite/die meistersinger von nürnberg
45 rpm issues: ABE 10097 (act 3 prelude only)/
409 106AE (act 3 prelude only)
further lp issues: ABL 3039/GL 5635/G03617L/
american columbia ML 4962
cd: sony SMK 89889

siegfrieds rheinfahrt/götterdämmerung
45 rpm issues: ABE 10016/409 019AE
further lp issues: ABL 3039/GL 5635/G03617L/
american columbia ML 4962
cd: sony SMK 89889

N 02136 L/symphonies by haydn

recorded in the kingsway hall london on 24 april and 1 june 1950 (no 93) and in abbey road studios london on 13-14 april 1951 and 8 october 1951 (no 94)

beecham
royal
philharmonic

symphony no 93
78 rpm issues: columbia LX 1361-1363/GQX
11472-11474/american columbia M 991
further lp issues: NBL 5037/GL 5632/G03614L/
columbia 33CX 1038/WCX 1038/FCX 328/
QCX 10032/american columbia ML 5437/Y-33285
cd: sony SMK 89890

symphony no 94 "surprise"
78 rpm issue: columbia LX 1499-1501
further lp issues: NBL 5037/GL 5632/G03614L/
S04623L/columbia 33CX 1104/FCX 328/
QCX 10060/american columbia ML 4453
cd: sony SMK 89890

N 02140 L/goldmark rustic wedding symphony
recorded in the abbey road studios london between 5-8 may 1952
beecham further lp issues: NBL 5041/GL 5719/G03631L/
royal columbia 33CX 1067/american columbia ML 4626
philharmonic cd: sony SMK 87780

N 02150 L/sibelius scenes historiques
recorded in the kingsway hall london on 28 september 1950 and in abbey road studios london in june and september 1952
beecham further lp issues: NBL 5030/GL 5718/G03630L/
royal columbia 33C 1018/QC 5014/american
philharmonic columbia ML 4550/Y3-35200
cd: sony SMK 87798/emi CDM 763 3972
excerpts
45 rpm issues: SBF 269/313 499SF/
columbia SEB 3504/SEBQ 115

S 04644 L/symphonies by mozart
recorded in the kingsway hall london on 9 march 1951 and in the abbey road studios london on 9 may 1951 (no 31) and in the kingsway hall london on 18 april 1950 (no 38)
beecham **symphony no 31 "paris"**
royal further lp issues: SBL 5226/S06685R/GL 5742/
philharmonic GBR 6525/G03643L/G05610R/EFL 2503/
699 023CL/columbia 33CX 1038/FCX 329/
QCX 10032/american columbia ML 4474
cd: sony SMK 89808
symphony no 38 "prague"
78 rpm issues: columbia LX 1517-1519/
american columbia M 934
further lp issues: SBL 5226/GL 5742/G03643L/
EFL 2503/699 023CL/columbia 33CX 1105/
FCX 235/american columbia ML 4313/
3216 0023/3236 0009
cd: sony SMK 87963

S 05648 L/beethoven symphony no 3 "eroica"
recorded in the abbey road studios london on 20-21 december 1951 and on 13 august 1952
beecham further lp issues: SBL 5233/columbia 33CX 1086/
royal american columbia ML 4698
philharmonic cd: sony SMK 89887

S 06624 R/schubert violin sonata d574
recorded in the église saint pierre prades in june 1952
szigeti further lp issue: american columbia ML 4632
hess *published on cd by music and arts and pearl*

S 06650 R/works by sibelius, grétry, berlioz and massenet
recorded in the town hall walthamstow between 7-18 december 1953 (sibelius, troyens march and massenet), 28 april 1954 (grétry) and 16 december 1954 (troyens prelude)

beecham **alla marcia/karelia suite**
royal further lp issues: SBR 6215/GL 5716/G03628L/
philharmonic 664 017ER/american columbia ML 5321/
Y-33288/61655
cd: sony SMK 87798
air de ballet/zémire et azore
further lp issues: SBR 6215/SBR 6245/S06710R/
GL 5713/G03625L/american columbia
ML 5029/PE 17
prélude/les troyens a carthage
45 rpm issues: ABE 10020/409 047AE
further lp issues: SBR 6215/GL 5714/G03626L/
american columbia ML 5321/Y-33288
cd: sony SMK 89807
marche troyenne/les troyens
45 rpm issue: ABE 10020/409 047AE
further lp issues: SBR 6215/GL 5714/G03626L/
american columbia ML 5321/Y-33288/
XSM 158111/61655
cd: sony SMK 89807
le dernier sommeil de la vierge
further lp issues: SBR 6215/GL 5713/G03625L/
american columbia ML 5321/PE 17/
Y-33288/61655

S 06665 R/orchestral works by delius
recorded in the abbey road studios london on 7 february 1950 (over the hills and far away) and on 27 october 1951 (in a summer garden)

beecham	**over the hills and far away**
royal	further lp issues: SBR 6242/GL 5713/G03625L/
philharmonic	columbia 33C 1017/american columbia
	ML 2133/ML 5268
	cd: sony SMK 89429/SX5K 87342
	in a summer garden
	further lp issues: SBR 6242/GL 5713/G03625L/
	columbia 33C 1017/american columbia 30056
	cd: sony SMK 89430/SX5K 87342

S 06708 R/sibelius symphony no 1
recorded in the abbey road studios london on 23 may 1951 and in november and december 1951 and in may 1952

beecham	further lp issues: SBR 6245/GL 5716/G03628L/
royal	columbia 33CX 1085/QCX 10071/american
philharmonic	columbia ML 4653
	cd: sony SMK 87798

S 06710 R/haydn symphony no 103 "drum roll"
recorded in the kingsway hall london between 29 january-1 february 1951

beecham	further lp issues: SBR 6253/S04623L/699 036CL/
royal	columbia 33CX 1104/FCX 329/QCX 10060/
philharmonic	american columbia ML 4453
	cd: sony SMK 89890

A 07186 L/weill die sieben todsünden
brückner-
ruggeberg
lenya, katona,
gollnitz, roth, pöttgen

L 09418-09420 L/weill aufstieg und fall der stadt mahagonny
recorded in the musikhalle hamburg between 3-11 november 1956

brückner-	further lp issues: american columbia
ruggeberg	K3L-243/M3X-37874/77341
ndr-orchester	cd: sony SM2K 77242/SM2K 91184
and chorus	
lenya, litz,	
sauerbaum,	
günter	

L 09421-09422 L/weill die dreigroschenoper
recorded in sender freies berlin between 11-15 january 1958

brückner-	further lp issues: ABL 3361-3362/american
ruggeberg	columbia O2L-257/O2S-201/Y2-32977/78279
sfb-orchester	cd: sony MK 42637
and chorus	*excerpts*
lenya,	further lp issue: S06715R
hesterburg,	
koczian, neuss,	
schellow	

664 023ER/works by chabrier, mendelssohn and bizet
recorded in the abbey road stusios london on 6 february 1950 (bizet), in the abbey road studios london on 7 february 1950 and kingsway hall london on 1 june 1950 (mendelssohn) and in the kingsway hall london on 24 april 1950 (chabrier)

beecham
royal
philharmonic

espana
78 rpm issues: columbia LX 1592/GQX 11539/ american columbia 73283D
45 rpm issues: CFE 15000/EFF 521/496 000CE/ 270 818EF/columbia SEL 1509/SEBQ 108
further lp issues: EFR 2029/CFL 1021/699 018CL/ GL 5692/G03636L/american columbia ML 5171

hebrides overture
78 rpm issue: american columbia 73281D
45 rpm issues: CFE 15004/EFF 517/ 496 005CE/270 814EF
further lp issues: EFR 2029/CFL 1021/699 018CL/ 699 037CL/GL 5692/G03636L
cd: sony SMK 87965

suite from la jolie fille de perth
78 rpm issues: columbia LX 8790-8791/ GQX 8033-8034/american columbia M 345
45 rpm issues: CFE 15059/496 043CE
further lp issues: CFL 1033/699 034CL/GL 5693/ G03637L/american columbia ML 2133

676 000KR/works by rimsky-korsakov and franck
recorded in the kingsway hall london between 9-24 january 1951 (rimsky) and on 9 march 1951 (franck)

beecham royal philharmonic	**suite from le coq d'or** further lp issues: KFR 4000/GL 5692/G03636L/ columbia 33CX 1087/QCX 10085/american columbia ML 4454 *excerpts* 45 rpm issues: CFE 15030/496 036CE further lp issues: CFL 1021/699 018CL/american columbia ML 5321/Y-33288/61655 **le chasseur maudit** 78 rpm issues: columbia LX 8813-8814/ GQX 11489-11490 further lp issues: KFR 4000/CFL 1042/699 014CL/ columbia 33CX 1087/QCX 10085/american columbia ML 4474 cd: sony SMK 87964

676 001KR/works by bizet and tchaikovsky
recorded in the columbia studios new york city on 21-22 december 1949

beecham columbia symphony	**suite from carmen** 78 rpm issue: american columbia X 333 45 rpm issues: CFE 15019/496 017CE/ american columbia A 1640 further lp issues: KFR 4001/GL 5720/G03632L/ columbia 33CX 1037/FCX 330/QCX 10012/ VCX 521/american columbia ML 4287/ 3216 0117/54035 cd: sony MH2K 63366 *excerpts* 45 rpm issue: EFF 512 further lp issues: CFL 1042/699 041CL/ american columbia AAL 27 **capriccio italien** 78 rpm issues: columbia LX 8924-8925/ american columbia X 334 45 rpm issues: CFE 15028/496 025CE further lp issues: KFR 4001/GL 5720/G03632L/ columbia 33CX 1037/FCX 330/QCX 10012/ VCX 521/american columbia ML 4287/ 3216 0117/54035 cd: sony MH2K 63366

676 002KR/berlioz harold en italie
recorded in the abbey road studios london between 12-15 november 1951
beecham	45 rpm issue: american columbia A 1074
royal	further lp issues: KFR 4002/GL 5715/G03627L/
philharmonic	columbia 33CX 1019/FCX 178/QCX 10005/
primrose	american columbia ML 4542/Y-33286/77395
	cd: sony MPK 47679

676 003KR/beethoven symphony no 6 "pastoral"
recorded in the abbey road studios london between 7-19 december 1951 and on 5 may 1952
beecham	further lp issues: KFR 4003/GL 5745/EFL 2505/
royal	697 201EL/columbia 33CX 1062/QCX 10020/
philharmonic	american columbia ML 4828
	cd: sony SMK 89888

697 201EL/symphonies by beethoven and schubert
recorded in the kingsway hall london between 15-24 january 1951, in the abbey road studios london on 9 may 1952 and in the kingsway hall london between 11-23 july 1952 (schubert)
beecham	**beethoven symphony no 6** *see 676 003*
royal	**schubert symphony no 8 "unfinished"**
philharmonic	78 rpm issue: columbia LX 8942-8944
	45 rpm issue: american columbia A 1070
	further lp issues: EFL 2505/CFL 1004/
	699 003CL/GL 5730/G03638L/columbia
	33CX 1039/FCX 236/WCX 1039/VCX 517/
	american columbia ML 4474/CB 21
	cd: sony SMK 87876/emi CDM 763 3982

697 209EL/symphonies by mozart
recorded in the kingsway hall london on 22 february 1950 (no 41)
beecham	**symphony no 40** *see 01230*
royal	**symphony no 41 "jupiter"**
philharmonic	78 rpm issues: columbia LX 1337-1340/
	GQX 11448-11451/american columbia M 933
	further lp issues: EFL 2518/GL 5747/GBR 6508/
	G03645L/G05668R/columbia 33C 1002/
	QC 5006/FCX 235/VC 805/american columbia
	ML 4313/3216 0023/3236 0009/54001
	cd: sony SMK 89809

699 001CL/mozart requiem
recorded in the town hall walthamstow on 13-14 december 1954 and in the abbey road studios london on 29 may 1956

beecham
royal
philharmonic
bbc chorus
morison, sinclair,
young, nowakowski

further lp issues: CFL 1000/american columbia ML 5160
cd: sony SMK 89808/theorema TH 121 151

699 004-699 005CL/delius a mass of life
recorded in the abbey road studios london 8 november-13 december 1952 and in january, april and may 1953

beecham
royal
philharmonic
lpo choir
fisher, raisbeck,
sinclair, craig, boyce

further lp issues: CFL 1005-1006/columbia 33CX 1078-1079/american columbia SL 197/ 61182-61183
cd: sony SM2K 89432

699 007CL/works by mendelssohn and handel-beecham
recorded in the kingsway hall london on 24 april and 28 september 1950 (handel-beecham)

beecham
royal
philharmonic

mendelssohn symphony no 4 *see 01329*
handel suite from the faithful shepherd arranged by beecham
78 rpm issue: american columbia M 990
further lp issues: CFL 1008/columbia 33CX 1105/ american columbia ML 5437/Y-33285
cd: sony SMK 87780
excerpts
78 rpm issue: columbia LX 1600
45 rpm issue: CFE 15031/496 037CE
further lp issue: american columbia ML 5226

699 018CL/works by mendelssohn, j.strauss, ponchielli, mozart, suppé and chabrier

recorded in the abbey road studios london on 16 march 1951 (ruy blas), 7 february 1950 (morgenblätter). 9 may 1951 (k605), in the kingsway hall london on 22 february 1950 (k249) and 24 april 1950 (suppé) and in the columbia studios new york city on 27 december 1949 (ponchielli)

beecham royal philharmonic	**espana; the hebrides overture** *see 664 023* **ruy blas overture** 78 rpm issue: columbia LX 1584 45 rpm issues: CFE 15004/EFF 534/496 005CE/ 270 809EF/columbia SEL 1501 further lp issues: CFL 1021/GL 5692/G03536L **morgenblätter waltz** 78 rpm issues: columbia LX 1322/american columbia 73053D 45 rpm issues: CFE 15000/EFF 516/270 010EF/ columbia SEL 1501/SEBQ 105 further lp issues: CFL 1021/GL 5692/G03536L/ american columbia ML 2134/AAL 6 **sleighride/german dances k605** 78 rpm issue: columbia LX 1587 45 rpm issues: CFE 15005/EFF 518/496 009CE/ 270 813EF/columbia SCB 106 further lp issues: CFL 1021/GL 5692/G03536L **march in d k249** 78 rpm issues: columbia LX 1340/LX 1587/ GQX 11451/GQX 11537/american columbia M 933 45 rpm issues: CFE 15005/EFF 518/496 009CE/ 270 813EF/columbia SCB 106/SCBQ 3011 further lp issues: CFL 1021/CFL 1042/699 041CL/ GL 5692/G03536L **morning noon and night in vienna overture** 78 rpm issues: columbia LX 1438/GQX 11508/ american columbia 73054D 45 rpm issues: CFE 15001/EFF 514/496 009CE/ 270 813EF further lp issues: CFL 1021/GL 5692/G03536L/ american columbia ML 2134/ML 5171/ML 5247/ AAL 6/CB 1
beecham columbia symphony	**danza delle ore/la gioconda** 78 rpm issue: american columbia 73052D 45 rpm issues: CFE 15001/EFF 515/496 001CE/ 270 808EF further lp issues: CFL 1021/GL 5692/G03536L/ american columbia ML 2134/ML 5171/ AAL 5/3216 0117 cd: sony MH2K 63366

699 019CL/mozart sinfonia concertante k364
recorded in the théatre municipal perpigan between 5-8 july 1951
casals further lp issues: CFL 1013/american
perpigan festival columbia ML 4564
orchestra cd: sony SMK 58983
stern, primrose *also published on cd by pearl and music and arts*
this recording was coupled with an american columbia recording of isaac stern playing and directing mozart violin concerto no 3

699 026CL/works by delius
recorded in the abbey road studios london on 14 february 1949 (north country sketches) and in the town hall walthamstow between 23-29 october 1955 and in the abbey road studios london in may and september 1956 (hassan)
beecham **north country sketches**
royal 78 rpm issue: columbia LX 1399-1401
philharmonic further lp issues: CFL 1020/GL 5691/G03635L/
 american columbia ML 4637/Y-33283/61354
 cd: sony SMK 58934/SMK 89429/SX5K 87342

beecham **incidental music for hassan**
royal further lp issues: CFL 1020/GL 5691/G03635L/
philharmonic american columbia ML 5268/61224
bbc chorus cd: sony MPK 47680/SC5K 87342
fry *excerpts*
 further lp issues: CFL 1033/699 034CL/GL 5673/
 G03637L/american columbia 30056

699 031-699 032CL/schumann manfred, incidental music
recorded in the town hall walthamstow between 13-23 december 1954 and in the abbey road studios london in may and october 1956 (overture)
beecham further lp issues: CFL 1026-1027/american
royal columbia M2L-245
philharmonic cd: somm BEECHAM 4
bbc chorus *overture*
 further lp issues: CFL 1042/699 041CL
 cd: sony SMK 87965

699 034CL/works by bizet, delius, rossini and nicolai
recorded in the abbey road studios london on 26 january 1951 (koanga), in the kingsway hall london on 28 september 1950 (cambiale di matrimonio), in the columbia studios new york city on 27 december 1949 (nicolai) and in the academy of music philadelphia on 3 february 1952 (semiramide)

beecham royal philharmonic orchestra and chorus	**suite from la jolie fille de perth** *see 664 023* **closing scene from koanga** 78 rpm issue: columbia LX 1502 further lp issues: CFL 1033/GL 5693/G03637L/ columbia 33CX 1112/american columbia ML 4915/Y-33284/61271 cd: sony SMK 58934/SX5K 87342
beecham royal philharmonic	**la cambiale di matrimonio overture** 78 rpm issues: columbia LX 1458/GQX 11498 45 rpm issues: EFF 535/270 811EF/columbia SEL 1509/SEBQ 108 further lp issues: CFL 1033/GL 5693/G03637L/ american columbia AAL 11/CB 1
beecham philadelphia orchestra	**semiramide overture** 45 rpm issues: CFE 15058/496 042CE further lp issues: CFL 1033/GL 5693/G03637L/ american columbia AAL 27/CB 1 cd: sony MH2K 63366
beecham columbia symphony	**die lustigen weiber von windsor overture** 78 rpm isue: american columbia 73051D 45 rpm issues: CFE 15031/EFF 548/ 496 037CE/270 821EF further lp issues: CGL 1033/GL 5693/G03637L/ american columbia ML 2124/AAL 5/CB 1 cd: sony MH2K 63366

appendix b: re-issue categories for lps drawn from the original philips european catalogue 1951-1969
information given in the following order: title of series/international numbering/ british numbering/stereo equivalent if applicable/approximate dates of availability

classical favourites 10-inch (25 cm): G05000R/GBR 5600/ 1955-1960
classical favourites 12-inch (30 cm): G03000L/GBL 5500/ GL 5700/GL 5800/837 000GY/SGL 5800/1959-1969

favourite music 10-inch (25 cm): S06000R/SBR 6000/1952-1959
favourite music 12-inch (30 cm): S04000L/SBL 4000/1952-1959

diskothek der meister 10-inch (25 cm): 610 000VR/836 000VZ
this german series overlapped with classical favourites G05000R

fontana 10-inch (25 cm): 663 000ER/675 000KR/EFR 2000/ KFR 4000/1959-1963
fontana 12-inch (30 cm): 697 000EL/699 000CL/EFL 2500/ CFL 1000/875 000CY/SCFL 100/1959-1965

pergola 12-inch (30 cm): 832 000PGY/1965-1969 *germany series included mainly reprocessed (artificial) stereo transfers*

fontana wing and mercury wing 12-inch (30 cm): 200 000WGL/ WL 1000/MGW 14000/SRW 18000/1968-1975
mainly for re-issues from mercury and vanguard but also including some early philips material; 200 000WGY series known in france as le cercle musical; SRW series were reprocessed (artificial) stereo

fontana special 12-inch (30 cm): 700 000WGY/SFL 14000/ 1968-1975/*known in italy as argento series*
fontana weltserie 12-inch (30 cm): 695 000KL/1970-1975
netherlands and germany
fontana grandioso 12-inch (30 cm): 894 000ZKY/1970-1975
netherlands and germany; also in italy as argento series

festivo 12-inch (30 cm): 839 000VGY/SFM 23000/1970-1975
fontana 12-inch (30 cm): 6530 000/6531 000/6570 000/1973-1980
universo 12-inch (30 cm): 6580 000/6581 000/6582 000/1973-1985
sequenza 12-inch (30 cm): 6527 000/412 0000/1982-1990

contour classics 12-inch (30 cm): CC 7500/2870 000/6870 000/ 1980-1990 *series also contained issues from deutsche grammophon and decca*

appendix c: index of conductors and orchestras

karel ancerl/wiener symphoniker
663 012	697 004	697 005	697 016
698 009	698 023		

volkmar andreae/wiener symphoniker
00273
malcolm arnold/royal philharmonic orchestra
10721
rudolf barshai/moscow chamber orchestra
2296   02297
serge baudo/orchestre lamoureux
02507
albert beaucamp/rouen chamber orchestra
802 710
david beckett/musica reservata
802 904
eduard van beinum/concertgebouworkest
00218	00219	00294-00295	00350-00351
00353	00373	00390	00398
00410-00411	00433	00434	00436
00437	00440	00441	00491
00502	00504	00720	00722
04032	05378	06150	09002
09007	835 003	835 006	835 009
835 013			

roberto benzi/orchestre lamoureux
02040	02053	02080	02229
03200	05431	610 119	

roberto benzi/paris opéra orchestra
02334   02386
roberto benzi/residentieorkest
02317
roberto benzi/london symphony orchestra
835 324
roberto benzi/bucharest philharmonic orchestra
802 700-802 701
birnbaum/unnamed orchestra
05468   698 509

karl böhm/concertgebouworkest
00318   00319   06141
karl böhm/wiener symphoniker
00357-00359   00435   02437   698 000
heinz bongartz/gewandhausorchester leipzig
835 388
ernest bour/concertgebouworkest
802 785
pablo casals/orchestre lamoureux
02067
see also entry under instrumentalists
marcel couraud/badische staatskapelle karlsruhe
02257   02265   02283   02336
03107   03117   03400
marcel couraud/stuttgart soloists
00571   00572   05424   09399
697 101-102   835 498
marcel couraud/stuttgarter philharmoniker
698 087
marcel couraud/rtf chamber orchestra
698 506
henryk czyz/cracow philharmonic orchestra
802 771-772
henryk czyz/warsaw philharmonic orchestra
839 701
colin davis/london symphony orchestra
02224   02225   02251   02253
02313   02363   02374   02378
02379   02384   02406   02418
02426   698 081   835 364   835 365
835 367   835 392   836 914   802 721-723
802 764   802 913   839 716-717 839 761
colin davis/bbc symphony orchestra
802 862   839 719-721   839 758-760
norman del mar/london symphony orchestra
02418
pierre dervaux/orchestre lamoureux
00638   00639   00663   00705
christoph von dohnanyi/wiener symphoniker
02243   663 019   698 040
christoph von dohnanyi/concertgebouworkest
02314

antal dorati/concertgebouworkest
00399	00545	00620	03066
09003-4	835 062		

antal dorati/residentieorkest
00154	00620	06036

antal dorati/wiener symphoniker
663 010	697 010	697 012	698 018

antal dorati/philharmonia hungarica
698 004

antal dorati/orchestre lamoureux
698 030

ohan dourian/orchestre lamoureux
200 024	200 028

cedric dumont/boyd neel orchestra
06052	402 029	402 030

jésus etcheverry/orchestre lamoureux
03482	03489	03498	697 009
698 507	835 497		

jörg faerber/württemberg chamber orchestra
00569	05468

erich fiala/amati orchestra
00501	02038

anatole fistoulari/london symphony orchestra
02262

oivin fjeldsted/wiener symphoniker
05421

oivin fjeldsted/oslo philharmonic orchestra
839 259

eduard flipse/rotterdam and brabant orchestras
00226-7	00297-8

jean fournet/orchestre lamoureux
00161	00188-9	00190	00192-3
00196	00228	00233	00246
00403	00420	00469	00509
00635	00636	00661	00661
00664	00669	00674	00703
00705	00706	00737	06022
06025	06104		

jean fournet/paris conservatoire orchestra
00160
jean fournet/orchestre pasdeloup
00701
jean fournet/concertgebouworkest
00536 835 064
jean fournet/wiener symphoniker
05371 05381 697 007
carlo franci/rai roma orchestra
839 791
john frandsen/danish radio orchestra
00764 06057 06060
louis de froment/instrumental ensemble
00792
alceo galliera/new philharmonia orchestra
802 719
alceo galliera/london symphony orchestra
835 351 802 728 802 881 802 882
839 755
franco gallini/orchestre lamoureux
00465
dimitri gebré/slovenian opera orchestra
00354-6
dimitri gebré/zagreb national opera orchestra
02014-6
ennio gerelli/milan chamber orchestra
02289 06083
alexander gibson/new philharmonia orchestra
836 919
hans gillesberger/wiener symphoniker
00460 02063
andré girard/orchestre national
835 494
szymon goldberg/netherlands chamber orchestra
00365 00459 00527 02063
02066 02085 03018-9 05441
05442 698 059 835 093
szymon goldberg usually directed from the violin
grebe/hamburger-telemann-gesellschaft
02357 836 912 802 816
ferdinand grossmann/wiener symphoniker
02252 02290 02312
odd grüner-hegge/oslo philharmonic orchestra
839 259

arrigo guarnieri/rai milano orchestra
00201
guller/chamber orchestra
00782
bernard haitink/concertgebouworkest

00546	02051	02052	02240
02263	02286	02299	02318
02339	02401	02408	02409
02410	02411	02412	02430
02435	02439	02455-6	02439
03066	05406	610 115	610 124
610 125	835 381	802 724	802 759-60
802 884-5	802 888	802 912	838 120
839 797-8			

bernard haitink/london philharmonic orchestra
802 892   839 788
pierre henry/electronic music group
00564   00565   00566   00567
maurice hewitt/hewitt chamber orchestra
00293   00346   00347   00349
john hollingsworth/royal philharmonic orchestra
10721
heinrich hollreiser/wiener symphoniker
03094   663 014   698 021   698 022
anton van der horst/netherlands chamber orchestra
00533
anton van der horst/netherlands bach society
02290   02362
milan horvat/zagreb philharmonic orchestra
02319   02387   610 803   700 130
700 200   835 318   836 927
samo hubad/slovenian opera orchestra
00329-30
eliahul inbal/concertgebouworkest
802 914
simon jansen/utrecht philharmonic orchestra
04590   422 520
see also entry under instrumentalists
eugen jochum/berliner philharmonisches orchester
00102

eugen jochum/concertgebouworkest
00604	00608	02034	02060
02072	02083	02222	02347-8
02502-5	802 810-802	839 777	839 778
839 779	839 780	839 781	839 782
839 783	839 784-5		

eugen jochum/sinfonieorchester des bayerischen rundfunks
02364-5   698 005   802 713-714

hein jordans/brabantsorkest
675 020   700 130   700 137   700 185
838 611

paul van kempen/berliner philharmonisches orchester
00177   00179   06054

paul van kempen/concertgebouworkest
00120   00141   00603   06015

paul van kempen/netherlands radio orchestra
00116   00119   00317   03147
06018   06025

paul van kempen/wiener symphoniker
00712

paul van kempen/orchestre lamoureux
00271   06054   06140

paul van kempen/santa cecilia orchestra
00284-5

hans knappertsbusch/orchester der bayreuther festspiele
02342-6

helmut koch/staatskapelle berlin
835 379

helmut koch/kammerorchester berlin
894 045

kyrill kondrashin/london symphony orchestra
00576

kyrill kondrashin/moscow philharmonic orchestra
02387

franz konwitschny/gewandhausorchester leipzig
698 033	698 034	698 035-6	698 057
698 058	698 076	698 077	200 004
700 131	700 141	700 143	700 143-4
700 157			

viteslav korunsky/europa-orchester
200 039

alexander krannhals/netherlands opera orchestra
00229-230

efrem kurtz/royal philharmonic orchestra
400 000
michel legrand/orchestra
839 801
fritz lehmann/berliner philharmonisches orchester
00111   00115
raymond leppard/english chamber orchestra
02337	02376	802 766-768	802 894
839 741-742	839 756	839 792-793	839 796

raymond leppard/new philharmonia orchestra
802 893	802 901	839 713

raymond leppard/london symphony orchestra
835 358
maurice leroux/orchestre lamoureux
697 011
bogo leskovic/slovenian opera orchestra
00331-2
bogo leskovic/wiener symphoniker
00423
wilhelm loibner/wiener symphoniker
00203	00266	00527	00629
00680	00693	00712	00713
00751	05435	05447	06005
06056	06075	06076	697 008
697 014			

lorin maazel/radio-sinfonie-orchester berlin
02473-4	02475-7	835 348-349	835 384
802 731	802 743	802 755	802 756
802 787			

charles mackerras/london symphony orchestra
836 909
fritz mareczek/stuttgarter philharmoniker
839 800
horst tanu margraf/orchester der händel-festspiele
698 051-054
igor markevitch/orchestre lamoureux
00457-8	00547	02041	02042
02043	02071	02075	02090-91

igor markevitch/london symphony orchestra
02239	02284	02371	02372
02377	835 327	835 390	802 702
802 703			

igor markevitch/new philharmonia orchestra
802 840   839 575
igor markevitch/concertgebouworkest
02433   802 785
igor markevitch/moscow philharmonic orchestra
02095-6
igor markevitch/ussr state orchestra
00559
igor markevitch/spanish radio orchestra
802 779   802 783   839 775   839 776
igor markevitch/instrumental ensemble
02306
jean martinon/orchestre lamoureux
00175   00370   00371   00748
03499
lothar mehler/danube symphony orchestra
200 016
willem mengelberg/concertgebouworkest
00150-53   09900   09901   09902
09903   09904   09905-6   09907
09908   09909   09910   09911
09912-13
joseph messner/wiener symphoniker
00470   00622-3
darius milhaud/orchestre lamoureux
00575
francesco molinari-pradelli/san carlo orchestra naples
00323-4   00444-5   02021-2   09000
francesco molinari-pradelli/orchestra of the teatro communale
00446
francesco molinari-pradelli/wiener symphoniker
03074
see also entry under instrumentalists
pierre monteux/london symphony orchestra
02261   02287   02323   02380
pierre monteux/concertgebouworkest
02247   02393
rudolf moralt/wiener symphoniker
00139   00163-4   00178   00183
00199   00210   00261   00280-82
00339   00367   00375   00386
00413-4   00417-9   00474   00630
00631   00634   00655   00667
00684   00687   00696   00732
00750   00780   04021   04031
06042   663 004

rudolf moralt/residentieorkest
00634
hans münch/stadtorchester basel
00738
vittorio negri/orchestra of la fenice venice
02431-2
vaclav neumann/gewandhaus-orchester leipzig
802 807-808   894 108
felix de nobel/netherlands chamber choir

00105	00127	00272	00312
00490	00678	00679	02223
06026	06055		

see also entry under instrumentalists
willem van otterloo/residentieorkest

00100	00101	00103	00107
00112	00114	00130	00132
00133	00134	00135	00138
00140	00144	00145-6	00149
00162	00198	00200	00249-50
00262	00263	00269	00286
00307	00370	00376	00377
00486	00487	00602	00651
00658-9	00662	00665	00689
00702	00709	00714	00718
00756	02047	04022	04024
04042	06008	06020	06036
06045	06159	663 001	663 002
663 003	663 008	698 008	698 029
698 031	698 032	835 062	894 126

willem van otterloo/concertgebouworkest
02392
willem van otterloo/wiener symphoniker

00176	00210	00249-50	00263
00290	00646	06115	06133
06134	610 116	663 005	697 006

willem van otterloo/berliner philharmonisches orchester
00123   00709
willem van otterloo/orchestre lamoureux
00191

tibor paul/wiener symphoniker
697 003　　　　698 024　　　　698 044　　　　700 169
anton paulik/orchester der wiener volksoper
02104
bernhard paumgartner/wiener symphoniker
00121　　　　00197　　　　00207　　　　00208
00211　　　　00213　　　　00244　　　　00258
00259　　　　00260　　　　00291　　　　00299
00305　　　　00313　　　　00315　　　　00340
00369　　　　00378　　　　00740　　　　00762-3
00771　　　　00777　　　　00778　　　　00781
02062　　　　02233　　　　02234　　　　02389
04020　　　　05468　　　　06031
bernhard paumgartner/camerata academica salzburg
00283　　　　00343-4　　　00367　　　　00374
00375　　　　00382　　　　00396-7　　　00493
00494　　　　00495　　　　00528　　　　00529
00768　　　　02217　　　　05317　　　　698 083
stanley pope/royal philharmonic orchestra
00783　　　　400 007
john pritchard/wiener symphoniker
00166　　　　00167　　　　00179　　　　00184
00235　　　　00239　　　　00657　　　　00668
see also entry under instrumentalists
ugo rapalo/san carlo orchestra naples
02018-20
kurt redel/pro arte orchestra munich
00557-8　　　02351-2　　　02400　　　　02445
kurt redel/lucerne festival orchestra
835 359-360
kurt redel/staatskapelle dresden
802 750-751
hans rosbaud/orchestre lamoureux
00363-4
hans rosbaud/concertgebouworkest
02086　　　　02263
manuel rosenthal/orchestre lamoureux
00563　　　　02309　　　　02375
manuel rosenthal/orchestre national
02301

witold rowicki/london symphony orchestra
02438 835 323 802 820 802 872
802 874 802 879 802 902 802 903
witold rowicki/warsaw philharmonic orchestra
02384 02388 02434
witold rowicki/wiener symphoniker
698 061
witold rowicki/residentieorkest
698 060
gennady rozhdestvensky/london symphony orchestra
02487
paul sacher/wiener symphoniker
00181 00212 00259 00288
00315 00626 00642 00675
00676
paul sacher/orchestre lamoureux
00251 00469 00749
paul sacher/kammerorchester basel
00214-5 00719
franz salmhofer/wiener symphoniker
00628 00685 00733 00754
02216 06186
heinz sandauer/wiener symphoniker
06014 06038
heinz sandauer/wiener tonkünstler-orchester
06162
wolfgang sawallisch/wiener symphoniker
00796 02024 02025 02027
02028 02029 02030 02258
02285 02293 02310
wolfgang sawallisch/concertgebouworkest
02026 02228 02237
wolfgang sawallisch/orchester der bayreuther festspiele
02211-3 02303-5
wolfgang sawallisch/new philharmonia orchestra
802 718 802 856-857 802 858
wolfgang sawallisch/staatskapelle dresden
802 797 802 798 802 799 802 800
802 801

hans schmidt-isserstedt/london symphony orchestra
835 330
tullio serafin/orchestra of san carlo naples
00393-5   00423-5   00463-5
borivoje simic/belgrade tv orchestra
02404
laszlo somogyi/wiener symphoniker
00544
alphonse stallaert/orchestre lamoureux
00688
eduard strauss/wiener symphoniker
00697   02216
otmar suitner/staatskapelle dresden
02230-1   894 041   894 046
otmar suitner/staatskapelle berlin
894 046
george szell/concertgebouworkest
00475   02436   802 769
kurt thomas/gewandhaus-orchester leipzig
698 047-8
luigi toffolo/trieste philharmonic orchestra
00428
federico morena torroba/agrupacion sinfonica zarzuela
00594-6   00995-6
edouardo toldra/orchestre lamoureux
00403
marinus voorberg/netherlands chamber choir
00692   00736   839 789
edo de waart/concertgebouworkest
839 757
edo de waart/netherlands wind ensemble
802 907   839 734
robert wagner/innsbruck symphony orchestra
02244   02282   03099   03113
03142   03401   03484   03485
03490   836 901
paul walter/wiener symphoniker
663 016   675 010   697 000   697 008
697 016

westermann/europa-orchester
200 031   700 183
helmut winschermann/deutsche bach-solisten
802 902   839 762   839 799
mogens wöldike/danish radio orchestra
836 750
carlo zecchi/concertgebouworkest
00342   00721   00723   06140
carlo zecchi/wiener symphoniker
00342   00526

appendix d: index of instrumentalists and chamber groups

isolde ahlgrimm/harpsichord
00155-6   00157-9   00169-171   00172-4
00185-7   00242-3   00265   00267-8
00300   00327   00335   00336
00415-6   00501   02038   02281
802 750-751   839 732
albrecht/organ
894 125
ilse von alpenheim/piano
00340
amsterdam piano quintet
00690
maurice andré/trumpet
00568   05468   802 710
willem andriessen/piano
06192
claudio arrau/piano
02259   02260   02314   02330
02335   02390   02391   02408
02409   02410   02411   02412
02429   835 380   835 382   835 383
802 706   802 729   802 730   802 741
802 746   802 793   802 906   839 709
839 743

felix asma/organ
00118 00147 00182 00241
00715 06109 06032-3
michele auclair/violin
697 006 698 087 836 901
dalton baldwin/piano
00461 02058 02059 02254-5
02256 02280 02324 02373
02382 802 765 802 870 802 919
839 733
daniel barenboim/piano
402 000
hubert barwahser/flute
00166 00208 00213 00306
00440 00695 02379 02406
frida bauer/piano
802 727
beaux arts trio
02422-5 835 393-394 835 395 802 747-748
802 802 802 833-834 802 916-918
phia berghout/harp
00440 00633 00695
bienvenu/piano
00225
stephen bishop-kovacevich/piano
839 702 839 722 839 761
trio di bolzano
00245
jacqueline bonneau/piano
00681
borodin string quartet
698 062
jan bos/horn
02085
yuri boukoff/piano
00517 00518 00544 00671
00673 00998 02039 02048
05371 05381
frederike bretschneider/harpsichord
00242-3 00501 02038
theo bruins/piano
00648
jack brymer/clarinet
02406

sas bunge/piano
802 882
robert casadesua/piano
02086
pablo casals/cello
00505   00506   00507   02208
see also entry under conductor
riccardo castagnone/piano
00348   00380   00499   06082
jacques cazauran/double-bass
802 757
charbonnier/harpsichord
00292
pierre cochereau/organ
00556   00568
eva czako/cello
802 757   802 895   802 905
leo czernak/bassoon
00369
georges cziffra/piano
02266   02267   02268   02301
02316
vasso devetzi/harpsichord
02297
jean doyen/piano
00233   00246   00509   200 009
836 924
leo driehuys/oboe
02389
maurice duruflé/organ
00749
ossian ellis/harp
02406
karl engel/oiano
00582   00592   02209   02210
06069   06102
jan eymar/piano
00381
leon fleisher/piano
00365

förstemann/organ
838 700   838 705
jean francaix/piano
802 805   835 316
maurice gendron/cello
02067   02243   02397-9   05420
835 316   835 358   802 805   802 818
802 892
grigory ginzburg/piano
663 025
paul godwin/viola
00299   00365
gousseau/piano
00251
cor de groot/piano
00106   00109   00114   00129
00130   00131   00133   00162
00200   00204   00290   00548
00613   00621   00632   00646
00718   00739   00756   00761
04042   06061   06115   06133
06134
arthur grumiaux/violin
00199   00228   00258   00313
00338   00348   00380   00400
00409   00412   00420   00422
00430   00432   00434   00465
00499   00750   00782   02051
02080   02205-7   02224   02236
02253   02264   02294   02309
02356   02375   02376   02378
05406   06082   610 124   802 708
802 719   802 757   802 785   802 803
802 848   802 895   802 905   839 747
839 757
werner haas/piano
02243-4   697 103   697 104   697 105
698 511-516   839 755
ingrid haebler/piano
00656   02321   02338   02438
02440   698 026   698 039   698 040
698 059   698 069   698 081   835 351
835 363   835 364   835 378   835 392
802 757   802 764   802 827   802 872
802 874   802 879   802 881   802 882
839 769   839 770   839 772   839 773

istvan hajdu/piano
02236	02264	02294	

adam harasiewicz/piano
02340-1	02402	663 015	698 011
698 021	698 022	698 028	698 041
698 068	698 073		

nikolaus harnoncourt/viola
00327

clara haskil/piano
00108	00134	00143	00259
00315	00338	00372	00400
00409	00412	00430	00432
00484	00724	02043	02071
02073	02075		

anton heiller/organ
00205-6	00223-4	00275-8	00308-311

alice heksch/piano
00112	00234	00244	00614
00691	06024	06027	06068

gerard hengeveld/piano
00645	00716	06023	06074

hans henkemans/piano
00142	00148	00184	00219
00237	00305	00339	00421
00478	00600	00627	00654
00758	00776		

hans hielkema/piano
00125	00339	00605	00700
06049			

hindar string quartet
839 241

ludwig hoffmann/piano
698 069	802 883

heinz holliger/oboe
839 740	839 756	839 786	839 787

holy/trumpet
05465

mieczyslaw horszowski/piano
00505	00506	00507

jolle huckriede/clarinet
00149
quartetto italiano
835 361   835 370   835 397   802 752-754
802 806   802 915   839 745   839 795
simon jansen/organ
836 000
see also entry under conductors
georges janzer/viola
02208   02209   802 757   802 895
802 905
jacques klein/piano
700 185
thom de klerk/bassoon
02085   02389
nap de klijn/violin
00112   00234   00299   00614
00691   06024   06027
robert köbler/organ
839 731
franz koch/horn
00369
johannes-ernst köhler/organ
698 047-8
pentti koskimies/piano
00560
detlef kraus/piano
838 704
hermann krebbers/violin
00132   00140   00209   00263
00487   04042   700 130   700 137
alexander lagoya/guitar
00570
maxence larrieu/flute
802 825-826   839 733
gustav leonhardt/harpsichord
00675
robert levin/piano
839 240
loewenguth string quartet
00304   00381
melita lorkovic/piano
00117

tibor de machula/cello

| 00107 | 00138 | 00231 | 00602 |
| 00687 | 04020 | 04042 | 06042 |

nikita magaloff/piano

| 00456 | 02061 | 02295 | 610 116 |
| 610 119 | 700 169 | 836 914 | |

thomas magyar/violin

| 00125 | 00238 | 00269 | 00605 |
| 00684 | 00700 | 00751 | 06049 |

adalbert meier/organ
02347-8

timo mikkilä/piano
00231

francesco molinari-pradelli/piano
00427

see also entry under condutors

mozarteum piano trio
00274

i musici

00301	00302	00303	00383
00384	00443	00447	00448
00449	00476	00488	00514
00516	00519	00539	02023
02037	02054	02057	02076
02077	02079	02098	02099
02220-21	02241	02246	02274
02275	02277-9	02320	02331-2
02333	02419-21	02428	835 025
835 355-356	835 388	802 715	802 725
802 733-736	802 761-763	802 796	802 864
839 740			

netherlands string quartet

| 00232 | 00306 | 00492 | 00615 |
| 00795 | 02064 | 05379 | |

neues wiener streichquartett
839 737-739

felix de nobel/piano
00104   00610   00625   00731
00746-7
see also entry under conductors
nowak string quartet
839 728-730
lev oborin/piano
02269   02270   02271   02272
02273
david oistrakh/violin
02269   02270   02271   02272
02273   02315   802 727
igor oistrakh/violin
663 025
theo olof/violin
00140   00219   00487
hans osieck/piano
00248
igor ozim/violin
610 803   700 130
theo van der pas/piano
00126   00609
erich penzel/horn
02234
arrigo pelliccia/viola
02378   839 747
sergio perticaroli/piano
02049   02074
pfersmann/flute
00265
philharmonisches oktett berlin
802 707   802 851   802 863   802 909
839 707   839 708   839 715   839 727
839 754
hans pischner/harpsichord
802 750-751
ida presti/guitar
00570
john pritchard/piano
00683
see also entry under conductors

eduard del pueyo/piano
00371 00388-9 698 015 698 016
698 043
rafael puyana/harpsichord
802 825-6 802 898
stephan radic/piano
835 318
sviatoslav richter/piano
00576 00581 00584 02307-8
02325 02326 02327
hans richter-haaser/piano
00325 00368 00474 02437
05418
mstislav rostropovich/cello
02307-02308
mstislav rostropovich/piano
02250
suzana ruzickova/harpsichord
802 750-1
peter rybar/violin
835 331
egida sartori/harpsichord
00333 00334 00385 00472
02349-50
annerose schmidt/piano
894 046
schnabel piano duo
00255 00326 00340 06046
richard schönhofer/clarinet
00369 05370
berl senofsky/violin
04021
harry sevenstern/trumpet
05468
sibinga/harpsichord
802 818
abbey simon/piano
00195 00689 04022
jan smeterlin/piano
00256-7

rosa spier/harp
00633
haakon stotijn/oboe
00527   02085
jaap stotijn/oboe
00527   00789   05379
karl suske/violin
894 046
paul szado/cello
02208   02209
henryk szeryng/violin
02487   835 330   835 331   836 919
magda tagliaferro/piano
00647   00664
pia tassinari/flute
00479
arne tellefsen/violin
839 240
louise thyrion/piano
00601   00666
evart van tright/oboe
02233
alexander uninsky/piano
00113   00124   00135   00136-7
00168   00370   00405   00429
00520   00651   00652   00653
00785   02050   02065   04024
09005   835 065
dinorah varsi/piano
802 908   839 718
sandor vegh/violin
00505   00506   02208   02209
ferruccio vignanelli/organ
00379
robert veyron-lacroix/harpsichord
835 389   802 750-751
luise walker/guitar
00626   00640
daniel wayenberg/piano
00688
janny van wering/piano
00611

bram de wilde/clarinet
00440   02085
wanda wilkomirska/violin
02388
adriaan van woudenburg/horn
05441

appendix c: index of singers

theo adam/bass-baritone
698 035-6   802 889-891
pierette alarie/soprano
00188-9   00363-4   00638   00663
00669
theo altmeyer/tenor
02257   02400   835 359-360   839 799
elly ameling/soprano
802 759-760   802 884-885   802 888   802 889-891
802 919   839 799
gianna d'angelo/soprano
02021-2
rolf apreck/tenor
02230-1
sari barabas/soprano
00178   02103
theo baylé/baritone
06025
ameliana beltrami/soprano
02018-20
margarete bence/contralto
09399   835 498
walter berry/bass-baritone
00121   00167   00260   00380-82
00357-9   00367   00375   00417-9
02062   02104   02252   03094
06186
liliane berton/soprano
02265
rené bianco/baritone
00188-9   02282   02283   03485

annette de la bije/soprano
02362   422 520   835 064
corrie bijster/soprano
00226-7   00312
arjan blanken/tenor
02362   422 520
ruthilde boesch/soprano
00396-00397   05317
laurens bogtman/bass
00746-7   04032
kim borg/bass-baritone
00560   02364-5
jean borthayre/baritone
02244   02276
géori boué/mezzo-soprano
03498
hans braun/baritone
00178   06186   02364-5
jean brazzi/tenor
02265
caspar bröcheler/baritone
00229-30
gré brouwenstijn/soprano
00119   00149   00284-5   00386
00413-4   00712   00713   03094
03147   06025
jacqueline brumaire/soprano
06025
grace bumbry/mezzo-soprano
02303-5
annelies burmeister/mezzo-soprano
802 889-891
annelore cahnbley/soprano
00367   05317
cora canne-mayer/mezzo-soprano
00312   00731
renato capecchi/bass
00323-4   00423-5   00444-5   02021-2
06200   09000
rosanna carteri/soprano
00385
rudolf christ/tenor
00121   00178   02062

franz crass/bass
02211-3   02226-7   02257   02502-5
03099   03107   03113   03117
835 359-360   802 810-812
oscar czerwenka/bass
00284-5   00413-4
irene dalis/contralto
02342-6
suzanne danco/soprano
00363-4   00427
ryland davies/tenor
802 862   839 758-760
xavier depraz/baritone
00188-9   00192-4   00347   00349
anton dermota/tenor
02437   698 000
cristina deutekom/soprano
839 791
helen donath/soprano
02475-7   802 713   802 856-7   802 862
walter dotzer/tenor
06014   06038   06047
ilona durigo/contralto
00150-3
otto edelmann/bass-baritone
00178   00266   00630   00680
karl erb/tenor
00150-3
deszö ernster/bass
00280-2   00417-9
andrée esposito/soprano
03484
lorenz fehenberger/tenor
00226-7
gerd feldhoff/bass-baritone
839 784-785
mario filippeschi/tenor
00393-5
birgit finnilä/contralto
839 799
res fischer/contralto
00226-7   02211-3

maureen forrester/contralto
802 711-712
jürgen förster/tenor
02230-1
carlo franzini/tenor
00201
gottlob frick/bass
00226-7   802 713-714
agnes giebel/soprano
02351-2   02431-2   02502-5   802 713-714
802 810-812
rita gorr/mezzo-soprano
00192-4
josef greindl/bass
02211-3
hilde güden/soprano
00457-8
andrea guiot/soprano
02053
horst günter/baritone
03142   835 359-360
ernst haefliger/tenor
00312   00410-11   00731   02475-7
04032   802 731   802 810-812
rotraud hansmann/mezzo-soprano
802 856-857
heather harper/soprano
802 721-723   839 719-721
judith hellwig/mezzo-soprano
02437
dagmar hermann/mezzo-soprano
00163-00164
annie hermes/contralto
00226-7
aafje heynis/contralto
00457-8   00460   00533   02063
02226-7   02362   02401   09007
802 884-885
andresz hiolski/tenor
802 771-772
guus hoekman/bass
802 759-760
marga höffgen/contralto
02431-2   02502-5   802 810-812
horst hoffmann/tenor
802 759-760
david hollestelle/baritone
00226-7   02362

ilse hollweg/soprano
00167   00260   00657   00781
02062
gerhard holthaus/baritone
00229-30
hans hopf/tenor
00266   00413-4   00732
hans hotter/bass-baritone
02342-6
maria von ilosvay/contralto
00145-6   00284-5   00649   00771
nina isakova/mezzo-soprano
02095-6
irene jaumillot/soprano
02244   02283   03400   835 497
siemen jongsma/bass
00229-30
sena jurinac/soprano
00280-82   00357-9   02351-2   835 359-360
patricia kern/mezzo-soprano
839 716-717
john van kesteren/tenor
02502-5
max kloos/baritone
09912-3
waldemar kmentt/tenor
00163-4   00167   00178   00197
00260   00413-4   00417-9   00435
00762-3   02062   02104   02252
03094   06075   06076   06186
06206   802 713-714   802 856-857
ernst kozub/tenor
03099   03107   03113   03117
03142   03203
annelies kupper/soprano
00226-7
bernard ladysz/baritone
802 771-772   839 701
albert lance/tenor
02053
adriana lazzarini/soprano
02018-20
evelyn lear/soprano
802 743   839 737-739

ilva ligabue/soprano
06083
wilma lipp/soprano
02226-7 04031
gisela litz/mezzo-soprano
02257 02445 03099 03107
03113
george london/bass-baritone
00280-82 02342-6
colette lorand/soprano
02282 03113 03117
christa ludwig/mezzo-soprano
00357-9 02216 802 743
suze luger/contralto
09905-6
melchiorre luise/bass
00444-5
erich majkut/tenor
00121 00367 00375 00395-7
02437 04031
luisa malagrida/soprano
00201
ira malaniuk/mezzo-soprano
00417-9 00435 02351-2
caterina mancini/soprano
00393-5 02018-20
jan van mantgem/baritone
00229-30
georg maran/bass
00343-4 00367
elisabeth margono/soprano
00611
lois marshall/soprano
02364-5
robert massard/baritone
02053
camille maurane/baritone
00192-3 00225 00349 00469
00669
nan merriman/contralto
00410-11 04032
joseph messthaler/bass
09399 835 498
joseph metternich/baritone
00163-4
janine micheau/soprano
00192-3 00347 00469

georgine von milinkovic/contralto
00163-4   00178
arnold van mill/bass
02230-31   03401
yvonne minton/mezzo-soprano
802 862
giuseppe modesti/bass
00423-5   00444-5
walter monachesi/baritone
02018-20
paolo montarsolo/baritone
06083
maría morales/soprano
00639
petre munteanu/tenor
00284-5   00323-4   00349
gustav neidlinger/bass-baritone
02342-6
gerd nienstedt/bass
802 862
wieslav ochman/tenor
839 701
julius patzak/tenor
04031
peter pears/tenor
02364-5
alois pernerstorfer/bass
00343-4
ivan petrov/bass
02095-6
miriam pirazzini/contralto
02021-2
gianni poggi/tenor
00463-4   02018-20   06191
tony poncet/tenor
02244   02276   02282   02283
02336   03400   03482   03484
03485   03498   835 497
hermann prey/baritone
02445
aldo protti/bass-baritone
02018-20

walter raninger/baritone
00367 00396-7 00493 00494
00762-3
willem ravelli/bass
00150-53 09905-6
liselotte rebmann/contralto
839 784-785
heinz rehfuss/baritone
00457-8 02282 02351-2 02400
anna reynolds/mezzo-soprano
02475-7 802 731 802 759-760
jane rhodes/mezzo-soprano
02053 02336
anton de ridder/tenor
839 784-785
margherita rinaldi/soprano
839 758-760
maria rivas/mezzo-soprano
02386
bruna rizzoli/mezzo-soprano
00323-4 00393-5 00444-5 09000
rosemarie rönisch/soprano
02230-1
hilde rössel-majdan/contralto
00762-3 06186 698 000
nicola rossi-lemeni/bass
00393-5
hans-joachim rotzsch/tenor
698 035-036 802 889-891
michel roux/baritone
00192-3 00749
friederike sailer/soprano
09399 835 498
antonio salsedo/baritone
00201
ivan sardi/bass
02021-2
chris scheffer/tenor
00229-30
hermann schey/bass-baritone
00103 00145-6 00150-3 00226-7
00312 00317 00625 00778

paul schöffler/bass-baritone
00357-9   02437   698 000
peter schreier/tenor
802 889-891
rosl schwaiger/soprano
02257   03094   03107
graziella sciutti/soprano
00280-2   00417-9   00705
michel sénéchal/tenor
00347   00681
john shirley-quirk/baritone
02475-7   802 721-723   839 716-7   839 719-721
839 758-760
dorothea siebert/soprano
00343-4
anja silja/soprano
02211-3   02342-6
léopold simoneau/tenor
00188-9   00280-2   00363-4   00638
00639   00740
to van der sluys/soprano
09905-6
gérard souzay/baritone
00461   02058   02059   02254-5
02256   02280   02324   02337
02373   02382   02507   802 765
802 870   839 733   839 762
ludovic spiess/tenor
802 700-701
mario spina/tenor
06083
erna spoorenberg/soprano
00145-6   00149   04032
maria stader/soprano
00738
ilona steingruber/soprano
06047
antonietta stella/soprano
00423-5   00463-4
teresa stich-randall/soprano
00376   00417-9   00435   00762-3
02437   06186   698 000

adele stolte/soprano
894 108
rita streich/soprano
00357-9   03142
reiner süss/bass
835 379
laszlo szemere/bass
00163-4   02104
giuseppe taddei/bass-baritone
00393-5   00423-5   00463-4
franco tagliavini/tenor
839 790
martti talvela/bass
02342-6   802 731
robert tear/tenor
839 716-717   839 758-760
jess thomas/tenor
02342-6
pauline tinsley/soprano
839 758-760
hertha töpper/mezzo-soprano
02364-5
richard tucker/tenor
02021-2
louis van tulder/tenor
00150-3   09905-6
fritz uhl/tenor
00457-8   02062   02211-13
giuseppe valdengo/bass
00323-4
cesare valletti/tenor
00423-5
vanovsky/tenor
02095-6
luisa villa/soprano
06083
jo vincent/soprano
00150-3   00610   09911   09912-3
galina vishnevskaya/soprano
00559   02095-6   02250
vivarelli/soprano
02282

corinne vozza/mezzo-soprano
00371
frans vroons/tenor
00119   00145-6   00226-7   00629
00706   00713   03147
jutta vulpius/soprano
02230-1
eberhard wächter/baritone
00280-2   00413-4   02216   02303-5
04031
john wakefield/tenor
802 721-723
helen watts/contralto
02439   802 721-723
ludwig weber/bass
00280-2
walburga wegner/soprano
00163-4
ingeborg wenglor/soprano
698 035-036
wolfgang windgassen/tenor
02303-5
rae woodland/soprano
02439
annie woud/contralto
00226-7
stefania woytowicz/soprano
802 771-772   839 701
zbyslaw wozniak/tenor
00229-30
fritz wunderlich/tenor
09399   835 498
hilde zadek/soprano
00207   00226-7   00266   00280-2
00288   00655   03099   04031
06062
ursula zollenkopf/contralto
698 035-036

Discographies by Travis & Emery:
Discographies by John Hunt.

1987: From Adam to Webern: the Recordings of von Karajan.

1991: 3 Italian Conductors and 7 Viennese Sopranos: 10 Discographies: Arturo Toscanini, Guido Cantelli, Carlo Maria Giulini, Elisabeth Schwarzkopf, Irmgard Seefried, Elisabeth Gruemmer, Sena Jurinac, Hilde Gueden, Lisa Della Casa, Rita Streich.

1992: Mid-Century Conductors and More Viennese Singers: 10 Discographies: Karl Boehm, Victor De Sabata, Hans Knappertsbusch, Tullio Serafin, Clemens Krauss, Anton Dermota, Leonie Rysanek, Eberhard Waechter, Maria Reining, Erich Kunz.

1993: More 20th Century Conductors: 7 Discographies: Eugen Jochum, Ferenc Fricsay, Carl Schuricht, Felix Weingartner, Josef Krips, Otto Klemperer, Erich Kleiber.

1994: Giants of the Keyboard: 6 Discographies: Wilhelm Kempff, Walter Gieseking, Edwin Fischer, Clara Haskil, Wilhelm Backhaus, Artur Schnabel.

1994: Six Wagnerian Sopranos: 6 Discographies: Frieda Leider, Kirsten Flagstad, Astrid Varnay, Martha Moedl, Birgit Nilsson, Gwyneth Jones.

1995: Musical Knights: 6 Discographies: Henry Wood, Thomas Beecham, Adrian Boult, John Barbirolli, Reginald Goodall, Malcolm Sargent.

1995: A Notable Quartet: 4 Discographies: Gundula Janowitz, Christa Ludwig, Nicolai Gedda, Dietrich Fischer-Dieskau.

1996: The Post-War German Tradition: 5 Discographies: Rudolf Kempe, Joseph Keilberth, Wolfgang Sawallisch, Rafael Kubelik, Andre Cluytens.

1996: Teachers and Pupils: 7 Discographies: Elisabeth Schwarzkopf, Maria Ivoguen, Maria Cebotari, Meta Seinemeyer, Ljuba Welitsch, Rita Streich, Erna Berger.

1996: Tenors in a Lyric Tradition: 3 Discographies: Peter Anders, Walther Ludwig, Fritz Wunderlich.

1997: The Lyric Baritone: 5 Discographies: Hans Reinmar, Gerhard Hüsch, Josef Metternich, Hermann Uhde, Eberhard Wächter.

1997: Hungarians in Exile: 3 Discographies: Fritz Reiner, Antal Dorati, George Szell.

1997: The Art of the Diva: 3 Discographies: Claudia Muzio, Maria Callas, Magda Olivero.

1997: Metropolitan Sopranos: 4 Discographies: Rosa Ponselle, Eleanor Steber, Zinka Milanov, Leontyne Price.

1997: Back From The Shadows: 4 Discographies: Willem Mengelberg, Dimitri Mitropoulos, Hermann Abendroth, Eduard Van Beinum.

1997: More Musical Knights: 4 Discographies: Hamilton Harty, Charles Mackerras, Simon Rattle, John Pritchard.

1998: Conductors On The Yellow Label: 8 Discographies: Fritz Lehmann, Ferdinand Leitner, Ferenc Fricsay, Eugen Jochum, Leopold Ludwig, Artur Rother, Franz Konwitschny, Igor Markevitch.

1998: More Giants of the Keyboard: 5 Discographies: Claudio Arrau, Gyorgy Cziffra, Vladimir Horowitz, Dinu Lipatti, Artur Rubinstein.

1998: Mezzos and Contraltos: 5 Discographies: Janet Baker, Margarete Klose, Kathleen Ferrier, Giulietta Simionato, Elisabeth Höngen.
1999: The Furtwängler Sound Sixth Edition: Discography and Concert Listing.
1999: The Great Dictators: 3 Discographies: Evgeny Mravinsky, Artur Rodzinski, Sergiu Celibidache.
1999: Sviatoslav Richter: Pianist of the Century: Discography.
2000: Philharmonic Autocrat 1: Discography of: Herbert Von Karajan [Third Edition].
2000: Wiener Philharmoniker 1 - Vienna Philharmonic & Vienna State Opera Orchestras: Disc. Part 1 1905-1954.
2000: Wiener Philharmoniker 2 - Vienna Philharmonic & Vienna State Opera Orchestras: Disc. Part 2 1954-1989.
2001: Gramophone Stalwarts: 3 Separate Discographies: Bruno Walter, Erich Leinsdorf, Georg Solti.
2001: Singers of the Third Reich: 5 Discographies: Helge Roswaenge, Tiana Lemnitz, Franz Völker, Maria Müller, Max Lorenz.
2001: Philharmonic Autocrat 2: Concert Register of Herbert Von Karajan Second Edition.
2002: Sächsische Staatskapelle Dresden: Complete Discography.
2002: Carlo Maria Giulini: Discography and Concert Register.
2002: Pianists For The Connoisseur: 6 Discographies: Arturo Benedetti Michelangeli, Alfred Cortot, Alexis Weissenberg, Clifford Curzon, Solomon, Elly Ney.
2003: Singers on the Yellow Label: 7 Discographies: Maria Stader, Elfriede Trötschel, Annelies Kupper, Wolfgang Windgassen, Ernst Häfliger, Josef Greindl, Kim Borg.
2003: A Gallic Trio: 3 Discographies: Charles Münch, Paul Paray, Pierre Monteux.
2004: Antal Dorati 1906-1988: Discography and Concert Register.
2004: Columbia 33CX Label Discography.
2004: Great Violinists: 3 Discographies: David Oistrakh, Wolfgang Schneiderhan, Arthur Grumiaux.
2006: Leopold Stokowski: Second Edition of the Discography.
2006: Wagner Im Festspielhaus: Discography of the Bayreuth Festival.
2006: Her Master's Voice: Concert Register and Discography of Dame Elisabeth Schwarzkopf [Third Edition].
2007: Hans Knappertsbusch: Kna: Concert Register and Discography of Hans Knappertsbusch, 1888-1965. Second Edition.
2008: Philips Minigroove: Second Extended Version of the European Discography.
2009: American Classics: The Discographies of Leonard Bernstein and Eugene Ormandy.

Discography by Stephen J. Pettitt, edited by John Hunt:
1987: Philharmonia Orchestra: Complete Discography 1945-1987

Available from: Travis & Emery at 17 Cecil Court, London, UK.
(+44) 20 7 240 2129. email on sales@travis-and-emery.com .

© Travis & Emery 2009

Music and Books published by Travis & Emery Music Bookshop:

Anon.: Hymnarium Sarisburense, cum Rubris et Notis Musicus
Agricola, Johann Friedrich from Tosi: Anleitung zur Singkunst. (Faksimile 1757)
Bach, C.P.E.: edited W. Emery: Nekrolog or Obituary Notice of J.S. Bach.
Bateson, Naomi Judith: Alcock of Salisbury
Bathe, William: A Briefe Introduction to the Skill of Song
Bax, Arnold: Symphony #5, Arranged for Piano Four Hands by Walter Emery
Burney, Charles: The Present State of Music in France and Italy
Burney, Charles: The Present State of Music in Germany, The Netherlands …
Burney, Charles: An Account of the Musical Performances … Handel
Burney, Karl: Nachricht von Georg Friedrich Handel's Lebensumstanden.
Burns, Robert (jnr): The Caledonian Musical Museum (1810 volume)
Cobbett, W.W.: Cobbett's Cyclopedic Survey of Chamber Music. (2 vols.)
Corrette, Michel: Le Maitre de Clavecin
Crimp, Bryan: Dear Mr. Rosenthal … Dear Mr. Gaisberg …
Crimp, Bryan: Solo: The Biography of Solomon
d'Indy, Vincent: Beethoven: Biographie Critique
d'Indy, Vincent: Beethoven: A Critical Biography
d'Indy, Vincent: César Franck (in French)
Fischhof, Joseph: Versuch einer Geschichte des Clavierbaues
Frescobaldi, Girolamo: D'Arie Musicali per Cantarsi. Primo Libro & Secondo Libro.
Geminiani, Francesco: The Art of Playing the Violin.
Handel; Purcell; Boyce; Green et al: Calliope or English Harmony: Volume First.
Hawkins, John: A General History of the Science and Practice of Music (5 vols.)
Herbert-Caesari, Edgar: The Science and Sensations of Vocal Tone
Herbert-Caesari, Edgar: Vocal Truth
Hopkins and Rimboult: The Organ. Its History and Construction.
Hunt, John: some 40 discographies – see list of discographies
Isaacs, Lewis: Hänsel and Gretel. A Guide to Humperdinck's Opera.
Isaacs, Lewis: Königskinder (Royal Children) A Guide to Humperdinck's Opera.
Lacassagne, M. l'Abbé Joseph : Traité Général des élémens du Chant.
Lascelles (née Catley), Anne: The Life of Miss Anne Catley.
Mainwaring, John: Memoirs of the Life of the Late George Frederic Handel
Malcolm, Alexander: A Treaty of Music: Speculative, Practical and Historical
Marx, Adolph Bernhard: Die Kunst des Gesanges, Theoretisch-Practisch
May, Florence: The Life of Brahms
Mellers, Wilfrid: Angels of the Night: Popular Female Singers of Our Time
Mellers, Wilfrid: Bach and the Dance of God

Travis & Emery Music Bookshop
17 Cecil Court, London, WC2N 4EZ, United Kingdom.
Tel. (+44) 20 7240 2129

Music and Books published by Travis & Emery Music Bookshop:

Mellers, Wilfrid: Beethoven and the Voice of God
Mellers, Wilfrid: Caliban Reborn - Renewal in Twentieth Century Music
Mellers, Wilfrid: François Couperin and the French Classical Tradition
Mellers, Wilfrid: Harmonious Meeting
Mellers, Wilfrid: Le Jardin Retrouvé, The Music of Frederic Mompou
Mellers, Wilfrid: Music and Society, England and the European Tradition
Mellers, Wilfrid: Music in a New Found Land: ... ... American Music
Mellers, Wilfrid: Romanticism and the Twentieth Century (from 1800)
Mellers, Wilfrid: The Masks of Orpheus: …… the Story of European Music.
Mellers, Wilfrid: The Sonata Principle (from c. 1750)
Mellers, Wilfrid: Vaughan Williams and the Vision of Albion
Panchianio, Cattuffio: Rutzvanscad Il Giovine.
Pearce, Charles: Sims Reeves, Fifty Years of Music in England.
Pettitt, Stephen: Philharmonia Orchestra: Complete Discography 1945-1987
Playford, John: An Introduction to the Skill of Musick.
Purcell, Henry et al: Harmonia Sacra … The First Book, (1726)
Purcell, Henry et al: Harmonia Sacra … Book II (1726)
Quantz, Johann: Versuch einer Anweisung die Flöte traversiere zu spielen.
Rameau, Jean-Philippe: Code de Musique Pratique, ou Methodes.
Rastall, Richard: The Notation of Western Music.
Rimbault, Edward: The Pianoforte, Its Origins, Progress, and Construction.
Rousseau, Jean Jacques: Dictionnaire de Musique
Rubinstein, Anton : Guide to the proper use of the Pianoforte Pedals.
Sainsbury, John S.: Dictionary of Musicians. Vol. 1. (1825). 2 vols.
Simpson, Christopher: A Compendium of Practical Musick in Five Parts
Spohr, Louis: Autobiography
Spohr, Louis: Grand Violin School
Tans'ur, William: A New Musical Grammar; or The Harmonical Spectator
Terry, Charles Sanford: Four-Part Chorals of J.S. Bach. (German & English)
Terry, Charles Sanford: Joh. Seb. Bach, Cantata Texts, Sacred and Secular.
Terry, Charles Sanford: The Origins of the Family of Bach Musicians.
Tosi, Pierfrancesco: Opinioni de' Cantori Antichi, e Moderni
Van der Straeten, Edmund: History of the Violoncello, The Viol da Gamba …
Van der Straeten, Edmund: History of the Violin, Its Ancestors… (2 vols.)
Walther, J. G.: Musicalisches Lexikon ober Musicalische Bibliothec (1732)

Travis & Emery Music Bookshop
17 Cecil Court, London, WC2N 4EZ, United Kingdom.
Tel. (+44) 20 7240 2129

© Travis & Emery 2009